My Life
and My Films

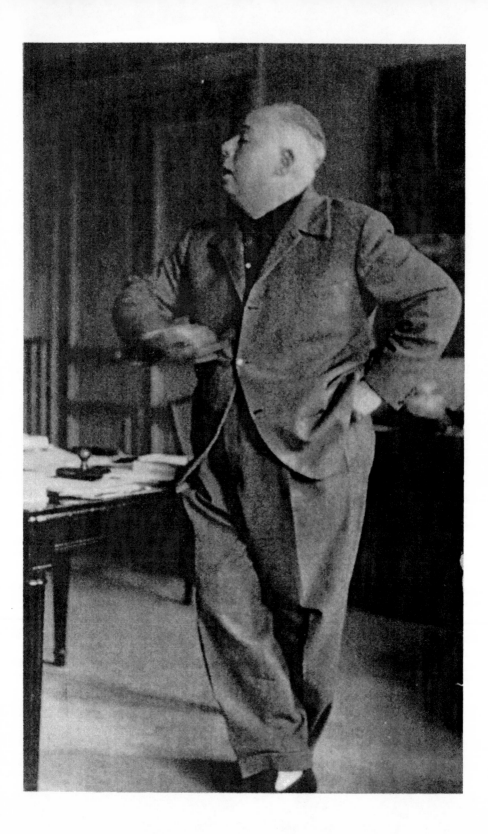

My Life
and My Films

by Jean Renoir

Translated by Norman Denny

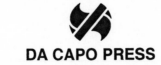

DA CAPO PRESS
A Member of the Perseus Books Group

Frontispiece: In my apartment on the Avenue Frochot

Library of Congress Cataloging in Publication Data

Renoir, Jean, 1894–
   [Ma vie et mes films. English]
   My life and my films / by Jean Renoir; translated by Norman Denny.
     p.   cm.—(A Da Capo paperback)
   Translation of: Ma vie et mes films.
   Reprint. Originally published: New York: Atheneum, 1974.
   Includes index.
   ISBN 0-306-80457-3
   1. Renoir, Jean, 1894–   . 2. Motion picture producers and directors
—France—Biography. I. Title.
[PN1889.3.R46A3 1991]   91-19626
791.43′0233′092—dc20   CIP

Originally published in French as *Ma Vie et Mes Films*
copyright © 1974 by Jean Renoir
English translation copyright © 1974 by Wm Collins Sons & Co Ltd
and Atheneum Publishers Ltd

10 9 8 7 6 5 4

Published by Da Capo Press, Inc.
A member of the Perseus Books Group

Contents

Illustration Acknowledgements

Mme G. Courtois-Doynel: Opposite page 49,
below. Opposite page 80, above. Between pages
136-137, right page centre. Opposite page 256,
above.
Bonnard: Opposite page 104.
Lourié: Between pages 136-137, right page below.
France Reportage: Opposite page 137, above.
William Vandervert: Opposite page 175, left.
RKO Pictures, Inc: Opposite page 208, below.
Frank Silvera: Opposite page 224.
Bernand: Opposite page 257, above.

I dedicate this book to those film-makers who are known to the public as the 'New Wave' and whose preoccupations are also mine.

Foreword

Everything that moves on the screen is cinema. I often hear people say: 'A very interesting film, no doubt, but not cinema.' I don't know why the use of pictures that move should be restricted to traditional melodrama or farcical comedy. A geographical film is cinema just as much as *Ben Hur*. A film designed to teach children the alphabet has as much claim to be considered cinema as a grandiose production with psychological pretensions. In my view cinema is nothing but a new form of printing – another form of the total transformation of the world through knowledge. Louis Lumière was another Gutenberg. His invention has caused as many disasters as the dissemination of thought through books.

The history of the cinema, above all of the French cinema, during the past half-century may be summarized as the war of the film-maker against the industry. I am proud to have had a share in that triumphant struggle. In these days we recognize that a film is the work of its maker, just like a novel or a painting.

But who is the maker of a film? In the heroic period of the American cinema it was generally the actor who put his stamp on it. As the industry prospered it became a medium for the manufacture of stars. The cinema of recent years has brought about the acceptance of the idea that the maker of a film is the director – a happy change, and in line with present-day artistic and literary tendencies. Today we have films signed 'Truffaut' or 'Jean-Luc Godard' just as we have novels signed 'Simenon' or 'André Gide'.

Many of my friends have urged me to write my auto-biography: and doubtless their interest is prompted by this new realization of the importance of the film-maker. It is no longer enough for them to know that an artist has freely expressed himself with the help of a camera and a micro-phone. They want to know who the artist is. For my part, I believe that every human creature, artist or otherwise, is largely the product of his environment. It is arrogance which leads us to believe in the supremacy of the individual. The truth is that this individual of whom we are so proud is composed of such diverse elements as the boy he made friends with at nursery school, the hero of the first tale he ever read, even the dog belonging to his cousin Eugène. We do not exist through ourselves alone but through the environment that shaped us. Of course it would be an exaggeration to claim that a potato, planted in suitable conditions, would yield strawberries; but it is certainly true that the yield of the plant in question will vary in taste and form according to the soil in which it is planted, the fer-tilizer that is used and the climate, to say nothing of the possibility of grafts which may produce a fruit quite differ-ent from its predecessors.

I shall not attempt to include in this book a catalogue of all my films. This has already been done, notably in the brilliant work by André Bazin, to which I have nothing to add. I have sought to recall those persons and events which I believe have played a part in making me what I am.

Mack Sennett

In the silent days the majority of films could be regarded as film-maker's films. The introduction of sound, by extending the technical range, hastened the death of that very simple system. This innovation also marked a step towards the non-interpretive reproduction of reality, or what was believed to be reality. I shall have a lot to say about that. It is a subject deserving of a volume to itself, and indeed volumes have been written about it. It embraces the whole problem of internal and external truth.

The earliest films were the direct expression of the dreams of the film-maker and bore his unmistakable signature, together with all the influences that had combined to shape him, English pantomime or popular melodrama, or, above all, the delightful American burlesque show.

Mack Sennett gathered his actors and technicians together on the steps of his office and planned the day's work with them. It happened in a commonplace little street in a Los Angeles suburb. The street was so steep that sometimes a car stalled and ran backwards – an admirable idea for a 'short'. The houses were all one storey high, with washing hanging out to dry in the gardens behind them. The sidewalks were sparsely shaded by young palm-trees. Mack Sennett had only to turn the handle of his camera to plunge the audience in a bath of genuine Americanism. His restricted finances compelled him to make the best he could of that America of humble people which, alas, we shall never see again.

An actor specializing in 'cop' roles would propose a

chase sequence in which the seal would play the leading part, for Mack Sennett owned a seal. There were also bathing beauties and clowns brought in from the circus and burlesque theatres. Everyone said what he thought, but they all respected the boss, and the films coming out of Mack Sennett's small studio were unquestionably Mack Sennett films, each bearing witness to the personality of the producer, director, gag-man – everything you can think of rolled into one. They were as much the work of a single man as a rare dish is the work of a particular chef or a Shaw play is a play by Bernard Shaw. And, which is important, the artists creating the work had no idea that they were producing masterpieces. They told simple tales and all they set out to do was to please their public, in exchange for which they earned a living. Of course there was more to it than that. When we think of any performance we must never ignore the religious element, a religion pursued by its devotees with a selfless passion.

An essential element in the quality of any work of art is simply the quality of the public from whom the artist gets his living. Mack Sennett's was an ideal public, a working-class public largely composed of newly arrived immigrants. Many of them knew very little English: the silent cinema exactly suited them. Today's public is composed of the children of those primitive audiences. They come from the university; they live in a world of advertising, newspapers and weekly reviews; they behave according to the principles instilled in them by the most effective publicity media, the most 'artistic' and the most entertaining. For their benefit the film-factories churn out heroism or love or, worst of all, psychology.

Throughout my life I have tried to make film-maker's

films, not from vanity but because God instilled in me the desire to establish my identity and proclaim it to an audience that may be large or small, brilliant or lamentable, enthusiastic or scornful. What I like about the film-maker's form of exhibitionism is that he does not manifest himself physically but modestly conceals himself behind the characters who bring his works to life. God has not made me a hero. I am afraid of violence and I find it highly convenient to send actors to suffer in my place. Subsequently I have to pay for this false security, but the fact that I have no contact with the public during the execution of the work fills me with daring. I own a dog who is like that. When he is with me he is heroically aggressive. Although he is only a miniature Basset he does not hesitate to defy the most impressive mastiff. But if I walk away he is seized with panic and runs to seek safety between my legs.

Where I am concerned, the conditions under which I display myself to the public are of no importance. All that matters is that I should display myself. I yield the more readily to this weakness since I am impelled to do so by the insistent questioning of youthful colleagues for whom everything that happened before the coming of sound seems as remote and mystifying as the ice ages. We ancients are held by them in an esteem similar to that accorded by modern artists to the cave drawings of Lascaux. It is a flattering comparison which causes us to feel that we have not wasted too many feet of film.

A Visit to Dufayel

Great loves are never premeditated. We are never on the lookout for the woman destined to transform our life. The girl we set out to conquer was the girl we knew at school; another one became our wife. Besides, a man never conquers a woman; it is the woman who conquers the man she has chosen, and her method is to persuade him that it was he who took the initiative. Later, in the course of married life, the situation is reversed. The woman allows herself to be possessed; she adopts the man's tastes and even his obsessions. She is truly Adam's rib. That is why a separation is more tragic for the woman than for the man, who, whatever the law may say, remains essentially polygamous.

My first experience of the cinema was in 1897. I was a little over two. My mother had decided to buy a whitewood wardrobe for Gabrielle's bedroom. Gabrielle, who was to become Renoir's model, was born at Essoyes, a village in Burgundy. She was my mother's cousin, and when I was born she came to live with us as a 'help'. The help consisted chiefly of looking after me and taking me for walks. She was then sixteen. I could not get on without 'Bibon', the nickname I bestowed on Gabrielle, which emerged from my vain efforts to pronounce her name. I was never able to get beyond the first syllable. After the 'Ga' I got muddled and the name became 'Gabibon', and finally I dropped the 'Ga'. My younger brother, Claude, seven years later completed the process of simplification by calling her 'Ga' and nothing else.

Our destination on this outing was the Dufayel depart-

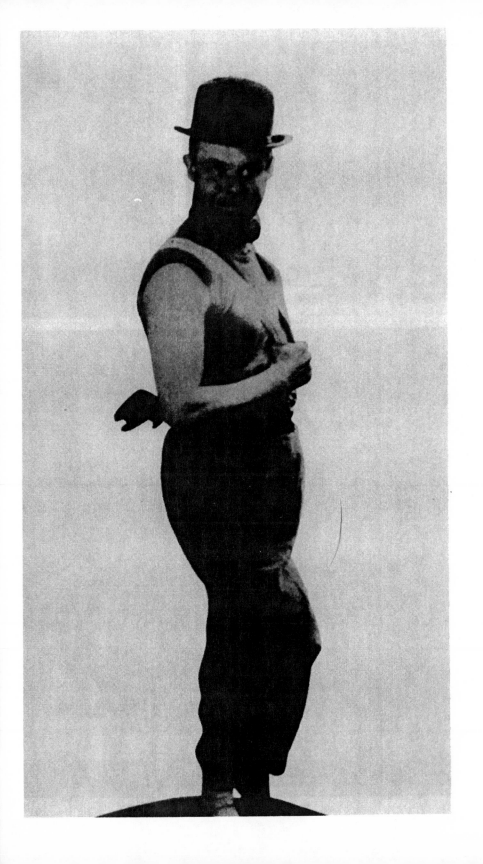

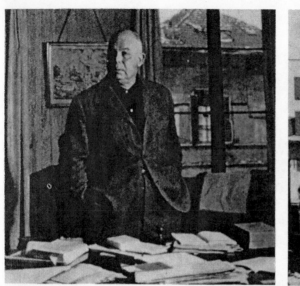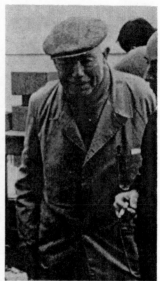
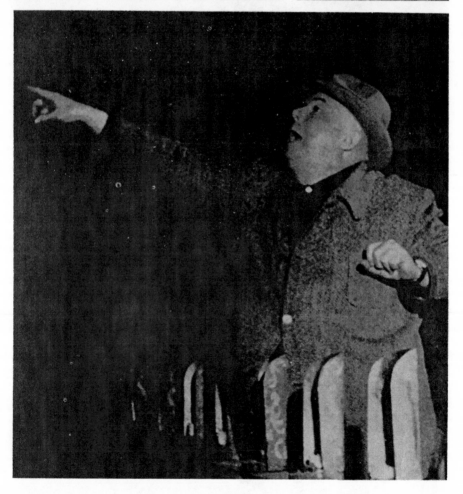

Above left: Avenue Frochot, my Paris home
for 37 years
Above right: During the shooting of *Le Petit
Théâtre de Jean Renoir*
Below: Rehearsing *Orvet*

17

ment store. I can only repeat what Gabrielle told me when,
at the end of her life, she came to join us in Hollywood. But
my memory goes far enough back for me to be able to recall
that the world in those days was divided for me into two
parts. My mother was the tiresome part, the person who
ordered me to eat up my dinner, to go to the lavatory, to
have a bath in the sort of zinc tub which served for our
morning ablutions. And Bibon was for fun, walks in the
park, games in the sand-heap, above all piggy-back rides,
something my mother absolutely refused to do, whereas
Gabrielle was never happier than when bowed down under
the weight of my small body. I was a spoilt child. Our
family life enclosed me in a protective wall softly padded on
the inside. Beyond this wall impressive persons came and
went. I would have liked to join them and be impressive
myself, but unfortunately nature had made me a coward.
Whenever I discerned a breach in the wall I uttered cries of
alarm.

All went well at the beginning of our visit to Dufayel.
The streets had a peaceful look – no sign anywhere of the
villains who steal children who wander away from their
mothers. At the entrance to the store a man wearing a
braided cap asked us if we wanted to see the 'cinema'. His
cap was rather like the uniform cap of the Collège de
Sainte-Croix, where my brother Pierre, the future actor,
had been sent as a boarder to make room in the home for
my cumbersome self. A man wearing such a cap could only
be on the side of the 'good', that is to say, those dedicated
to safeguarding the small fragment of the world which was
the only one I knew. It was therefore in a spirit of comparative confidence that I allowed Bibon to take me into the
projection room.

The Grands Magasins Dufayel were in the forefront of progress. They had been the first to sell on credit. The building, with its walls of real stone and large glass windows shedding their light on imitation Henri II sideboards, gave to those privileged to enter that temple of mass-produced goods an impression of solidity capable of withstanding anything. The free cinema was another of their daring innovations. Gabrielle's account of the incident was terse and lacking in detail. Scarcely had we taken our seats than the room was plunged in darkness. A terrifying machine shot out a fearsome beam of light piercing the obscurity, and a series of incomprehensible pictures appeared on the screen, accompanied by the sound of a piano at one end and at the other end a sort of hammering that came from the machine. I yelled in my usual fashion and had to be taken out. I never thought that the staccato rhythm of the Maltese cross was later to become for me the sweetest of music. At the time I did not grasp the importance of that basic part of both camera and projector without which the cinema would not exist.

So my first encounter with the idol was a complete failure. Gabrielle was sorry we had not stayed. The film was about a big river and she thought that in a corner of the screen she had glimpsed a crocodile.

The Camel's Coat

Intolerable infant that I was, I had reached the point of allowing no one to touch me when I was in Gabrielle's arms, as though some contagious germ had attempted to invade my private domain. I gazed at the intruder in terror and yelled, '*A tou Dan*,' which meant, 'He has dared to touch Jean.'

I was furiously possessive of the small, softly padded world in which I noisily grew up and from which I excluded all outsiders. Of course I had to bear with the irruption of the butcher's boy with his basket on his head, the man who brought firewood, the milkman, clad in white as his calling required, and the small baker's boy who brought us hot croissants every morning. I tolerated the presence of hawkers in the streets, they were a part of my kingdom. I remember their cries. '*Chand d'habits*,' proclaimed the sonorous voice of the old-clothes man. '*Du mouron pour les petits oiseaux*,' sang the seller of chickweed, whose tongue had been injured in a railway accident so that his cry became, '*Du mou'on pou' les p'ti' oi'eaux*.' This kind of language, directly related to '*A tou Dan*,' seemed to me the only civilized speech. The rag-and-bone man intoning in a sepulchral voice, '*Chiffons, ferraille à vendre*,' was equally entitled to his rank as citizen in the world of Bibon, as was the seller of watercress, '*Bon cresson de fontaine. La santé du corps*.' I accepted them during their brief visits, but they must not presume to address me. 'Such a pretty baby!' said the washerwoman, and my response was to stamp my foot.

My father loved to paint my hair, and his fondness for the

golden ringlets which came down to my shoulders filled me
with despair. At the age of six, and in spite of my trousers,
many people mistook me for a girl. Street urchins ran jeer-
ing after me, calling me 'Mademoiselle' and asking what I
had done with my skirt. I impatiently awaited the day when
I was to enter the Collège de Sainte-Croix, where the regula-
tions required a hairstyle more suited to middle-class ideals.
To my great disappointment my father constantly postponed the date of my entry, which for me signified the bliss-
ful shedding of those locks. I may add that he had a horror
of 'education' to the point of sympathizing with the boys
who played truant. He liked Sainte-Croix because of its
extensive grounds, considering the quality of the air more
important than the quality of the mathematics master. His
scepticism where schooling was concerned was summed up
as follows: 'In Protestant schools you become a pederast,
but with the Catholics it's more likely to be masturbation.
I prefer the latter.'

On a morning like many another my father announced
that he was going to paint my portrait. I protested, pre-
tending that I had a sore leg, and to prove it I limped
ostentatiously. But my father was determined to paint me,
and the whole household, not wishing him to be put off,
tried to persuade me. Suddenly Gabrielle had an idea. I had
a camel which I adored, not a real one of course, but a toy
one no bigger than my hand which came, not from Africa
but from the toyshop in the rue d'Amsterdam, near the
Gare Saint-Lazare. Gabrielle said between two of my sobs:
'You ought to make a coat for your camel. The weather's
getting cold and it will soon be winter. Your camel simply
must have a coat.' The idea delighted me. I sat down in
front of my father's easel and began sewing. Renoir, with

his terror of sharp-edged or pointed implements, was greatly perturbed. He started to paint, muttering: 'Your hand slips and the needle goes into your eye and you're blind for life.' But my hair that morning had a glow which pleased him, and in his absorption with the problems it presented he forgot about the danger of the needle. Rinsing his brush in a glass of turpentine he murmured, 'Pure gold.' I realized that he was talking about my hair, and by degrees pride in being crowned with gold became more important to me than the discomfort of acting as a model. In any case I was better off than the children of many painters. Renoir did not insist on absolute immobility. Indeed, I still have a feeling that he feared it.

Magagnosc

The paintings by my father which covered the walls of our apartment were an essential part of the background of my small life. When my mother took me to visit a collector I was shocked to find that pictures I had seen at home were now hanging in alien territory. In my father's kingdom, which was also that of my mother and of Bibon, the bouquets of flowers, the nudes and the landscapes were as much a part of the domestic scene as the doorknobs, the umbrella-stand in the lobby, the cane chairs bought from Thonet and the oil-lamp, for my father mistrusted the inflammability of kerosene.

How had these pictures, the companions of my daily life, come to leave that paradise? Probably they had been stolen. The distinguished gentleman with his scented beard who was ostensibly posing for his portrait might well be the leader of a gang of robbers. Those pictures were part of my own private kingdom, and their removal from our walls threatened to lead to terrible consequences, as though someone had stolen the frying-pan in which the *'boulangère'* – incidentally another of my father's models – cooked her marvellous fried potatoes.

The *boulangère* was like one of the family. She was not really a baker-woman but had got the nickname from her intimate association with a young man working for a local baker who went by the entirely esoteric name of 'Tè-Tè', a nickname of which no one knew the origin. Tè-Tè loved to 'lend a hand'. Directly he had finished work at the bakery he would come round to us and enjoy himself doing odd jobs, such as peeling vegetables, oiling locks and beating carpets. Meanwhile, the *boulangère* would be frying potatoes. There were no specialists in my father's establishment and we thought it normal for the potatoes to be fried by one of his models. Generally speaking, the frying-pan plays no part in a child's artistic formation, but in my life it was of the first importance.

I did not look at my father's pictures but I was aware of them. I knew that if I were to be deprived of them disaster would follow – a flood or an earthquake, a plague of locusts, even the disappearance of my father and mother and Gabrielle. This thought froze the blood in my veins and I would sometimes stand trembling at the front door, await-ing the return of one or another of them. Then, directly the bell rang, I would fly into one of my fits of rage. I made no bones about behaving odiously in the presence of my defenders. A moment earlier, solitary and deserted, I had been trembling with fright. I was born a coward.

My father's was an errant kingdom. The need to seek new qualities of light impelled Renoir frequently to change his dwelling. By turns I was a Burgundy urchin, rolling my 'r's', a lisping Parisian and a deep-voiced Meridional.

A setting which greatly influenced me was a villa near Grasse which my father rented for the winter of 1900. Its owner had a passion for tropical plants. The garden might have been conceived by Douanier Rousseau. It took only a small effort of the imagination to picture it populated with lions, tigers and snakes. I had several times seen a green lizard, come to enjoy its damp shade, and this harmless creature, magnified a hundred times, became in my imagina-tion a most satisfactory crocodile. Gabrielle was enchanted: she had a particular love of lions, and surely these were to be met with in a place where one found crocodiles. I became so used to the 'croco', the name we bestowed on the lizard, that I started to collect reptiles. I had a glass cage full of lizards, glow-worms and salamanders, made for me by the son of the owner of the villa, who was a cabinet-maker. I kept them in my bedroom and always carried one around with me hidden under my shirt.

This led to a painful incident which I have never forgotten. We were travelling back to Paris by train, Gabrielle, my father and mother, and me. A very thin English-woman entered our compartment at Saint-Raphael and could not take her eyes off my golden locks. 'Such a sweet little girl, such pretty hair!' she exclaimed with a strong English accent. A small lizard which I was taking with me to Paris popped its head out of the middy-blouse of which I was particularly proud – there were no girls in the Navy. At the sight of it the English lady uttered a piercing shriek. Renoir did his best to soothe her, but in vain. She rushed out into the corridor and came back with the guard, who insisted on the animal being handed over to him. He took it from me without gentleness. A lizard's skin is very sensitive and the grasp of a rough hand must be painful to it. The guard mercilessly flung my small pet out of the window. The English lady, relieved, settled back in her corner and, indifferent to my sobbing, began to read the Bible.

Our stay at the villa near Grasse was for me ideal, but it did not last long. There were too many stairs to suit my father's legs, which were already becoming paralysed. It remains deeply imprinted in my memory not only because of the lizards but because of Jeannot Lapin. Jeannot Lapin was a real rabbit. Thanks to my prayers and promises never again to fly into a rage, he had escaped the stew-pot. He lived in a packing-case in the dining-room, and every day we took him for a walk in the hills. We put him on the ground and formed a circle round him consisting of my father and mother, Gabrielle, the cook, the gardener and the son of the owner, who, according to Gabrielle, was paying court to a girl who lived near by. One day I came across the couple in the gardener's shed, lying on top of one another and groaning as though they were in pain. I was frightened and ran away. Soon afterwards I found them seated in the kitchen drinking a glass of wine. I was afraid to ask if they were feeling better, but the incident caused me to suspect the existence of a world of which I had hitherto known nothing. To me 'making love' meant hand-kissing and reciting poetry. It was my first glimpse of the hollowness of appearances.

Our villa was situated on a hillside. The kitchen, to be level with the street, was on the first floor. This position was particularly convenient for Antoinette, a housemaid who went out that way to join her lover, a magnificent sergeant in the Chasseurs Alpins. Sometimes the great man took me to have a meal with his platoon. He put his béret on my head and let me touch his rifle. To me this was glory, Napoleon pinching the ear of one of his grenadiers. Not until about a year later did I discover delights capable of surpassing even that exalted state. I am thinking of my future passion for the soldiers of the Empire and the Musketeers.

That sense of admiration, which I have never been able clearly to define, takes with me the form of a kind of ecstasy, a lump in the throat and a tightening of the face muscles. It is more physical than spiritual, as though the object of my admiration had hypnotized me. When the fit is at its height I am no longer myself but the incarnation in my outward frame of someone else. I was truly a sergeant in the Chasseurs Alpins, decorated with a colonial medal and with an authentic lustre emanating from my small person. I forgot about my long hair, although I hated it to the point of weeping. But my father loved to paint it, and thus far it had resisted all my attacks. I would sooner have been bald.

I was constantly assailed by contradictory feelings. Where humans were concerned this always began with hate-filled mistrust. I saw nothing but faults, including physical defects. At the start of our acquaintance Raymond Aubert, the son of the local café proprietor, had a nose that was too short, over-thin lips, very small eyes, and his face as a whole expressed malice. His huge hands were those of a murderer and his flat feet gave him an ungainly walk. That was my first impression. It took all Gabrielle's persuasion to bring me to the point of allowing him to touch my clockwork train. He was fifteen years old and I was six, and he treated me like a child. But there was one thing in his favour. He never referred to my hair. At the end of a few days Raymond Aubert's nose had lost its sharpness and his mouth was normal. At the end of three weeks he was the personification of masculine beauty.

Raymond Aubert, in my eyes, was a figure of unlimited luxury. His parents, his sisters and brothers, and his home were symbols of boundless wealth. His grandfather was the proprietor of the Café des Amis at Magagnosc, a humble establishment where lovers of absinthe and Chambéry-Fraisette were accustomed to foregather of an evening. Magagnosc was a village near Grasse, its inhabitants at that time being peasants, smallholders whose wives worked in the scent distilleries. The part of Grasse in which our villa was situated was, on the other hand, a rich quarter, one without shops or peasants or, indeed, any genuine inhabitants. Its opulent dwellings were rented to strangers who passed their time in incomprehensible excursions or playing strange games, such as tennis. At Magagnosc they played *boules* and generally rode on donkeys. There were already a few motor-cars to be seen in Grasse, and my father said they poisoned the air of the district. When they drove past, Raymond Aubert would exclaim, '*Ça pue . . . à boire*' – 'That stinks . . . fit to drink.' I still don't know what he meant by it.

A peasant cottage was to let in the centre of Magagnosc, only a few yards from the Aubert café. My father decided to rent it. Once again Renoir found himself living among real human beings, people whose daily bread was directly related to their calling. One may ask why living in a middle-class suburb is so monstrous. Why is the wine-grower or chair-mender so interesting, whereas their neighbour, the notary, is such a bore? The notary is far better educated than the chair-mender. He has travelled and seen places. His conversation should be the echo of a larger world. I have often asked myself that question, but my father never bothered to ask it. He was often to be seen on the terrace of the Café des Amis, listening to the talk of his neighbours as they told about mildew discovered in their vines or a granddaughter who had just been to her first communion.

I sometimes played with the local boys. 'Do you smoke?' one of them asked. I said that I smoked chocolate cigarettes, thinking this was clever. 'You're a nit,' he said to me.

Raymond played the clarinet and his father owned a tricycle. When his father was in a good humour he would let him ride on that weird vehicle, which was still commonly used in France. 'The little queen' – the French name for the bicycle – was destined to drive it inexorably off the roads. Sometimes Monsieur Aubert would let me cling to the saddle of the tricycle while he gave me a ride. I would not have called Rothschild my brother.

I knew all the regular customers of the café and all the members of the Aubert family. The Café des Amis, with its terrace flanking the main road, the dog Médor, Tante Nanette, whose beef stew my father particularly relished – all the several fragments of that peaceful setting combined together to make me one with themselves. When my mother bore me off to Paris to go back to school I was over-whelmed with despair, but I had no idea how far my grief was justified. I was to see none of it again – the peace of Magagnosc, Père Aubert's tricycle, the slow, weighty stride of the peasants. No one will ever see those things again. The world has changed for the better and for the worse. One thing is certain, that the calm of evening has vanished from this present world of which the keynote seems to be purposeless agitation.

Guignol

When I was about five years old Gabrielle introduced me to *Guignol*, the French equivalent of the English Punch-and-Judy show. I became a passionate lover of that form of entertainment, but my fondness for it was highly selective. I did not care for the Champs-Elysées *Guignol* whose characters, clad in shimmering silks, seemed to me the expression of an effeminate luxury. My ambition in those days was to become a Napoleonic grenadier. I possessed a number of grenadiers, lead ones, of course. I called them my '*Soltats t'l'Empire*'. God alone knows why in this case I substituted 't' for 'd' – no doubt the former letter seemed to me more masculine.

My godfather was Georges Durand-Ruel, the son of the great art-dealer who is so closely linked with the history of the Impressionists. I remember my outburst of rage when, as a Christmas present, he brought me an almost life-sized Polichinelle clad in shiny satin. This was, in my view, a material that could only be worn by a girl; above all, I detested the ribbons.

As opposed to the Champs-Elysées *Guignol* the one in the Tuileries appealed to me by its greyish settings which formed a background for characters in drab garments. When I try to recall that little theatre I associate its style with the paintings of Braque and Chardin. Even now, when I pass through the town of Lyon, the quays of the Saône with their austere houses, their grey façades and the unvarying rectangle of their windows, recall the beloved Guignol of my childhood. If the town of Lyon had given nothing but the Guignol Lyonnais to the world it would have deserved for this alone to be remembered by posterity.

Guignol, who was conceived in the eighteenth century, was dressed like the artisan of his day, in a grey jacket with his hair tied back with a black ribbon. Mademoiselle Henriette wore no frills. One may wonder how she could have excited the passion of the 'doctor', the 'proprietor', the 'gendarme' and the other characters tirelessly whacked by Guignol's cudgel.

The most delightful moment was the one before the curtain went up. Its very material seemed to quiver at the sound of the accordion coming from the wings. Then came three knocks, as at the Comédie Française. Gabrielle said I got so excited that I sometimes greeted the rise of the curtain by wetting my pants. I can well believe it: even today I find that moment of suspense before the curtain rises, if the performance promises to be a good one, deliciously exciting. My father told me that he felt the same during Mozart's overture to *Don Giovanni*. For my part, I know that this sensation is the infallible sign of a masterpiece, and the one which for me falls most instantly into the diuretic class is Stravinsky's *Petrushka*.

Guignol certainly contributed to my artistic education. The one at the Tuileries at the end of the last century caused me to fear brutal contrasts. At the beginning of my career in the cinema I exaggerated these contrasts. It was a mistake, not the kind of cinema that suited me. Guignol also endowed me with a fondness for simple tales and a profound mistrust for what is generally called psychology.

I was about nine when my second meeting with the cinema occurred. I was a pupil at the school of Sainte-Marie de Monceau. The head of the school invited us every

Sunday to a film display in the parlour, of which the shutters were closed to obtain the requisite darkness. The projectionist was a gentleman with a large moustache who wore a long grey overall and a bowler-hat that seemed to be glued to his head – it was impossible to imagine him without it. He set up his machine at one end of the room and hung a white screen at the other. The music-master, wearing a flowing bow tie, played the piano. I do not remember to what order the monks who taught at Sainte-Marie belonged, but in their selection of programmes they displayed a taste foreshadowing that of the Surrealists – a third of a century ahead of them.

The part of the performance which we awaited most eagerly was a short film played by a burlesque comedian known as Automaboul. Automaboul wore a goatskin of which the hair had been starched, so that he looked like a hedgehog. His face was hidden behind huge spectacles and surmounted by a magnificent cap. The films were always more or less the same and we never wearied of them. Automaboul entered a field where there was a ramshackle car. He tried to start it, but without success. The car would only start when he had given up trying. His attempts were accompanied by a variety of explosions, shuddering on the part of the car, backward starts when he wanted it to go forward and so on. These happenings very effectively placed Automaboul in a world of magic inasmuch as, the film being silent, the most resounding explosions could only be represented by the smoke and flames pouring out of the machine. I don't know if Automaboul would delight me as much today as he did when I was a child, but however that may be, one of the ambitions I never achieved, when I myself became a maker of films, was to make 'shorts' based on mechanical jokes. Life is a tissue of dis-appointments. Certain colleagues whom I admire and envy realized that dream, among them René Clair and Mack Sennett.

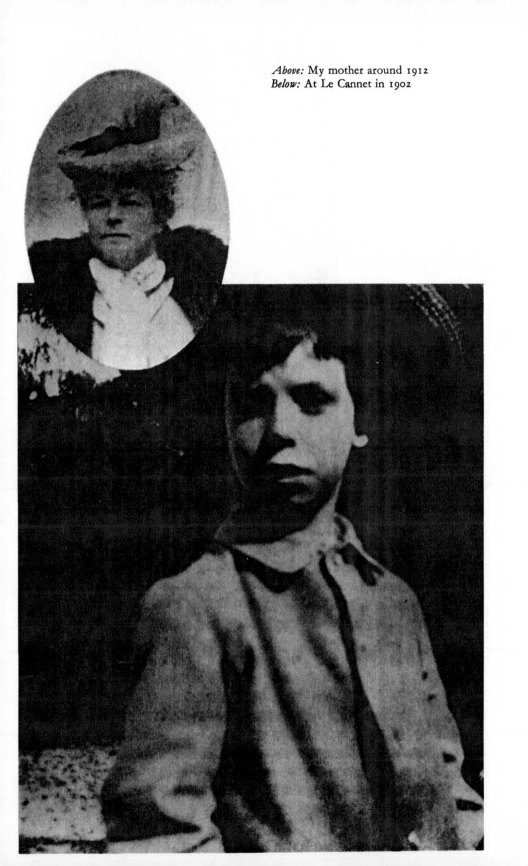

Above: My mother around 1912
Below: At Le Cannet in 1902

Above: Making my camel's
coat
Below: Gabrielle

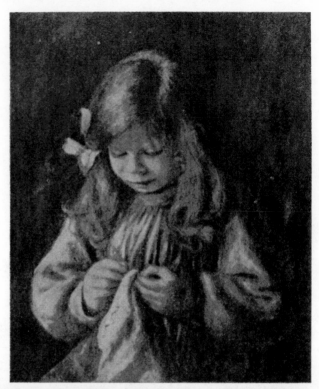

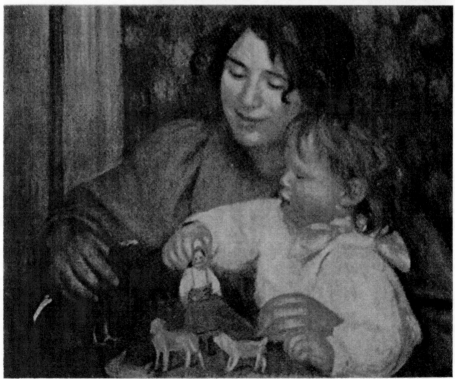

The Musketeers

To the '*Soltats t'l'Empire*' were added the Musketeers. I discovered Alexandre Dumas when I was about ten. I am still discovering him. The Musketeers restored the dignity of long hair – it is impossible to imagine d'Artagnan with a crew-cut.

But the Musketeers were not merely a matter of hair: first and foremost they were an affair of honour. Without putting it into words, I went through life saying to myself, 'I am a man of honour.' I walked the streets in search of orphans to be saved and travellers in danger, attacked by bandits whom I drove off with magnificent flourishes of my sword. Under my breath I repeated the defiance of Gauthier d'Aulney, the hero of Dumas' melodrama, *La Tour de Nesle*. Confronting a gang of footpads, he cried: 'Ten ruffians against one gentleman – that's five too many!' But all that was outward show, a display of heroism and lordly gesture. Inwardly, and not far below the surface, I remained a complete coward. Explosions terrified me. On July 14 I ran away from the street-boys' fire-crackers and hid behind the closed door of my bedroom.

It was Gabrielle who taught me to adore melodrama. This kind of show had been driven out of the fashionable theatres by the psychological drama. Oh, Freud, what crimes have been committed in thy name! No longer acceptable at the Vaudeville or the Théâtres du Gymnase, de la Renaissance, de la Porte Saint-Martin, etc., the melodrama of the Boulevard du Crime continued to draw floods of tears from the audiences in the few theatres that remained faithful to it, among them the Théâtre Montmartre. This last, which later went intellectual and changed its name to the Théâtre de l'Atelier, was near my parents' home. The 'Boulevard du Crime' was the name bestowed on the part of the boulevards where the Place de la République is now situated. Nearly all the theatres in Paris were situated in a stretch of half a kilometre. The most popular pieces were bloodthirsty melodramas – hence the name, Boulevard du Crime.

Among those which most impressed me I must cite *Le Bossu, Henri III et sa Cour, La Tour de Nesle, Les Deux Orphelines, Les Deux Gosses, Le Fils du Diable, ou les Trois Hommes Rouges* and above all *Jack Sheppard, ou les Chevaliers du Brouillard*. Gabrielle and I must have seen that last piece half-a-dozen times, and we were always carried away by the huge burst of laughter from the audience at the conclusion of the following scene: Jack Sheppard has been brought up by child-stealers who have taught him only one thing in life, the art of picking pockets. In the course of the plot he is adopted by an honest, well-meaning old woman who sends him out one day to do the shopping. He comes back loaded with supplies, but when he gives the old woman the change she finds that it amounts to more than she gave him. The delight of the audience was shared by Gabrielle and me.

The settings of *Jack Sheppard* impressed me by their romantic unreality, notably the Thames Embankment where the effect of fog was achieved by veils let down from the flies. The costumes and props, like the scenery, were parts of a whole, belonging, with the actors, to a world that was clearly make-believe but which nevertheless possessed the quality essential to any work of art, namely unity. I realize now that the effect of those melodramas on the public was produced chiefly by the dialogue. The following is one of the lines that most moved me, taken from *Les Deux Orphelines*. One of the orphan girls is held prisoner by a family of lawless ruffians, wretches whose function in the romantic theatre is to depict absolute evil. They murder and do no work, beg and get their living by foul play. They do not practise rape, however, for the romantic theatre was pure: the disgrace of sexual debauchery was reserved for the great lords of pre-revolutionary days, and even these were exceptional and traitors to their class. There are two brothers in the orphan's 'family', one a vicious brute who beats and starves her, the other a cripple who is madly in love with her and ready to protect her at the risk of his life. When the wicked brother threatens the girl, the good one snatches up a huge kitchen knife and drives him back. The bad one says – and this is where my quotation comes in – 'You wouldn't dare.' The good brother's reply is to turn and address the audience: 'He knows the secret of my soul and he wonders if I would dare!' At this challenge, delivered in vibrant tones, the audience, seized with intense emotion, remained silent for some moments: then it burst into wild applause.

We have moved a long way from realism, and that fashion of bringing the public into the play was the forerunner of the audacities of modern stage direction. But in those days there was no director. An experienced actor advised his fellow-players, showing them how to achieve the best effect and advising them where to stand so as to catch the light. This way of doing things was childish in its simplicity. The floats and footlights provided most of the lighting. Small individual spotlights were unknown. There were virtually no scenic effects or contrasts. What would seem to us today a grey drabness was quite enough for the lover of that kind of show.

Superior minds regard this kind of theatre as 'false'. They have replaced it with the so-called realistic theatre, which to my mind is as false as the theatre of romanticism.

Godefer's Shoes

Most people associate the stages of their lives with events –
'It was the year Lindbergh flew the Atlantic . . . The year of
the Exhibition . . . The year the talkies came in.' But my
calendar is related to friends. Every period of my life has
been dominated by the figure of a friend.

I am not referring to my father and mother. Their influence was exercised in spite of school, in spite of con-
vention and the whole framework of lies which encompasses
our lives. Nor am I referring to Gabrielle, my beloved
Bibon, who for me was the criterion of everything that was
good. For me my native land was summarized by Gabrielle;
beauty was her steadfast face, which I find even firmer in my
father's paintings than it was in life.

Then there was Godefer. I saw him at Essoyes every
summer. His father was a farm labourer and very poor.
Godefer shared a wooden shack with a dozen brothers
and sisters. Every so often the police poked their noses
in and declared that it must be evacuated for sanitary
reasons.

Godefer's great ambition was to wear a pair of shoes. Not
to own a pair, but simply for a few hours of a single day to
know the glorious sensation of being 'rich'. He said to me:
'Ask your father. He thinks well of me.' I tried to explain to
him that the rich were not necessarily smothered in bank-
notes, and he said: 'If you're really rich you must have
pennies.' . . . 'I haven't got any pennies,' I said . . . 'Well
then, shillings.' And I had to admit defeat.

It was I who profited by our exchanges. Godefer gave

me numerous presents and I gave him nothing. For instance, he taught me how to make a sling and how to use it to break window-panes. Having a respect for property, my exploits were confined to the family windows. He taught me how to climb a fence without being seen and steal chickens from farmyards, but I must confess that when it came to this latter operation he failed completely.

On one occasion, to square the debt between us, I gave him a pair of new shoes which my mother had just bought me. I had not yet worn them. Godefer instantly went and displayed them in the Place de l'Eglise, where honest citizens promptly persuaded him to return them to their rightful owner. 'In any case,' they said, 'they'll only make his feet sore.' This incident caused me to be classed among the eccentrics of the neighbourhood like Clampin the satyr, Bordaloue the drummer, and P'tit Duc, the freshwater poacher.

In talking to Godefer we used the local patois, an expressive language which the young people of today no longer understand. One phrase remains fixed in my mind. Godefer would arrange to meet me with the words, '*Valton. En bas les bouchots,*' which simply meant, 'By the tree-trunk under the willows.'

Godefer knew the ways of the river-pike. He knew their secret paths and the tunnels of swirling greenery in which the small fry they lived on flowed into their mouths. P'tit Duc the poacher, Lord of the river under God, tolerated his competition, and from time to time Godefer, to keep in his good graces, would tell him where a plump prey was to be found. Godefer came for me in the early morning, whistled three times and waited for me in the street. We went down to the river and chose one of the moored boats – padlocks held no secrets for Godefer. We lay flat on the bottom and let the boat drift with the stream. It was wonderful, as wonderful as the rise of the Guignol curtain.

Gabrielle knew of these expeditions and did not approve. She was afraid I would get drowned. She was awakened one morning by Godefer's whistle, which was perhaps a little more piercing than usual. Without bothering to put on a petticoat, she ran to the front door and stood in her night-dress beckoning to us to come back. Then she called my mother who organized a round-up. We were captured and Godefer was sent home. I never saw him again. My mother was generous and Godefer père did not want to offend this source of alms.

An Actor Named Charlot

The event which most greatly influenced the Frenchmen of
my generation was the First World War. It is doubtful
whether western civilization will survive its present madness, but if our species does not wholly disappear, and if
historians still exist a few centuries hence, they will be able
to divide the chronicle of our time into two stages – before
and after 1914. For me that war marked a considerable
diminution of the influence of the Musketeers and the
'*Soltats t'l'Empire*'. My break with those symbols was, however, only a partial one, and I am bound to confess that it is
not yet quite complete. Where I am concerned, that war
taught me the creed of man for himself, man starkly
naked, stripped of all romantic trappings. Those who were
educated in that school of total discomfort, wet feet, cold
stew and infrequent sleep, will have learnt that our social
values are of very little worth. One soon learns that a comfortable bed after one has got outside a good steak and
chips is nearer to reality than a bank account. The motherland and the national honour are noble ideals, but to someone crouching in the bottom of a trench they are not worth
a pair of dry boots.

My friends during the war did not wear swords hanging
at their side like the Musketeers, or bearskin caps like
Napoleon's grenadiers. Their language was simple, with
none of the picturesqueness favoured by the reporters behind the lines. I never heard the word *poilu* used in the
trenches, or the word *Boche*. We referred to the Germans as
'*Fritz*', and they gradually became '*les Fridolins*'.

My time in the trenches was cut short by a German bullet. I was wounded in the leg, and this had a great influence on me. I was destined to limp for the rest of my life. Paradoxically, I consider this an advantage. A person who limps does not see life in the same way as someone who does not limp. But I directed films as much with my legs as with my head, and the result of that wound, which never healed, was that four years ago, at the age of seventy-five, I had to abandon a career which, to my mind, was only just beginning.

After vicissitudes I found myself in a bomber squadron where I became friendly with a remarkable young man. He was the son of the celebrated Professor Richet, Nobel Prizewinner and the discoverer of anaphylaxis. My fellow-members of the squadron and I were blind admirers of Professor Richet. None of us knew what anaphylaxis was.

Upon his return from leave Richet said to me: 'My father took me to see a film made by a remarkable actor. He says it's the best thing he has seen for many years, and he rates this actor higher than Sarah Bernhardt and Lucien Guitry. His name's Charlot.' Richet went on to say that Charlot had restored to the art of the cinema a simplicity in these days forgotten, concentrating upon the basic emotions of fear, hunger, envy, joy and sadness.

On my next leave I went to Paris determined to see a Charlot film. But first I called on my elder brother, Pierre, whom I had not seen since the beginning of the war. He had had his arm smashed by a German bullet and had been demobilized. Professor Gosset, a surgeon of genius, was trying to restore the partial use of his right hand by bone-grafts taken from other parts of his body. Pierre was in great pain, but he never complained. He hoped, thanks to Gosset's skill, to be able to resume his career as an actor.

In the end they devised a special apparatus to support his arm. He learnt to know the movements which betrayed his infirmity and to avoid them.

He was married to the actress Vera Sergine. Scarcely had I taken off my cap and greatcoat than he asked me, 'Have you seen Charlot?' I told him what Professor Richet had said. 'That doesn't surprise me,' said Pierre. 'Greatness attracts greatness' – and we went to see a Charlot 'short' in a little cinema near the Place des Ternes. To say that I was enthusiastic would be inadequate. I was carried away. The genius of Charlot had been revealed to me.

The name of 'Charlot' was the one by which Charlie Chaplin was known to most Frenchmen. It was years before I learnt my idol's real name, which was eventually told me by a Scotch officer on a leave train. He also introduced me to his native whisky, and the two discoveries gave me equal pleasure.

When my leave was over I rejoined my squadron and learnt that in response to my request I had been transferred to the flying-school at Amberieu to take a pilot's course. Hitherto I had been only an observer, which I had not enjoyed at all. I was in love with machinery, and to be ferried about in the air by another man gave me a feeling of being shown a toy which I was not allowed to play with. Toys are only interesting if one can take them to pieces.

At the end of my course I underwent my pilot's test and was turned down: I weighed five kilos too much. I subjected myself to a week's diet which was the more painful because I was naturally greedy: I enjoyed wine even more than good food. I shall never forget that wretched week; but I was rewarded by passing my test with honours. On the same evening I gorged myself with sauerkraut washed down with

Alsatian wine. I was posted to a reconnaissance squadron with which I remained until a bad landing put an end to my career as a flier. French aviation lost little by this. I was not a very good pilot.

After several temporary postings I was sent back to base. My new duties kept me in Paris and allowed me plenty of spare time. I had not forgotten Charlot. I saw every film of his that was shown in Paris again and again, and my love of him did not grow less. I began to be interested in other films and became a fanatical cinema fan. Charlie Chaplin had converted me. I reached the point of seeing three feature films a day, two in the afternoon and one in the evening. The cinema was beckoning to me.

I shall always remember an afternoon session in a boulevard cinema called Parisiana. It had once been a successful café-concert where such stars as Spinelli had appeared. I had gone there to see an American film, preferring to avoid French films, which were too intellectual for my taste. I was the only person there, or at least I thought I was; but after some minutes I had a feeling that someone else was seated not far away from me. I stood up, resolved to get to the bottom of the mystery. The film was about the ghost of a murdered woman who haunted her murderers. They hid in the most unlikely places but the ghost invariably found them. I half expected to encounter some denizen of the other world; but instead I found a large rat crouched on a seat apparently following the performance. It was startled by me and fled. I went back to my ghost.

D. W. Griffith

This period of my discovery of the cinema occurred before I met Catherine Hessling, my future wife. My heart was free and ready to be given. It was given to the cinema, but of course only as a spectator. I would not have dared to suppose that I might join that company of demi-gods who brought life to the world's film-screens. I worshipped the actors, and still more the actresses. I dreamed of Pearl White, Mary Pickford, Lilian Gish, Douglas Fairbanks and William Hart, and it did not occur to me that actors and actresses, male and female, were the living embodiment of the musketeers and grenadiers of my childhood. Old-fashioned melodrama was cunningly undermining its conquerors, the discursive plays and drawing-room comedies, the boulevard-theatre in general. Literary theatre occupied the centre of the road, but the cloak-and-dagger heroes were not done for and only awaited their chance to come out of hiding. This chance was what the American cinema gave them. The cowboy was a reincarnation of the Royal Musketeer, that was all. It was this direct descent from the Boulevard du Crime, more than its novelty, that ensured the triumph of the cinematograph.

I soon began to realize that in addition to the talent and physical appearance of the actors there had to be someone who put the whole thing together, devised the settings and probably instructed the players. My brother Pierre told me that this was the director.

Pierre was a stage actor, successful in the boulevard plays which I so abominated. He was a wise man. His view was that an actor must act even if the play is not to his taste. As for the French cinema, his opinion of it could be summed up in a very few words – it didn't exist. 'The cinema doesn't suit us,' he said. 'Our burden of literature and drama is too heavy for us to follow that particular line. We must leave cinema to the Americans.' And he concluded: 'French dramatic art is bourgeois, whereas the American cinema is essentially working-class. Between ourselves, I envy my colleagues over there who have that kind of public to work for – Irish or Italian immigrants who scarcely know how to read.' The Boulevard du Crime public of the beginning of the nineteenth century must have been like the American silent film public. They adored figures of heroism, and would have taken no interest in our realistic reproductions of daily life.

I began to note differences of style in the films made by different directors. It was a new stage in my development. I followed the work of Griffith with intense interest. The marvel of marvels was the close-up. I have never changed my opinion about this. Certain close-ups of Lilian Gish, of Mary Pickford and of Greta Garbo are imprinted on my memory for life. The enlargement enables us to delight in the texture of the skin, and a slight quivering of the lip tells us something about the inward life of the idealized woman. I am ready to bear with the most tedious film if it gives me a close-up of an actress I like. And in my passion for the close-up I have sometimes inserted perfectly irrelevant sequences in my films simply because they allowed me scope for a really good one.

The first ones I saw were in films by Griffith. Twenty-five years later I was to meet him in Hollywood. I found myself confronted by a very well-preserved elderly man. His excellent state of physical and mental health caused him to resent the way the studios neglected him. Hollywood wanted no more of him. The strictly commercial period was at its peak and the industry had no use for an individualist such as he. This attitude on the part of a town which he had partly created greatly distressed him. His had been the first films to go beyond the limits of the fairground booth. From the technical point of view we owe him something like the 'reinvention' of the cinema and its complete separation from the theatre.

This visionary who had created a new art-form was a bitter man, and I can understand why. A group of Hollywood producers decided to hold a banquet in his honour. At the end of the meal he was invited in the traditional manner to make a short speech. He stood up and, contemplating the assembled tycoons, he spoke as follows: 'Can anyone here lend me five dollars?' Then he sat down, while the orchestra burst into light music.

I had the good fortune to see him frequently before his death, either in my own home, where he sometimes came to dine, or in that of Lilian Gish, with whom he remained on terms of close friendship.

Catherine

Happy is the man who, knowing nothing about the cinema, is content to admire other men's films: it is restful, but only provided he has not himself tasted the forbidden fruit. The cinema has brought me many setbacks and disappointments, but the happiness it has given me far outweighs the miseries. If it was all to do again, I would again make films.

I met the future Catherine Hessling during a leave which I spent at Les Collettes, the property near Nice owned by my parents. Her name in those days was Dédée. She was the last present given to my father by my mother before her death. My father was looking for a blonde model for his big painting, *Baigneuses*. My mother applied to the Nice Académie de Peinture and discovered Dédée. Then she died, of diabetes according to the doctors; but I knew that she had died of the nervous strain of a journey to the front after I had been seriously wounded and conveyed to a hospital close behind the lines.

Dédée came from Nice by train every morning except Sunday, and her arrival was like the touch of a magic wand. My mother's death had plunged the house and its inmates into a state of utter gloom. Despite her corpulence, my mother was the soul of gaiety. Everything grew bright around her and while she was alive Les Collettes could be seen as a symbol of quiet happiness. With her departure the gaiety had fled, and with the arrival of Dédée it was restored. Dédée adored my father, who returned her love. In the morning she would come dancing into the studio where he awaited her, and while she made herself ready to pose she would sing popular songs at the top of her voice. This delighted Renoir, who maintained that a house without song was a sepulchre. After his death in 1919 I married Dédée. Our shared passion for the cinema played a large part in our decision to link our lives together. Only when she had decided to become a film-actress did it occur to us that she should have a stage name. We chose Catherine Hessling. I forget why.

My father wanted me to go in for pottery. He had installed a studio and an oven for me and my younger brother Claude (the 'Coco' of the pictures) in an old building a few yards from our house. Dédée, it goes without saying, was part of the scheme. Renoir thought her very gifted, and hoped that we would work together in modelling and decorating useful objects. He had no use for callings in which the hands played no part. He mistrusted intellectuals. 'They poison the world. They don't know how to see or hear or touch.' The painter, Albert André, and his wife, Maleck, joined Dédée and me in this enterprise. Albert André had been like another son to my father.

At Renoir's wish we did everything by hand. We got our clay out of fields where the soil looked to us particularly heavy and mixed it with sand which we got from the bed of a stream. Then came the spinning. Our wheel was an old-fashioned one operated by a treadle. The baking was done in a wood-oven and took ten hours. In the evenings, while keeping a check on the temperature of the oven by means of a small hole bored in the door, we listened to records and ate *pissalat*. This is an old Provençal dish composed of anchovies steeped in olive oil, but the most important part of the meal was the bread, good black country bread, and the wine, which came from our own vine.

Dreaming of *The Three Musketeers*

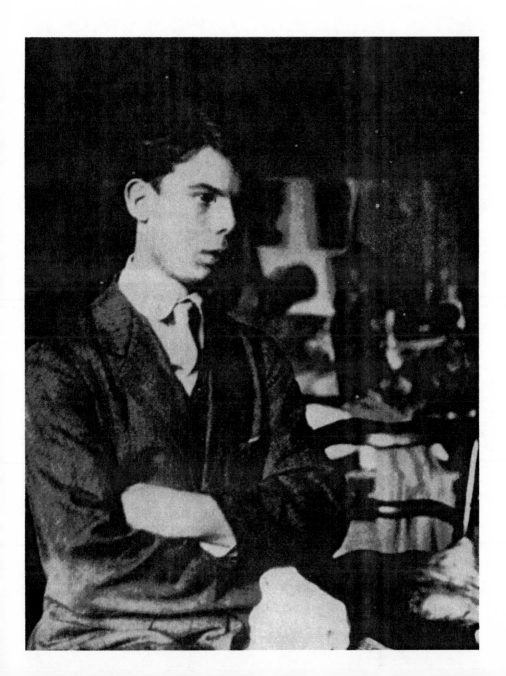

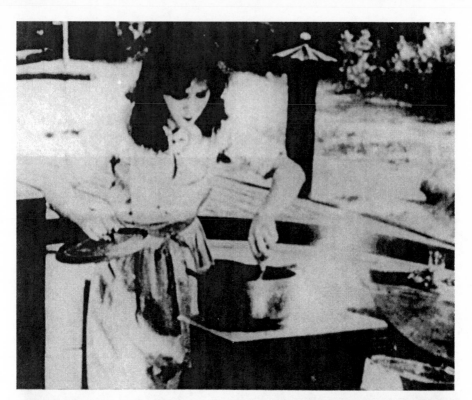

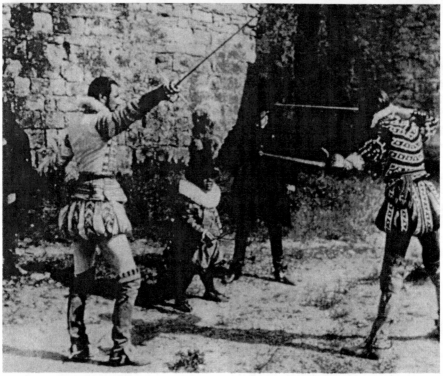

Above: Catherine Hessling in *La Fille de l'Eau*, 1924   **49**
Below: Le Tournoi dans le Cité, 1928: one of my
rare costume films

Dédée and I continued for some years to live at Les
Collettes after we were married. It is there that our son
Alain was born. I met Pierre Champagne there and also the
writer Basset, who was living in Nice and who taught me
to know Dostoievsky. In the company of that gentle genius
I entered a new world, seeing Prince Mishkin at every
street corner. Basset's life was punctuated with quotations
from Raskolnikoff. He called himself Dimitri after the hero
of *The Brothers Karamazov* and he had christened his dog
Grouchégnka – a charming fox-terrier bitch with an expression of perfect bourgeois calm, quite unaware of the
associations of the name her master had given her.

Our love of the cinema drew Dédée and me inexorably
into that calling. Dédée was very beautiful. Everyone told
her this, and it was difficult for her to ignore it. We went to
the cinema nearly every day, to the point that we had come
to live in the unreal world of the American film. It may be
added that Dédée belonged to the same class of woman as
the stars whose appearance we followed on the screen. She
copied their behaviour and dressed herself like them.
People stopped her in the street to ask if they had not seen
her in some particular film, always an American film. We
thought nothing of the French cinema. So it was very easy
for us to believe that Dédée had only to show herself to be
accepted as another Gloria Swanson or Mae Murray or
Mary Pickford. I called upon the help of my friend Pierre
Lestringuez, who was a writer and had contacts in the
cinema. As for myself, I was resolved to have no part in the
business except on the financial side. This was to prove
disastrous.

I must insist on the fact that I set foot in the world of the
cinema only in order to make my wife a star, intending,

once this was done, to return to my pottery studio. I did not foresee that once I had been caught in the machinery I should never be able to escape. If anyone had told me that I was to devote all my money and all my energies to the making of films I should have been amazed.

Since the stories proposed by Lestringuez did not satisfy Catherine, I myself came up with a little tale that reflected all my admiration for American films. Catherine played the part of an innocent young girl pursued by a villain. I trust that no trace still lingers of that masterpiece of banality. Albert Dieudonné, who played Napoleon in the Abel Gance film, agreed to direct it. It was a total failure. Proudly entitled *Catherine*, it was never shown in any cinema. I had no artistic pretensions, but all the same I was disappointed. I hasten to acknowledge that Dieudonné did his utmost to make me see reason. None so deaf as he who will not hear.

The bug of film-directing had now taken root in me and there was no resisting it. I felt the need to express myself through the ingenuity of my own products, whether they were china vases or films. Catherine and I decided to embark upon a new venture – *La Fille de l'Eau*.

Later I was often to think nostalgically of our tranquil life at Les Collettes under the big olive-trees, and the good smell of wood smoke that accompanied our work. Dédée, pressed against me, would look up at the stars, and we would rejoice together in the contemplation of limpid skies. In Paris one seldom looks at the stars.

For Catherine and me the cinema was a medium of expression that deserved a life of its own. We felt in those days that it was worthy of something better than the business of reproducing literary and stage works, which was all that most audiences expected of it. The actors in the early French films, to my mind, were hammy. There were, of course, exceptions, the films of Abel Gance, Louis Delluc and the admirable Max Linder, and the productions of Feuillade – in a word, there were masterpieces. But the run-of-the-mill cinema, the daily offering to the masses, was nothing but a popularization of the *théâtre du boulevard* or the Porte Saint-Martin style of melodrama. Catherine and I dreamed of developing a French cinema free of all theatrical or literary encumbrances. We also hoped to foster an American style of action, derived more from the direct observation of nature than the French style was.

I was to discover in the course of my career that bad acting is the same the whole world over and that when an actor has talent, this too is universal. In the course of my experience as a director I was also to learn that there is no such thing as over-acting: an actor plays 'false' or he plays 'true'. If he plays true he may allow himself all manner of exaggeration. It has often happened that, delighted with an actor's performance, I have urged him to go to the limit without worrying about being called a 'ham'.

I was principally concerned with the pictorial aspect, and in this was well served by Catherine Hessling. Her success would have been dazzling if it had been less of a novelty. The public is scared of novelty. One has to use cunning to induce them to swallow it, disguise it under the semblance of the commonplace. Catherine's acting was a form of mime. She had taken a great many dancing lessons and her body possessed a professional suppleness. With her we had conceived a mode of expressing the emotions which had more to do with dancing than with the cinema. I had got it into my head, and into her head, that since the moving picture depended on the jerks of a Maltese cross it must be played jerkily. I also thought that the photography of French films was too soft. I wanted films based photographically on sharp contrasts. I went so far as to restrict Catherine's make-up to an extremely thick white base, with all the other tints rendered in black, including the pinks and reds. Her mouth and eyes were made completely black. She became a kind of puppet – a puppet of genius, be it said – entirely black and white. I thought: 'Since the cinema is black and white, why photograph other colours?'

While we were making the film *Catherine*, of which I was the producer but not the director, I could not restrain myself from constantly interfering with the director. Dieudonné needed the patience of a saint to put up with the two of us, Catherine and me. I made experiments with our second cameraman, Bachelet. I had a notion that the monstrous enlargement of details would help the viewer to enter a dream world.

My greatest success in this line was the realization of my childhood dream, making a close-up of a lizard fill the screen, so that it looked like a ferocious crocodile. As you know, I had always had a weakness for crocodiles. I have it still. My son has inherited this passion, which certainly originated with Gabrielle. When he was five years old and I was entertaining guests, he appeared holding a lizard in each hand, with a blind-worm draped round his neck and a frog on his head. He explained the performance by saying: 'I am the friend of animals.' But for '*bêtes*' he said '*bêdes*'. This confusion of 'd' and 't' is, as you see, hereditary in our family: but whereas he preferred the former, I prefer the latter.

Those enlargements of mine were in fact an attempt to

escape from photographic realism. The fairy-tale took its place alongside the Musketeers and the *'Soltats t'l'Empire'*. The realization of this was to lead me to what is still my greatest aspiration, the discovery of magical elements in the most commonplace circumstances and settings.

In Search of a Grammar

La Fille de l'Eau was born in 1924 of the strange juxta-position of Catherine Hessling and the Forest of Fontaine-bleau. I· had a house at Marlotte, on the edge of the forest, and Catherine and I together discovered the enchantment of that mysterious countryside. The trees in the Forest of Fontainebleau are of course real trees; nevertheless they provide a background of disturbing unreality, especially the beeches with their straight trunks rising to the ceiling of the forest in a bluish light. One might be at the bottom of the sea, surrounded by the masts of sunken ships.

It was in this setting that I filmed a part of the dream of *La Fille de l'Eau*. One day a party of walkers caught me in the act of hanging Pierre Champagne by his feet from the branch of a tree. One of them asked me: 'What are you filming there?' . . . 'It's a dream,' I replied. . . . 'A dream!' he exclaimed in astonishment. 'Well, why don't you fake it?' He could not understand the use of physical means for filming a dream.

Oddly enough, the mysterious quality of that splendid setting taught me that I could do very well without it. To a film-director who will take the trouble to use his eyes, everything that constitutes our lives has its magical aspect. A métro-station can be as mysterious as a haunted castle. I think I now have a better understanding of the relation-ship between the film-maker and the viewer. The latter is grateful to the former for having shown him that the stair-way in his house may lead to the castle of the Sleeping Beauty.

La Fille de l'Eau was a tale without literary importance. Lestringuez and I had devised the scenario to display Catherine Hessling's photogenic qualities, in which we were helped by the magic of the Forest of Fontainebleau. The plot was a secondary consideration, simply a pretext for purely visual imagery. We were doing battle with the attitude of the intellectuals, who give first priority to the theme and consider the content more important than the container. They admire Géricault's *Raft of the Medusa* but for the wrong reasons. It is a magnificent painting, but few people realize that its greatness arises out of a balanced symphony of form and colour. What it depicts is of secondary importance. What matters is that its creator wholly expressed himself, giving himself to the subject with a sort of exaltation.

A work of art is only worthy of the name if it offers the beholder the chance of uniting with the creator. To gaze at the *Raft of the Medusa* is like having a conversation with Géricault. The rest, in particular the account of the situation, is simply literature. It is the same with art as with life. One enjoys a story because one is in sympathy with the story-teller. The same tale, told by someone else, would be of no interest. André Gide has summed it up in a very few words: 'In art all that matters is the form.'

In the dream of *La Fille de l'Eau*, and later in *La Petite Marchande d'Allumettes* (The Little Match-girl) I really let myself go: shots with the camera turning in reverse, characters suddenly appearing, Catherine riding a horse galloping through the clouds, and above all Catherine's fall through the sky, which was particularly successful.

I had made those two films with the simplest possible technical appliances. At that time superimpositions were not yet done in the laboratory. Objects had to be photo-graphed directly against the background. On a large stage in the Gaumont studio at Buttes-Chaumont I had had a canvas cylinder some twenty metres in diameter constructed. The interior of the cylinder was painted jet black, as was the floor. Catherine was dressed in white and mounted on a white horse. She had to gallop against this black back-ground, far enough away from it to avoid casting a shadow. The camera, installed in the centre of the cylinder on a rotating platform, followed the gallop in a perfect pan shot. The whole thing was done in two stages on the same film. First Catherine was photographed on her horse, and then, without the film having been developed, a background of clouds was photographed.

Devices of this kind delighted me, and they delighted the little troupe, partly composed of amateurs, which I had collected for the purpose of 'renovating' the French cinema. The cameramen, Gibory and Bachelet, and some of the technicians were professionals. Most of the actors were my personal friends. My friend Pierre Champagne saw to the transport of the photographic equipment. His wife, Mimi, and Catherine made the costumes.

I went into the film business with very definite ideas. I did not believe in the importance of the subject-matter. I recognized the necessity for it, but denied it the privilege of influencing the course of the narrative. What mattered to me was a fine close-up. It so happened that if they were to accept a close-up the public had to be given a story. I bowed to the necessity, but with reluctance. Needless to say, I was firmly opposed to the adaptation of literary works for the screen. 'We'll have nothing to do with that,' we said. A crazy resolution.

I believed in improvisation in the studio or on location, and I still do. The human imagination is dangerously limited. It tends to resort to nothing but clichés. Direct contact with the actors, the scenery and the props is what opens our eyes to aspects which we did not foresee. At the same time I was afraid, and still am, of photographing Nature as it is. I think one has to look very hard, and by means of camera-angles and lighting enlarge the significance of a setting, a countryside or a human face.

Rapid cutting fascinated me. Some of the shots in *La Fille de l'Eau* consisted of no more than five frames. The dazed audience feels as though it has been hit in the eye. I was not the only person to practise this kind of editing. Abel Gance used it superbly in his *Napoléon*. Editing of this sort, as well as distorted images, generally from below looking up, must have been in the air at the time, because his use of them coincided with that of the Russians, without anything having been concerted between them. Rapid cutting is simply an attempt to convey the speed of the actor's reactions by the speed of the picture: by repeating the actor's expression in short jerks one can give an impression of intensity. This device did not last long and was confined to a few so-called avant-garde productions. It was in any case only one aspect of the conflict between the artificial and the natural, and it was to make a brilliant reappearance half a century later in American television variety programmes such as 'Laugh-In'. I was soon to give up this kind of experiment, and I now consider that the best editing is the kind that is not noticed. I think the best camera-angle is that determined by the height of an average human being. In a close-up the lens should be level with the performer's eye.

My approach to the business of acting was precisely the opposite of what it later became. I wanted the actors to be simply automatons, giving nothing to the film except their physical appearance. I refused to allow them any emotion. What they called 'feeling' a part seemed to me nothing but a pretext for stagey grimacing. I shall always remember my absurd meddling with a particular close-up of Catherine. Despite my injunctions, that true actress, moved by the situation, shed real tears. I stopped the camera, sent her off to repair her make-up, and re-shot the close-up with glycerine tears.

The laboratory work fascinated me. I enjoyed following the different stages in the development of my films. I soon discovered that by suitable adjustment an outdoor scene shot on a grey day could give splendid night effects. This was the method I used later in *La Nuit du Carrefour*. Bit by bit the camera was to teach me that I must submit to the law which has governed every philosopher known to history, from Aristotle onwards – that of the happy medium. It is easily exemplified in photography. Jet black can only be used to produce certain definite effects. The same is true of pure white: a very bright light destroys other lights.

I considered that the world, and especially that of the cinema, was encumbered with false gods. It was my task to overthrow them, and, sword in hand, I was ready to devote my life to it. But the false gods are still there. My persistence during half a century of film-making may perhaps have shaken one or two. But it has also taught me that not all the gods were false and that some did not deserve to be shaken.

One false god which remains omnipotent is that which is known as 'good taste', which in fact is nothing but a taste for mediocrity. Society opposes every attempt at novelty in the name of good taste. My friends and I sturdily aligned ourselves on the side of bad taste. Other expressions exasperated us – for instance, 'It's exaggerated,' which simply expressed people's embarrassment at being confronted with something which was beyond them.

As opposed to the terror of exaggeration there was the fatuous approval of false realism. With Lestringuez we invented a word which summed up all these attitudes. It was '*hostellerie*' (pronounced hosse-tellerie). In the theatre it could be applied to the actor who, when playing a countryman, adopted a provincial mode of speech to make it sound more natural. The wine waiter, clad in a blue smock and with a mock cellar-key slung round his neck, who serves you wine out of an imitation antique flagon is *hostellerie*. The modern fortified castle with a drawbridge built by a retired tradesman is *hostellerie*: as a rule the guard-tower houses a lavatory.

But the most solidly installed false god, public enemy number one, is the cliché. By cliché I mean an image, an opinion, a thought which has been furtively substituted for reality. There are clichés which endure for centuries. Here are a few: 'the good old man', 'love which conquers all', 'the faithful servant', 'military bravery', 'the English sense of humour', 'southerners dressed in gay colours', 'the end justifies the means'. Life teaches us that there are bad old men, that love is often conquered, that servants are not always faithful, that some soldiers are utter cowards, that there are English people totally devoid of humour, that most people living in southern parts dress in black, and that there is no end which justifies murder. I may add that the blonde and scented leading ladies on the screen have little in common with the leading ladies in real life. To fit the cliché they are bewigged with golden locks. I should like to believe that this pursuit of the cliché does not fool anyone; but alas, the public, stuffed with lies, clings to its conventions and wallows in the falsity of a world manufactured for its diversion.

Technical Tricks

Catherine Hessling's make-up in our first films is an example of the insecurity of my convictions. I abandoned my search for exaggerated contrasts, the desire to pass without transition from absolute black to the most dazzling white, on the day I discovered the existence of panchromatic film. You see how ignorant I was! I had made my first films without knowing that every cameraman in the world used orthochromatic film for interiors – that is to say, film almost without shading, of absolute black and white. But the moment they went out of doors they substituted panchromatic film which has a great many shades, so that reds, blues and yellows, all the colours of the spectrum, are conveyed by greys of varying density. The fact was that the lighting equipment of the studios dated from the earliest days of the cinema and consisted chiefly of mercury-tubes which did not suit panchromatic film. Real sunlight possesses a different quality to which its shading reacts.

It did not take me long to adapt my taste to shaded photography. My reversal was complete. I saw the possibility of close-ups of a magical softness. Unfortunately there was no system of lighting equipment suitable for panchromatic interiors, and two years went by before it occurred to me to make it myself. Jean Tedesco, the leading spirit at the Vieux Colombier avant-garde cinema, who thought this an excellent idea, came to my assistance. By this time I had made *La Fille de l'Eau, Nana, Sur un air de Charleston* and *Marquitta*. Lack of funds had already forced me to give up all ideas of financing my own productions.

An old friend of mine, Raleigh, who acted as my technical adviser, strongly supported my scheme, and Bachelet, who was now my chief cameraman, was equally enthusiastic. The problem was not difficult. We had found by experiment that panchromatic film was sensitive to the light of an ordinary bulb burning a slightly higher voltage, so it was simply a matter of adjusting the voltage.

The use of panchromatic film entirely was, for me, a step in the direction of colour film, which I was not to use until twenty years later, in *The River*. The need for panchromatic film occurred at almost the same time to the film technicians across the Atlantic, and before long they, too, were using panchromatic film for interior shots. There was no plagiarism in this: ideas spread like epidemics. The harsh contrasts of orthochromatic film were suddenly relegated to the past; they became one of our memories of the pioneering stage, along with accelerated motion to produce comic effects. This new kind of photography, because it better expressed reality, paved the way for a different kind of script and a new style of acting – in fact, for that dream of the lover of realism, the talking film.

Artistic developments are in practice the direct outcome of technical improvements. The most striking example of this known to me is the Impressionist revolution in painting. Before Impressionism painters used colours contained in small cups which were difficult to carry about. The paint ran out of them, and this made outdoor work impracticable. But after someone had had the idea of storing paint in tubes with screw tops the painters of the new school could take their colours with them and paint directly from nature. It is true that the Impressionist revolution was conceived in the minds of the painters, but it would not have taken the same form if they had not been able to take their paint-boxes into the Forest of Fontainebleau. Although it did not have all the repercussions of paint in tubes, the use of panchromatic film represented an immense forward step. Most of the screen masterpieces were made in black and white on panchromatic film.

Raleigh, my associate in this business, was a remarkable film-technician. He was an Englishman who had come to end his life in Paris. He had worked all over the place and had developed the first Mary Pickford and Douglas Fairbanks films in Hollywood. In 1912 he had come to France as the representative of American Biograph. The camera they used took a larger film than the one used by Pathé. By way of launching American Biograph, Raleigh acquired the exclusive right to film the Jeffries-Johnson boxing match. It earned him a small fortune. Just before the 1914 war he made a documentary on the French and German armies. The film was cut in halves down the middle, with the French on the left and the Germans on the right, so that the French were shown as attacking to the right and the Germans to the left.

Raleigh's reason for settling in Paris was his attitude to sex. 'The English and Americans know nothing about it,' he said. 'Here in Paris they understand it.' He was well over seventy when he said this.

He suggested that we should convert the attic of the Vieux Colombier theatre into a studio for panchromatic film. We ourselves made tin reflectors and the appropriate rheostats. Current was supplied by a generator driven by an engine taken from a damaged Farman truck. The development laboratory was set up in Raleigh's kitchen, and he himself made the wooden basins and frames. We set the scene for group shots on the stage of the Vieux Colombier.

The result was *The Little Match-girl,* a fairy-tale that came off quite well, in which Catherine Hessling was very moving and remarkable. She played Andersen's heroine in the manner of a ballet. This had always been her ambition, and I am happy to think that I helped her to realize it in that film, the last one we made together, in 1928. The close-ups, shot with our handmade material, are superb.

With *Marquitta* I reached the climax of my passion for technical innovation. I had devised a track for a moving camera which reduced the jolting that is so difficult to overcome on a system of rails. 'Zooming' was still unknown. My device was a wooden laminated track, the gaps between the sections being carefully smoothed with sandpaper. The planks were waxed. The camera was mounted on a chassis of which the wheels had been replaced by cushions. The results were highly satisfactory. It needed only the touch of a finger to move the camera along the track, and by widening the track astonishing effects could be achieved. This contrivance, which delighted Jean Bachelet, was despised by most film-technicians, perhaps because it was so out of keeping with the aesthetics of film apparatus. There was also the fact that the studios insisted on using their own equipment. Moreover, the machinists were accustomed to the railway system, and this kind of cushioned carpentry seemed to them ridiculous.

Another of my notions was a scheme for presenting the actors against a miniature background. I worked it in *The Little Match-girl.* The method was to photograph the miniature setting in a mirror. The actors had to stay in positions carefully decided in advance. The part of the mirror backing corresponding to these positions were scratched out. The

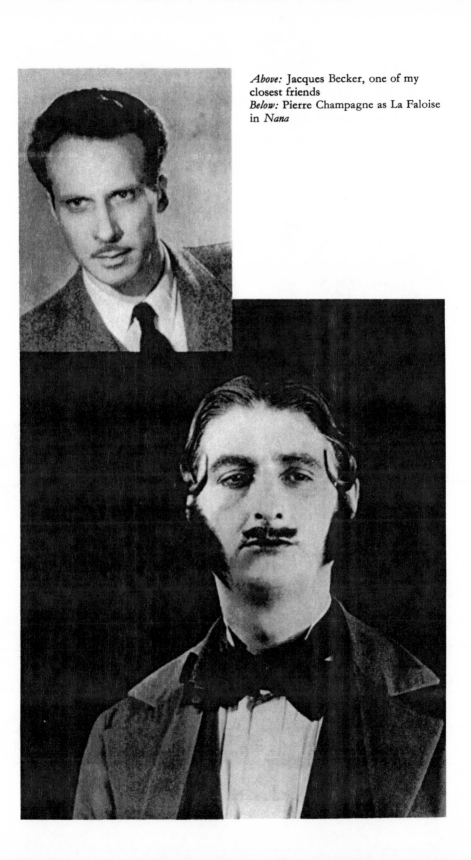

Above: Jacques Becker, one of my closest friends
Below: Pierre Champagne as La Faloise in *Nana*

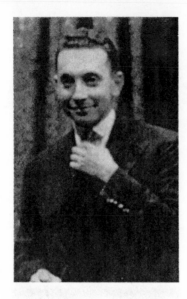

Above: Pierre Braunberger in his
Berlin days
Below: With Pierre Lestringuez on my
left, my hero Douglas Fairbanks
on my right, and Edmund Corwin,
chief cameraman of *Nana*

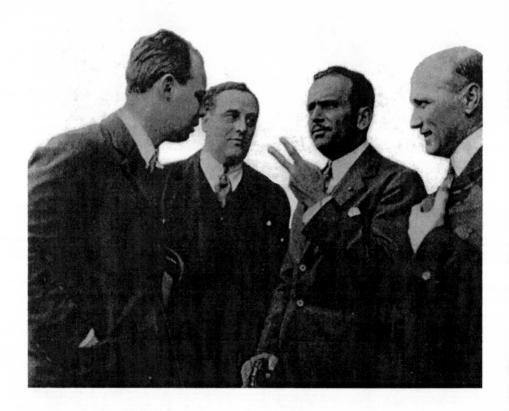

life-sized actors performed in these gaps against a miniature background behind the camera which was reflected in the mirror facing the camera. In *Marquitta* the miniature background represented the Barbès-Rochechouart intersection with the pillars of the métro-station and trains passing over the bridge. Naturally there was a fragment of lifesized setting immediately behind the actors corresponding to the miniature setting. The danger was that if the actor made a movement extending outside the fragment of real setting he went into the miniature setting and found himself minus an arm.

The intricacies of this device caused me to swear that I would never use it again; but the surprising thing is that it was technically a success. The actors kept within the pre-scribed limits while a model electric train running above their heads genuinely made it look as though we were at Barbès-Rochechouart. Another advantage was that one could bring the lighting closer to the actors, which im‑ proved its quality and was also more economical. I was to learn later that in Germany the cameraman Karl Freud had devised a system on similar lines and that Abel Gance had also experimented with it. As you see, there is no such thing as plagiarism.

One of the technical achievements which most delighted me was the shot of a banquet in *Le Tournoi dans la Cité*. The problem was to photograph the guests at a large banquet without using a series of close-ups. Nor did I want to use a camera travelling along one side, which would have given me an unattractive row of backs. I had a narrow banqueting-table made, about twenty metres long and one metre wide. I then had a kind of bridge constructed, mounted on four bicycle wheels. The camera was suspended from the middle of this bridge and was pushed to the centre of the table. The lens was just above the heads of the actors, and while shooting was in progress the technicians removed any props which would have got in the way of this gantry. The device was successful. Films were silent in those days, and this enabled me to do something which I detest and would never do now, namely to give instructions while shooting was in progress. I realized that one must not make the actor's job too difficult by involving him in technical complexities which were no concern of his.

Friendship

A thing that has unquestionably influenced my development as a creator of films is water. I cannot conceive of cinema without water. There is an inescapable quality in the movement of a film which relates it to the ripple of streams and the flow of rivers. That is a clumsy way of describing a feeling. The truth is that the affinity between the film and the river is the more strong and subtle because it cannot be explained. Lying on the bottom of the skiff with Godefer, with the branches brushing our faces, I had a thrill very near to what I feel when watching a film which moves me deeply. I know we cannot go back upstream, but I am free to relive in my own fashion the sensation of leaves stroking the end of my nose. For me that is what a good film is, the caress of foliage in a boat with a friend.

The importance of Godefer in my life was repeated twenty years later in the person of Pierre Champagne. He, too, was an innocent. Pierre Champagne was never happy unless he could dedicate himself to something. When we were shooting *La Fille de l'Eau* he did a bit of everything. He was my personal assistant and he also played a part as an actor; he drove the cars and helped the cameramen to carry their equipment. But his major role, where I was concerned, was simply to be himself.

His innocence was accompanied by an infallible flair, and his feeling for truth was only exceeded by his obstinacy. He was an absolute mule! A friend of his once told me the following story. He had got engaged to a girl whom his father did not consider a suitable wife for him. She came of a very good family and was what is called a good match, but old Monsieur Champagne had already made up his mind. After a furious altercation Pierre went out on to the balcony of their fifth-floor apartment and put a leg over the balustrade, announcing that he was going to jump. 'Since I can't live without Mimi I might as well put an end to everything. That would solve the whole problem.' The sight of that big body hanging over a five-storey drop attracted notice in the street and before long a crowd had gathered. Women screamed, and one even rolled on the ground as though in an epileptic fit. The objection to Pierre's marriage to Mimi was promptly withdrawn.

The second passion in his life, the first being the cinema, was motor-cars. Pierre Champagne owned a garage, and when anything went wrong with my old Napier I took it along to him. Mimi Champagne was like a pretty little brown mouse. She came from Agen, as her accent proclaimed, and never ceased to protest at the extent to which the garage interfered with their private life. She did so in vain. It happened quite often that her husband would dismantle an engine on the dining-room table and amuse himself for hours adjusting the valves by hand. 'Well, at least leave room for me to lay the table. The leg of mutton will be overdone.' Sometimes she was reduced to tears. 'You know you like leg of mutton to be rare. By the time you've cleared the table it'll be cooked to a frazzle!' Pierre Champagne would take her in his arms and hastily transfer his engine and tools to the sideboard.

For Pierre the High Priest of his motor-car religion was Ettore Bugatti. He would sometimes stop alongside a Bugatti and address its owner. 'Excuse me, Monsieur. Would you mind if I raised the bonnet of your car?' The owner would stare at him in astonishment. 'But what do you want to do that for?' . . . 'Just to have a look at it.' . . . He was tall and thin with a profile like an eagle's beak. He looked like Don Quixote. The owner of the car would smilingly consent. One has to humour the insane. Pierre would raise the bonnet, stroke the engine, check the level of oil, congratulate the owner on the admirable lubrication of the brake-pedal and go on his way, leaving the owner charmed by their encounter.

The Champagnes spent the summer in their cottage on the river Garonne. I was always invited and went to them in May. I did not want to miss the shad-fishing expedition which took place in the spring when those fish go upstream to spawn. These were large-scale operations. The son of a neighbouring farmer had a net large enough to cover a whole arm of the river. On a moonless night we would wade in water up to our waists and stretch this net across the pathway of the shad. We brought back enormous quantities of fish. Then we called on all our friends in the neighbourhood bearing gifts. It must be said that shad is a delicious fish; rather too many bones, but with an exquisite flavour. Those parties had the attraction of forbidden fruit. The gendarmes and fish-wardens were suspicious and kept a close watch on the river.

When Pierre Champagne drove down from Paris he had scarcely got out of his car before he caught the local accent. He was proud of it. Had it not been the accent of Henri IV? He even went so far as to adopt the same oaths as the most illustrious of the Béarnais line, adorning his speech with such sonorous expletives as *ventre d'ânesse'* – an admirable example of the influence of environment.

People were astonished by my persistence in using Pierre

as a performer. They could understand my need to associate with a 'simple' man, but to go so far as to admit him to the noble profession of acting was excessive. The truth is that I did not find Pierre Champagne as simple as all that. He had a unique perceptiveness in the assessment of men and women, an instant discernment of vulgarity and also of nobility. He himself was an aristocrat.

It was perhaps because he so loved dogs that Pierre had acquired something of their nature. When we were talking about a dog-owner he never named the individual in question but always referred to 'Macaron's master' or 'Mirza's mistress', identifying the owner by his dog. I had noticed that Gabrielle did this too. For both of them the dog was what mattered, far more than the owner.

In Pierre Champagne's world it was not only dogs which existed outside the social hierarchy. All animals and even plants were entitled to the same esteem. The rustic who robbed a tree of its fruit was as guilty as the brute who beat up an old woman for her handbag. This kind of total egalitarianism delighted me. It does so still, but alas, only in memory.

As to Pierre's acting career, this was obviously confined to my films. He was incapable of transposing himself; he could only transform himself. It was like his Gascon accent; the change came from his affection for the people around him. It was not the mask which an actor assumes when he enters the stage, but a step towards the metamorphosis of the individual under the influence of his surroundings.

One had to take or leave Pierre as he was. Such as he was, he invested the parts he played with an unanswerable authenticity. Unfortunately it was not an authenticity which applied to the characters he thought he was interpreting.

He did not 'act'. Whether he was playing La Faloise, a snobbish dandy in *Nana*, or Justin Crépois, a ruffianly peasant, in *La Fille de l'Eau*, he was always Pierre Champagne, and this inability to change himself obviously worked to the detriment of the plot. When he appeared on the screen it was as though one were watching another story. I did not let this trouble me. I deliberately disregarded all the rules of the drama. What mattered to me was to reproduce faces for their own sake. And besides, Pierre loved the cinema nearly as much as I did, and this shared passion constituted a bond between us as powerful as that existing between drug-addicts or the neophytes of a religious sect. Since love of the cinema and for motor-cars could only be abstract passions, Pierre expressed them in his love for me. His devotion to me was absolute.

A quarter of a century later, when I was making *The River* in India, I was to discover a similar kind of affection, and perhaps it was this that caused me to become so deeply attached to that country. The word 'friendship' does not suit India, one has to say 'love'. One may love or one may hate. Indian friendship consists in enjoying the presence of a friend without a word being spoken. A dog likes to sit at its master's side, although they don't talk. Besides which, there is neither master nor servant in a truly affectionate relationship. Western friendships, on the other hand, are often based on some form of barter. One is fond of a man because he is useful in one's business, or because he is an entertaining story-teller, or simply because one admires him. In India one comes across people who love one another for no reason. One friend calls upon another, going silently into the room where he is sleeping. He will squat down on the floor without a word and watch the other live a few hours of his life; and finally he will get up and go away, fortified by the visit.

A dog stretches out and dies on its master's grave. It is not a matter of devotion or gratitude, but simply because its master's absence has created a void in which it cannot breathe. Indian friendship goes further than disinterest. It is a physical need, as though there existed between two persons who feel an affinity for one another a kind of wireless system whereby they communicate in a fashion that our mathematical brains cannot grasp. Pierre Champagne had that gift. Sometimes he would come and sit beside me. We would not talk. We would each enjoy the presence of the other as one enjoys a ray of autumn sunshine or a breeze coming from the sea.

Fate was to brand with the mark of tragedy my departure from the phase of amateurism. When, after *Marquitta*, in which he played the part of a taxi-driver, Pierre Champagne at last realized his ambition to own a Bugatti (but, mark you, no ordinary Bugatti, one of the 'Brescia' type), his first thought was to take me out for a trial spin. He drove at full speed along one of the roads through the Forest of Fontainebleau. A car in front of us had had an oil-leakage and left a slippery patch behind it. The Bugatti went out of control on this patch of oil and spun round, flinging us both out. Pierre landed on a heap of stones and was killed instantly. I landed on a grassy bank and woke up to find myself in a van filled with game. It belonged to two poachers who were going to sell their bag in Paris, at Les Halles. In going out of their way to take me to hospital they risked being arrested. I am profoundly grateful to them. Moreover, I owe them the idea for my stage play, *Orvet*.

In contrast to Pierre Champagne there was Pierre Lestringuez, a perfect example of what Diderot in the eighteenth century called '*l'honnête homme*'. He was more than a childhood friend; he was a friend from before childhood. Our fathers had been intimate. Lestringuez' father was a hunchback and he put me in mind of an incarnation of the Devil. He was one of a group of people interested in sorcery who experimented with magic, and he described his experiments in a resounding voice which enhanced the mystery of his recital. It happened several times that I was lurking unnoticed in a corner of my father's studio, and I heard things that terrified me. Renoir was the last person to be impressed by that kind of foolery. He roared with laughter, and I laughed too, feeling reassured. Renoir's very French sense of logic had no room for those demoniac manifestations. His comment on Lestringuez' claim that his communications with the Devil were genuine may be summed up as follows: 'The whole lot of it isn't worth a well-shaped bottom.' It may be added that this reaction did not represent my father at his most profound.

The younger Lestringuez was a highly talented writer, a friend of Jean Cocteau, who belonged to the same select circle. Apart from his literary talent, he possessed a quality which was at once his triumph and his downfall: he was a faun, a womanizer, which left him little time to spare for writing. He was built like a faun, with a marvellous face resembling the portraits of Fragonard or Boucher, a noble, severe countenance that frequently glowed with the light of concupiscence. I could imagine him clad in animal-skins pursuing nymphs amid the columns of an abandoned temple, and it was surprising to find that he did not possess cloven feet. Louis Jouvet said of him: 'Pierre has not had the literary success he deserves, but that will come because God has blessed him with a core of wisdom.'

One of Lestringuez' great friends was Jean Giraudoux. We often foregathered in pleasant bistros, Pierre Lestringuez, Giraudoux, Louis Jouvet and myself. The game we played consisted in trying to define the occult influence which Lestringuez possessed over women. He was not in the least interested in the demons which had so fascinated his father. On the other hand, his dealings with the other sex always moved us to astonished admiration. Without a word or gesture on his part they 'knew'. Men who are 'women's men' go through life wearing a halo that other men cannot see. When Lestringuez entered a restaurant it was like a cock entering a hen-roost. The ladies simpered and preened themselves and literally melted.

Giraudoux and Jouvet have their place in this account of people who have influenced me; in fact, they are among the very few who have influenced me directly. I thought a great deal about Giraudoux while I was writing *La Règle du Jeu*, and about Jouvet with his system of rehearsal in the Italian manner.

Another Pierre who played a basic part in my development as a maker of films is Pierre Braunberger, the man who was to become my associate in many film projects, and who was destined, a quarter of a century later, to play an essential role in the inception of the Nouvelle Vague. He is a man bubbling with imagination and teeming with ideas; a highly-strung creature constantly skipping from one foot to the other, chewing the blotting-paper on his desk in moments of impatience (he has even been known to eat a cheque) and consumed, as he still is, with a violent passion for the cinema. I could easily imagine him being eaten by lions rather than repudiate his divinity. Carl Koch, another of my 'accomplices', seriously maintained that Pierre Braunberger was a reincarnation of Harlequin. He was quite right. Braunberger would have been magnificent in Goldoni's comedies. His function in our little group was to try to market my films. He was one of the few people to find in *La Fille de l'Eau* virtues capable of attracting customers. Unfortunately they were highly esoteric virtues, and perhaps it was this that appealed to Pierre Braunberger.

During the week when the Germans were electing a new Chancellor, Braunberger and I were in Berlin trying amid great difficulties to set up a new film. I have spent my life trying to raise money for my films. Except in one or two rare cases I have been successful only through the intervention of Divine Providence. I have no aptitude for what is called 'business' and Braunberger's fantastical mind did nothing to compensate for my deficiencies. His idea of trying to find money in Berlin in the year 1933, when the votes of the German people put Hitler in power and decided the fate of the world, was a notion truly worthy of Harlequin. No worse moment could have been chosen, but Harlequin knew that he could duck out with a pirouette.

Cinema Madness

Today the actor is the first of my preoccupations. My work as a director starts with the actor. He is what the public sees and hears, and it is he who will determine our success or failure.

But I had not reached this point with *La Fille de l'Eau*. What mattered to me at that time was the pictorial quality of the film. I called in a number of amateurs whose faces enchanted me. The painter, André Derain, was the proprietor of Le Bon Coin, the bistro in the film. Van Doren, a young American who was spending the summer at Marlotte, where I had my house, took on the rôle of *jeune premier*. Pierre Lestringuez, under his stage name of Pierre Philippe, played the villain, and I can assure you he was thoroughly villainous. My brother Pierre, a real actor, played a peasant.

I did not expect to stand the film market on its head with that low-budget film, and indeed I was prepared to make a present of it to any exhibitor who was prepared to show it. The simple tale told in the film could shock no one. It depicts the misfortunes of a young orphaned girl, the daughter of a bargeman, who is hated by the villagers and persecuted by her uncle, who seeks to violate her. She takes refuge in the forest to escape from her persecutors and has a dream. It was this dream, I fancy, which aroused the misgivings of the exhibitors. A girl galloping in the sky on a white horse, and the same girl surrounded by deformed beings who terrify her – this was not true to life. The sequence which most shocked them was that in which a rope twined round the neck of the wicked uncle turns into a snake. This, they considered, was treating the public as though they were children . . . Well, whatever the reason, *La Fille de l'Eau* was unanimously rejected by the representatives of the profession.

The only benefit I derived from it was that it forced me to recognize a truth that was all too obvious, namely that I had nothing in common with the film business as it then existed. If one wishes to achieve what is commonly considered as success in this life, one does not go into battle single-handed. One has to be one of a group. Woe to the loner! My tastes and ideas were and still are totally opposed to those of the people who lay down the law in the business. At the outset I believed that audiences could not remain indifferent to my immense sincerity and desire to please them. To touch their hearts was everything, but this could only be done with the help of the cinema proprietors. It is all very well to make a fine film, but you have to show it. So the problem was to get into the cinemas; and seeing that I did not own one myself, and that the people who did own them took no interest in me, the sensible thing was to give up films and busy myself in some field of activity where the customers would respond to my efforts. Why not go back to pottery? My kiln was still there, waiting for me to use it. It would not take long for my hands to recover their skill in handling clay.

But that was another pipe-dream. The customers who had been interested in my work when I was producing pottery had been solely attracted by the name of my father. They hoped to be able to boast equivocally, 'I have a Renoir vase,' which flattered their vanity. I was obliged to admit that in their hearts they did not like the things I made.

With a view to earning money by trade I opened an art shop. It was a very pretty shop in a good position near the Madeleine, and I considered the goods I offered for sale extremely handsome. Among other things there were some materials painted by Albert André's wife, Maleck, which I thought marvellous. This was also the opinion of the audience at the Casino de Paris, for which Maleck had done a great many of her paintings on cloth; but it was not a view shared by my customers. The sad but inescapable fact is that I was not born to be a shopkeeper. I'm incapable of selling anything. But in the film business one has to be a salesman. Above all, one has to sell oneself. I could see only one way out of the situation and that was to become a layabout, a difficult calling for which Catherine and I had had little training.

It was in this frame of mind that we surveyed our future. If we were to go on making films we needed to have money, a great deal of money, which we did not possess. Catherine was heartbroken, while I, toiling away in my art boutique, tried to pretend that the cinema did not exist. Every morning when I awoke I repeated to myself, 'There's no such thing as the cinema.' But Catherine, with the admirable obstinacy of creators, continued to make plans. The kind of cinema she envisaged was even more closely related to the dance than our fruitless first attempts.

One day, wandering aimlessly along a Montmartre street, I ran into my friend Jean Tedesco. He had recently turned the Théâtre du Vieux Colombier into an avant-garde cinema where he found it possible to show good films and make a little money. It had indeed become a centre for people interested in 'real' cinema. Jean Tedesco told me that he had included the dream sequence from *La Fille de*

l'Eau in a programme of film excerpts. 'You should come
and see it,' he said. At first I was indignant, asking him what
right he had to arbitrarily extract a part of a film from the
whole, and this without having secured the author's consent. I considered, and still do, that a film is a whole, and
that only the author has the right to edit it. Tedesco
listened to me with a quizzical smile and simply said, 'Well,
come along to the Vieux Colombier one evening and then
tell me what you think.' Although I had sworn to have
nothing more to do with the cinema, even as a spectator, I
told Catherine about this meeting.

Our curiosity was aroused. That same evening, after
eating a sandwich at Dominique's, the Russian provision
merchant in Montparnasse, we went to the Vieux Colombier, never dreaming that this visit was to determine the
course of our lives. The programme started with a rather
tedious documentary about a power-station, and the lights
went up again on a scene of general boredom. The audience
seemed to us even hostile, and determined not to be interested in anything. We were dreadfully put out by this. The
dimming of the lights scarcely reduced the babble of conversation. The title, 'Extracts from *La Fille de l'Eau*,'
appeared on the screen. The pianist played a few intro-
ductory chords and accompanied the opening scenes with
very soft music, followed by an improvisation in the heroic
style for the riding sequence. The images succeeded one
another with what seemed to me desperate slowness. Did
they like it or didn't they? But after five minutes the
audience was gripped. Several sequences were followed by
applause. Catherine and I found that our first agonies were
followed by a glow of happy excitement. When Catherine
slipped from her horse and was dragged into an endless fall

there was a loud burst of applause, and when the lights went up again and the screen was bare this was repeated with a warmth that left no room for doubt. It was a continuous ovation, and for the first time in my life I knew the sweet smell of success. Jean Tedesco had placed us in the middle of the auditorium, in a position where the whole audience could see us. Catherine was recognized and the applause broke out again. The whole audience rose spontaneously to its feet. No, decidedly, we weren't going to give up film-making!

The outcome of this change of heart was *Nana*, filmed in 1926. Why *Nana*? Simply because Pierre Lestringuez and I had a profound admiration for Zola's novel. I talked to Catherine about it and she at once began to mime Nana in her own fashion, so that we got a new version of Nana every day. Moreover, from the commercial point of view *Nana* could hardly fail: with that title we were, we thought, bound to break through the barrier separating us from the commercial cinema. In order to finance *Nana* I had to borrow money. It was going to be an expensive film, but no matter, it was in the bag. We did it in a big way. The Leblond-Zola family helped us to acquire the film rights and was co-operative in every respect. It was a good augury. *Nana* was made in conjunction with a German film company which bore a part of the cost of shooting in Germany. The reason why we worked in Berlin was that the cast included a number of German actors, the most important being Werner Krauss and Valeska Gert.

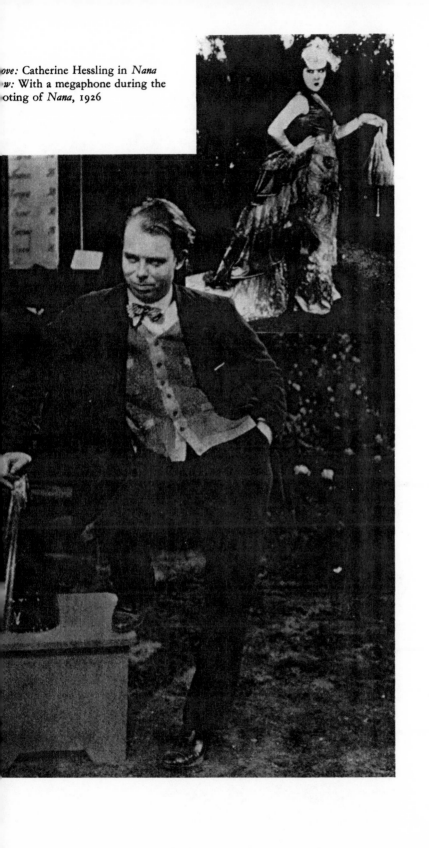

ove: Catherine Hessling in *Nana*
w: With a megaphone during the
oting of *Nana*, 1926

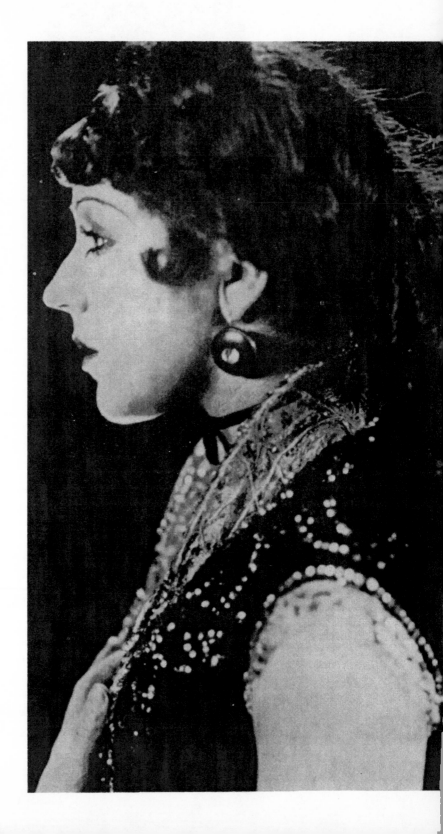

'*Nana*'

It was Werner Krauss who taught me to understand the importance of actors. I greatly admired him and that is why I asked him to play the part of Count Muffat in *Nana*. My admiration dated from *Caligari*. I had also seen him in other films and in a stage production of Ibsen's *Wild Duck*. What impressed me about him was in the first place his technical skill, his knowledge of make-up and the use he made of small physical peculiarities. After a number of experiments he devised a Count Muffat which was not Werner Krauss and yet was him. Later on I was to realize that this skill in the physical presentation of a character is not the root of the actor's business, and that although a convincing outward appearance is certainly a help, it can never be more.

Werner Krauss was at the height of his fame. He had already become what he has since remained, the finest actor in the German language. He took pity on my inexperience, treated me with friendship and understood my problems. After we had been working together for some weeks a great degree of frankness had sprung up between us. He admitted to me that he made use of clichés. In particular he had invented his famous walk seen from behind. To the enthusiastic audience, that bowed head and those drooping shoulders, laden with all the cares of the world, were the expression of their own unhappiness. The director had to find an excuse for using that walk in all his films, and I did not fail to do so in *Nana* . . . 'At the beginning of my career,' Werner Krauss said to me, 'that walk was entirely spontaneous. The movement of my legs and the forward droop of my body were prompted by the fact that I really did feel the sorrows of the character I was playing. Now I put it on in the way one does an old coat; but I can do so honourably because I forget about it as readily as one forgets an old coat. I use it as a prop. It isn't what really matters. What really matters is what I feel, and that is expressed by reactions of which I am not the master.' But he genuinely believed that audiences were charmed and delighted by the clichés. The public looks for a particular reaction on the part of an actor in a given set of circumstances, and if it is not humoured it resents it and the actor may fall out of favour. When one considers the difficulty of succeeding in the actor's profession one can hardly blame actors and directors for safeguarding their real substance by dishing up this kind of pre-digested nourishment.

Safety, for the honest author as for the honest actor, consists in presenting an outward show so acceptable that the real intention remains hidden except for a few particularly clear-sighted spectators. It often happens that the film-maker himself is unconscious of the deeper meaning of his work. An example of this is *La Grande Illusion* which was warmly received by the trade and the public, who thought of it simply as an escape film. Later the real theme, which was that of human relations, was understood and accepted; but the way for this had been paved by its success, when the unorthodoxy with which I had filled it was applauded by even the most thick-headed spectators. It is hypocritical, I admit, but if one wants certain home truths to be swallowed one must sugar the pill. The same applies to certain Indian sweetmeats, the first mouthfuls of which are deliciously suave; but one takes another bite and comes upon a spice that makes the hair stand on end.

Quality cannot be made to order. The actor who creates a masterpiece does so unwittingly. Too many people believe that one can decide the quality of a work in advance. One does not say, 'I am about to create a masterpiece' – or, if one does, one is more likely to produce a flop. The masterpiece may emerge of its own accord out of a production conceived on purely commercial lines. We are confronted by what in English is termed a 'blueprint'. I shall have a good deal more to say about the perils of the 'blueprint' civilization. I will not go so far as to maintain that a masterpiece can be born only of an idea that is crudely commercial. It is born of the inspiration of its creator; and this, in the cinema, may be an actor, a writer or a director. I personally believe that it should be the director. He is the only one who can shape the film by kneading its different elements, in the way that a sculptor kneads clay. In *Nana* I had the assistance of highly talented actors and technicians, but, as was the case with *La Fille de l'Eau*, there was not a movement, not an expression, not a prop that I did not discuss and finally decide upon.

Nana was a mad undertaking. The budget was a million francs, without counting the German contribution, and this was enormous in those days. Claude Autant-Lara, my designer at that time, adorned the production with a richly decadent setting in which authenticity and fantasy were mingled. I have often wondered if that film was not made before its time. It was, of course, in black-and-white, although it really needed colour, and also, since we are wringing our hands, it needed a sound-track. The contrast between the luxury of the setting and the language used by the heroine would have enhanced its baroque nature. But it is no use crying over spilt milk. Commercially *Nana* was doomed to failure, and this was because of the character of Catherine Hessling. I have talked already about stylization. In *Nana* she carried it to the uttermost extreme. She was not a woman at all, but a marionette. The word, as I use it, is a compliment. But this was a transfiguration which, alas for us, the public could not accept. People like to be able to say, when the play is over, 'How true . . . That's how it must have been . . .' not realizing that realism of detail generally conceals falsity of feeling.

Nana was given a terrific world *première* for which I had prepared the way with a riot of publicity. The walls of Paris were covered with posters of Catherine Hessling, and the Press heralded the event with a fanfare of trumpets. I had hired the big hall of the Moulin Rouge, together with its excellent orchestra. The place was packed, the audience being divided into two opposed parties – devotees of the classic cinema on the one hand, who, without knowing why, looked upon me as a wicked revolutionary, and on the other hand, upholders of the avant-garde cinema, who, also without knowing why, considered me a daring innovator. The film ran to an accompaniment of whistles and catcalls punctuated with bursts of hearty applause. People took sides and exchanged abuse. The wife of the most noted film-director of the day screamed repeatedly: 'They're all Boches! It's a Boche film! Down with the Boches!' That first night was the epitome of my whole career. It has been my destiny always to be caught between the extremes of rebellion and orthodoxy, with never a safe middle way: but at least audiences of that kind have the merit that they are not indifferent.

I thought this reception meant that the film would play to

packed houses. But in fact it failed, as I know to my cost, because I lost my million. *Nana* won a few supporters for Catherine Hessling and perhaps for myself, but the larger public would have none of it, and the trade still less.

At the risk of sounding sordid I cannot refrain from dividing my career into two purely material halves, during the first of which I paid to make films, whereas in the second I was paid to do so. Since my private means consisted essentially of the pictures bequeathed to me by my father, my excursions into cinema were marked by the disappearance of canvases which were like a part of myself. It was as though a conversation between my father and me had been for ever discontinued. I was living a new version of Balzac's *Peau de Chagrin* and I spent the days brooding over my shame. Every sale seemed to me a betrayal. At night I wandered about my house at Marlotte, of which the walls were being slowly but inexorably stripped bare. I had kept the frames. They were like gaping outlets to a hostile world. Never had I felt myself so closely linked to my father's memory. The time came when only a few pictures were left, and one night I asked Catherine to come and talk to me in the drawing-room. I don't remember exactly what happened. All I can say is that, surrounded by those empty frames, we felt like homeless orphans. We resolved to give up the cinema and at all costs to hang on to the few of my father's pictures that still remained. But it was too late. I had to pay the last bills for *Nana*.

A few days later there was a phone-call from my sister-in-law, Marie-Louise Iribe, who had just launched a film company. Her aims were strictly commercial. She wanted me to direct a film entitled *Marquitta*. The script was by Lestringuez, who had sardonically loaded it with every conceivable cliché and banality. I pondered for a day and a night, but in the morning I had come to the logical conclusion. To direct *Marquitta* would be to cross the frontier into the world of the commercial cinema, that is to say, the world in which producers and distributors tinkered with scripts, chose the cast and generally took it upon themselves to represent the so-called 'public taste', which in fact is simply their own taste. The public's real taste is something that no one knows and that will always be an enigma. If one did know it, the business would be wonderfully simple . . . To direct *Marquitta* would be to give up all idea of 'making' a film in the way that one writes a poem or composes a sonata. True; but on the other hand one had to go on living and the fee would help me out of a difficult situation. So I accepted, and deserted the ranks of the avant-garde cinema for those of the industry.

There was something else about *Marquitta* which was very important to me. It was the first film I directed without Catherine, the first in which I was working for my own success and not that of my wife; and this recollection of my beginnings prompts me to ask the following question: 'Is it possible to succeed without any act of betrayal?' The demon of cinema had taken possession of me, and after a few weeks behind the camera my scruples were borne away on the flood of my new preoccupations.

At the time when it was proposed to me that I should direct *Marquitta* I received another offer which was, to say the least, unexpected. Madame Regina, the proprietress of a number of 'houses' in the Midi, including a very luxurious one in Nice, had seen the dream sequence in *La Fille de l'Eau* and discussed it at length with Lestringuez, who was a friend of hers. She suggested that I should make a number of films for her establishments, and she showed us one or two that she had had made by a local film-man. All one can say of them is that they showed a lamentable lack of eroticism – and yet, what a limitless field eroticism presents! Those films, alas, never rose above the level of pornography. The best of them – that is to say, the least bad – was entitled *The Baron*. It depicted the adventures of a baron who joins in the romps of two ladies, without, however, causing them to discontinue their own activities. I asked Madame Regina how she had managed to find a man of such enormous potency and she told me that the Baron had been very skilful in the use of rubber contrivances. The film was lent a touch of comedy by the fact that the Baron never removed his tail-coat, his bow-tie or his top-hat. Lestringuez and I devised some wonderful stories. We even thought of adapting the Marquis de Sade. Madame Regina, a very well-read woman, followed our debates with interest. But I had to start work on *Marquitta*, and so I gave the Marquis de Sade a miss.

Jacques Becker

Before proceeding further with my personal recollections, I must speak about my assistant, Jacques Becker. I cannot get used to the idea that Jacques is dead. He was my brother and my son; I cannot believe that he is now rotting in his grave. I would sooner think that he is waiting for me in some corner of the next world, waiting for us to make another film together.

When Jacques Becker first came to see me he was a youngster and the perfect embodiment of everything that I most dislike – a member of the French upper class, well acquainted with bars and night-clubs and given to the pursuit of elegant sports. But when I had got past that veneer I found myself confronted by someone who was both lovable and ardent. His enthusiasm for the films which I also liked, notably Stroheim's *Greed*, and above all his approach to his fellow men definitely rid me of the idea that he was a snob. He loved mankind not in any generalized, theoretical way but directly and in terms of the individual. He had no prejudices in his choice of friends, being as capable of sturdy attachment to a plumber as to a noted writer.

I made his acquaintance through Paul Cézanne, the son of the painter. Renée, Paul's wife, was the daughter of Georges Rivière, a lifelong friend of my father and author of the book *Renoir and his Friends*. Renée had lost her mother when she was still a child, and had been partly brought up by my own mother. I give these details to convey something of the family atmosphere in which Jacques Becker now and then immersed himself. The Cézannes had a magnificent old house at Marlotte, where Catherine and I had settled. It was called La Nicotière and dated apparently from the time of Jean Nicot, who introduced tobacco to France.

Sundays at La Nicotière are among my happiest memories. Aline and Jean-Pierre Cézanne were still children; but it may be said that in the company of Paul and Renée Cézanne we all became children. Paul, though growing old, still resembled the portrait of him as Harlequin painted by his father. He was very short-sighted, but physically exceptionally strong; indeed, his general appearance was rather that of a weight-lifter performing on the Boulevard Rochechouart. At the end of the afternoon, the process of digestion being completed, we drank apéritifs under the chestnut trees, and the numerous guests, while they sipped white wine, played *boules*. Paul's lack of skill was outstanding. While this was going on the children drained the heel-taps in the glasses – and Renée laughed.

Paul Cézanne presided over these bohemian gatherings in which harmless games were mingled with philosophical discussion, culinary experiments and mildly off-colour stories. The keynote of a day spent with the Cézannes at Marlotte was absolute liberty, and to me, as I recall them, they represented the *fêtes galantes* of the cultivated middle-class.

To come back to Jacques Becker, he was passionately interested in my film undertakings, but always with the conviction that they were nothing to do with him. He saw no way of escape from his own way of life, which was that of an honest manufacturer of accumulators. He was then aged twenty and possessed a talent for elegance. He understood fashion and knew how to adapt it to his own personality. I am not thinking only of clothes, but of the modes of thought and action, of seating oneself, of paying the waiter who serves the drink in a café, which were current among the small group of people who were 'in the know'. In all the ritual gestures of life he was ten years ahead of his time.

During the making of *La Grande Illusion* we had decided to live together. The affection between us went far beyond the bounds of normal friendship, so much so indeed that had it not been for our physical aspect ill-intentioned minds might have suspected a relationship of quite another kind. And why not? I am a firm believer in loving friendships in which there is no sexual element. The relationship between Rauffenstein and Boieldieu in *La Grande Illusion* was simply a love story. Our friendship was to last eight years until we were separated by the Second World War. When I returned to France, Jacques Becker had become a leading film director in his own right. He followed his line as I followed mine. His film *Casque d'Or* remains one of the masterpieces of the screen.

Apart from films, we liked the same things – sports cars, American safety-razors and, above all, jazz. At the age of eighteen he had got a job with the shipping firm, La Compagnie Générale Transatlantique, so as to be able to go to New York and call on one or two of his gods, especially Duke Ellington.

By chance he got to know Doucet, the pianist, who in association with Weiner was trying to found a French school of jazz. Doucet played him an American jazz record, a Brunswick record if I remember rightly. The players were a Chicago group who went by the name of the Mound City Bluebirds. Jacques was so excited that he borrowed the record and played it to Catherine. I came home that evening to find my wife and Jacques sitting on the floor with a portable gramophone, drowned in noise of a most strident and unexpected kind. My first reaction was one of annoyance with the record that had caused my dinner to be late, but then I was carried away by the strangeness of the music. It made me think of animals in a virgin forest whose cries conjured up a picture of monstrous plants and brilliantly coloured flowers. But then exoticism gave way to modern life, and the record became for me a representation of Chicago, the city from which it sprang. Needless to say, not the real Chicago but the Chicago of the crime-thrillers, street-walkers in short skirts, glaring lights bathing the wooden façades of speakeasies – in a word, the Chicago which might be imagined by a young Frenchman after the First World War.

Catherine and I went out with Jacques Becker nearly every evening. He introduced us to Johnny Higgins, a black dancer from New York. Johnny had come to Paris with a touring company and had decided not to go back to the States. Paris in those days was the Mecca of black people.

This was after the failure of *Nana*. In a gesture of farewell to the cinema I indulged myself in the luxury of using up the considerable unused footage from that film to make a 'short' in which there would be no concessions. The story was set in the future and afforded a pretext for a dance by Catherine and Higgins. The idea was one of the utmost simplicity. A black scientist from another planet pays a visit to the earth, where all civilization has been destroyed by an inter-planetary war. He lands near a Morris pillar, all that is left standing in the desert, and is found by a savage woman who, not knowing his language, can only communicate with him by dancing. When the dance is over the visitor returns to his own planet, taking her with him.

This film, *Charleston*, was never quite finished, to my regret. The few metres of it which remain seem to me interesting, and Catherine herself is dazzling. Curiously enough, the film, or rather, the fragment, which was deliberately avant-garde, born of my enthusiasm for jazz, was favourably reviewed by the Press; but this did nothing to open the doors of the popular cinemas.

The great black revue which brought us Josephine Baker had just come to Paris. Members of the company, after giving their performances at the Ambassadeurs or the Théâtre des Champs-Elysées, drifted into certain Paris night-clubs and delighted their patrons, ourselves among them, with their most typical compositions. I don't think they did it for money. Jazz was a religion which attracted devotees. I am happy to have lived through that period when the great exponents of hot jazz were discovering themselves. After leaving the night-club Catherine and I, always in company with Jacques Becker, would go home and revel in interpretations of Red Nichols and Duke Ellington. Our hero was Louis Armstrong, 'Satchmo', who was then quite young. He toured France with a band of half-a-dozen musicians; but he had less success in Paris than we had hoped. This was certainly due to the choice of theatre, the big hall at the Théâtre des Champs-Elysées. Armstrong fans would have preferred a less solemn setting.

I wondered how he would get on in the provinces. The first thing that caught my eye, when I arrived in Marseilles, was a placard announcing his appearance at the Palais de Cristal. That theatre is enormous, apart from which I could not believe that the Marseilles public was capable of understanding that kind of music. I was wrong. His visit was a triumph. On the first night there was a reasonably good house, but on the second they were turning people away. The audience wildly applauded a performer of a kind quite new to them playing music that was utterly strange. I think I can understand why. American jazz comes from New Orleans, a seaport like Marseilles, inhabited by the kind of people who belong in seaports. There is a community of taste which extends beyond the Mediterranean and the Gulf of Mexico. I am sure that a docker in Vladivostok would find that he has much in common with his opposite number in Naples or Constantinople.

Berlin — Other Influences

I am a man of 1914 and, like many of my ex-combatant contemporaries, I am attracted by the spirit of Germany. I owe a great deal to the Germans. I owe them Karl Koch, without whom *La Grande Illusion* could not have been what it is.

To me Germany is the carnival of the Rhine-towns: sober citizens plunged into wild debauchery because it is the carnival season – a cliché. Germany is also Grunewald's triptych at Colmar, in contradistinction to the diabolical fantasies of Nietzsche: that is the anti-cliché. To me Germany was, and still is, a fascinating enigma. Her outward aspect hinted at an intense secret life.

I took advantage of a visit to Berlin to make the acquaintance of Alfred Flechtheim, the art-dealer, artist and writer whose personality intrigued me. I rang the door-bell at his gallery and was confronted by a curiously effeminate young man in a chauffeur's uniform whose duties appeared to include opening the door. He made me repeat my name several times, and then, gazing mistrust-fully at me, asked me to wait. He vanished into the depths of the gallery, and I learned later that he announced me as follows: 'There's someone at the door who calls himself Renoir. Next time it'll be Rembrandt.' Being finally admitted by this sceptical Cerberus, I found myself in the presence of the master of the establishment. With his long, lean body and his beak of a nose he was a sort of Jewish Pierre Champagne. He was talking to a visitor whose ultra-correct attire impressed me. It was Paul Klee, the painter, and this meeting alone justified my trip to Berlin.

I left Pierre Braunberger to his dinners with film-distributors, and embarked with my new friends, Flechtheim and Klee, on a voyage of exploration of a Berlin that was new to me. Flechtheim was a contributor to *Querschnitt*, the satirical review which originated an ironical style that conquered the world. I cannot better convey the nature of that paper than by describing one of its two-page spreads. On the left-hand page there was a photograph of a review of the Prussian Guard – men in immaculately fitting uniforms presenting arms to an officer with the precision of mechanical toys. On the right-hand page was a picture of an inspection of page-boys at the Hotel Adlon: equally immaculately clad and looking as military as the soldiers.

Flechtheim was familiar with the curious aspects of the town. It is true to say that the fashionable entertainments in Berlin between the wars were boxing and homosexualism. Sodom and Gomorrah were reborn there. I cannot resist describing an evening at the Grosses Balhaus on the Alexanderplatz, which was remarkable, not for what happened but for what did not happen. It was a huge hall packed with a dense crowd of male and female dancers, but on looking a second time one realized that the 'females' were males in 'drag'. What was disconcerting was their air of respectability. I knew homosexual establishments in Paris where the regulars wore astonishing dresses and outrageous make-up. There was nothing of this sort here. The man was undoubtedly a clerk or factory foreman, and the 'lady' looked like a salesgirl, a model of lower middle-class orthodoxy, modestly dressed with a skirt long enough to conceal any excessive display of leg and, of course, no make-up.

We sat down at a table and one of the couples soon joined
us. We chatted about the weather and the indecency of the
revue at the Admirals Palast, the Folies Bergère of Berlin –
'Girls with cleavage down to their navels – well really!'
One sensed, in this odd pair, a craving for order and con-
vention. That evening convinced me of something that I
already knew, namely that defeat had thrown these people
completely off-balance. Wounded pride can be dangerous!
What is certain is that the Berliners hid their resentment
under a mask of absolute indifference. The face of Berlin in
those days, under the display of sardonic ribaldry, concealed
a monumental despair. Berlin was the fertile climate in
which the best and the worst flourished. The best was the
work of painters such as Paul Klee, plays such as those of
Bertold Brecht, films like *The Cabinet of Dr Caligari*, *Die
Freudlose Gasse* and *Nosferatu, the Vampire*. The worst was
prostitution, both female and male, which extended even
to members of the strict Prussian bourgeoisie.

Defeat had corrupted Germany, but no more than so-
called victory had corrupted France. I can see now that,
win or lose, no nation can escape the decadence engendered
by war. War destroys in a matter of months what a slowly
evolving culture has taken centuries to create. 'Thou shalt
not kill' is a moral law which in principle all men respect;
but from the moment war is declared it becomes commendable to slaughter one's fellow man on the grounds that he
belongs to a different group of humanity from one's own.

This distortion of moral values principally affects the
young. The age of delinquency is growing dangerously
lower. A few more wars and it will begin in the cradle.
Personally, I have nothing against youthful debauchery,
but I think of the terrible boredom that will overtake the

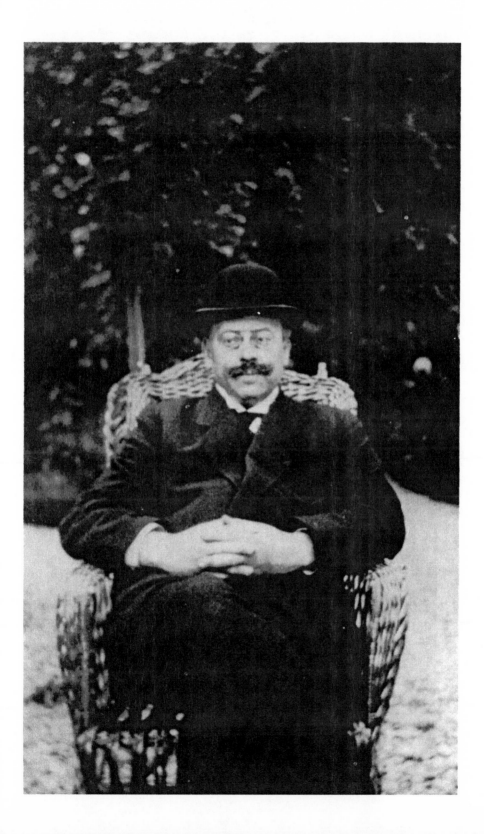

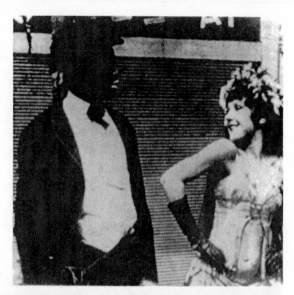

Catherine Hessling and
Johnny Higgins in *Sur un Air de
Charleston*, 1926

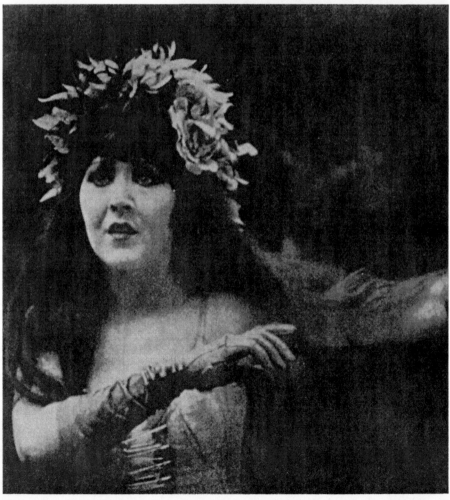

precocious debauchees when they have reached years of discretion. There will be nothing new for them to discover – a miserable state of affairs!

Hitler was elected. I decided to stay in Berlin, thinking to witness historic events. In fact what I witnessed was something abominable. A gang of athletic young men in brown shirts forced an elderly Jewish lady to go down on her knees and lick the pavement, saying that this was the only work suitable for Jews. I begged Braunberger to come to Paris with me, before the restrictions which were inevitable in the circumstances made it impossible. But he refused to leave Berlin. His state of tension led him to acts of the wildest provocation. I saw him plant himself, obvious Jew that he was, in front of a huge uniformed Nazi and make the Hitler salute with one hand while he covered his nose with the other. Frantic gestures of this kind seemed to me futile. I thrust him almost by force into a Mitropa sleeping-car, and the next day he rang me up to report his safe arrival. A few days later I, too, decided to leave.

The end of my visit was marked by a tragi-comical incident. I was in a taxi driven by an old Berlin driver. Berlin taxi-drivers are a race apart. One has a feeling that they weigh you up before accepting your custom, and their colourful speech expresses their determination not to be put upon by anyone. My driver during this trip never stopped grumbling. The quickest route to the address I had given him was by way of the Kanzleiplatz, that is to say, past the residence of the new German Chancellor, Adolf Hitler. We found the square surrounded by guards forming a cordon to keep back the hysterical crowds massed in the adjacent streets. One of them tried to prevent my cab from entering the square. My driver, enraged at being given orders, put his foot down and drove on into the empty square, ignoring him.

As it came opposite the entrance to the Chancellery a huge open Mercedes drove out. Standing erect beside the uniformed chauffeur was a personage whom I could not fail to recognize – Adolf Hitler. Quite unperturbed, my driver kept level with the Führer's car, and we continued thus, a few yards apart, amid the clamorous plaudits of the crowd, which Hitler acknowledged with the Nazi salute. Women went down on their knees as the car passed, and men wept with emotion. The whole demonstration seemed to be directed at me, and I was by no means happy about it. The generals in the back seat of the Mercedes glared suspiciously at me, obviously wondering who I was. They probably decided that I was a newspaper man vouched for by some other department. Hitler himself was far too busy saluting to pay any attention to trifles. My chauffeur did not even bother to look at the great man. Eventually we came to an intersection and Hitler turned left while I turned right.

Is the Cinema an Art?

To the question 'Is the cinema an art?' my answer is, 'What
does it matter?' You can make films or you can cultivate a
garden. Both have as much claim to be called art as a poem
by Verlaine or a painting by Delacroix. If your film or your
garden is a good one it means that as a practitioner of
cinema or gardening you are entitled to consider yourself
an artist. The pastry-cook who makes a good cake is an
artist. The ploughman with an old-fashioned plough creates
a work of art when he ploughs a furrow. Art is not a calling
in itself, but the way in which one exercises a calling, and
also the way in which one performs any human activity. I
will give you my definition of art: art is 'making'. The art
of poetry is the art of making poetry. The art of love is the
art of making love.

My father never talked to me about art. He could not
bear the word. If his children chose to go in for painting,
acting or music, they were free to do so, but they must
never be pushed. The urge to paint a picture must be so
powerful that it could not be resisted. My father said of
Mozart, whom he worshipped, 'He wrote music because he
could not prevent himself,' to which he added, 'It was like
wanting to pee.' He considered that the mode of expression
was unimportant. If Mozart had not made music he would
have written poems or planted gardens.

My father's influence on me is undeniable, but it is manifest principally in the details of my everyday life. The truth
is, I think, that the influence of one person on another can
never be defined. It has to do with the smell of the body, the

colour of the hair, the bearing and above all the kind of invisible and unanalysable wireless in which I firmly believe and of which the effects are beyond scientific explanation.

Although he did not seek to influence his children my father did most decidedly influence us by the magic of the pictures covering the walls of our home. We came unconsciously to believe that his was the only possible kind of painting. I can only remember one occasion when Renoir uttered what might pass for a word of advice from master to pupil. He was talking to a young friend of his, the painter Albert André. 'One has to fill out,' he said. 'A good painting, a good novel or a good opera makes its subject burst at the seams.' Albert André observed that there were splendid pictures with empty spaces in them, in particular those by painters at the beginning of the Italian Renaissance. Renoir's reply to this was that what Albert André supposed to be empty spaces were as filled with life as the parts crammed with matter. A pause in music can be as resonant as a fanfare by a dozen military bands. This law of content enclosed in a containing framework is one of the few pieces of artistic advice that my father gave me, albeit indirectly, and it astonishes me that my young mind, stuffed with nonsense about the '*Soltats t' l'Empire*' and the Musketeers, should have remembered it.

I have spent my life trying to determine the extent of the influence of my father upon me, passing over the periods when I did my utmost to escape from it to dwell upon those when my mind was filled with the precepts I thought I had gleaned from him. When I started to make films I went out of my way to repudiate my father's principles; but, strangely, it is precisely in the productions where I thought I had avoided Renoir's aesthetics that his influence is most apparent. I use the word 'aesthetics' because I cannot think of a better. My father would not have approved. In fact, it was a philosophy which he practised as much in life as in painting. He considered that the world is a whole, comprised of parts which fit together, and that its equilibrium is dependent on every piece.

This belief in the one-ness of the world manifested itself in Renoir in his love of all living things. When he walked through the fields he would do a curious dance to avoid crushing a dandelion. He believed that in destroying an ant one might be upsetting the balance of a whole empire. It is my subconscious faith in the clear-sightedness of Renoir that causes me to be attracted to those beings whom the world calls 'simple', but who probably possess a small fragment of the eternal wisdom – for example, Pierre Champagne.

In practice Renoir's belief in balance expressed itself in his love of proportion. He cited the Parthenon, that small Greek temple of which the perfect proportions make it one of the world's great buildings. On the other hand, he regarded the Arc de Triomphe on the Champs-Elysées as a failure, a big-bellied monster perched on skinny feet. But the Carrousel Arc de Triomphe entirely satisfied him, with its good, sturdy legs supporting a non-intellectual head.

From Silent Films to Talkies

Following *Marquitta*, which caused no sensation but made money, I thought I had definitely joined the profession. How wrong I was! The next three films I made were all privately financed, without recourse to the film industry. Where I am concerned, I was helped on more than one occasion by the oldest profession – that is to say, prostitution. Financiers knowing nothing about films took a gamble to gratify a mistress. At first this outraged me, but by degrees I came to find the system normal and even commendable. It had its good side. After all, there is no reason why a rich man's mistress should know less about the cinema than the commercial 'regulars'.

Although I had chosen none of the stories, I can claim that after a few weeks' work on the scripts I made them my own and came to take pleasure in them. Once again I was made to realize that in art the subject is less important than the execution. *Tire au Flanc*, made in 1928, which was based on a military farce, rewarded me with a handsome present. It put me in touch with Michel Simon.

Tire au Flanc also reminds me of a delightful actress who played a small part in it. She was kept in luxury by several immensely rich lovers. When she arrived at the studio in the morning she was always stopped by the concierge who was anxious to see the jewels which she enjoyed showing off. 'Who gave you that one?' he would ask, pointing to a large diamond. She had an answer designed to baffle inquisitive persons hoping to hear a famous name. 'It was Arthur.' The next day it would be a rope of pearls, but the donor was again Arthur. It was always Arthur, until finally the concierge asked in bewilderment: 'But who is this Arthur?' . . . 'My ass,' was the reply.

It became more and more clear to me that a film-director can only choose his subjects if his reputation in the trade is overwhelming. Although I did my best with the work that came my way, it was a great disappointment to me not to be able to make the films I had in my head. After *Marquitta* I tried hard to find a producer for an idea which Lestringuez and I both cherished. It was a story called *La Belote* which bore us up to Paradise by means of a slot-machine. God the Father was presented as wearing a bowler-hat of which he was very proud. We offered it to supposedly avant-garde producers, but in vain, none would accept it. I do not mention this reverse, which was one of many, because I consider myself ill-treated. After all, *La Belote* might have been a flop. I am simply thinking of all the young directors, some of whom are certainly bursting with ideas, who have no means of breaking into the fortress. It is a queer sort of system which restricts the right of self-expression to the possessors of a bank account or an influential relation. The productions I made at my own expense were financial failures, but at least I possessed sufficient private means to make *La Fille de l'Eau* and *Nana*. Although neither brought me fame or money, they drew attention to me; and it is thanks to them that I was engaged to direct *Marquitta*.

And in 1929 a monster was born which was to stand the whole business on its head – the talkies. I welcomed it with delight, seeing at once all the use that could be made of sound. After all, the purpose of all artistic creation is the knowledge of man, and is not the human voice the best means of conveying the personality of a human being? I

In 1915 I was wounded and sent home on convalescent leave. It gave me the opportunity to spend some delightful hours with my father, who told me stories of his early days

contacted a number of producers with proposals for a film based on a novel by La Fouchardière, *La Chienne* (The Bitch); but without avail. This time *Le Tournoi dans la Cité* was held against me; it had been made two years previously and had cost a great deal of money. I had used lavish settings for that film, extravagant costumes, hundreds of horses hired from the Cavalry School at Saumur – in short, a great many luxuries which were not considered possible in a talking film. Even without so much elaboration the shooting of a talkie was found to be a very slow business, and in the cinema, as in all industries, time is the biggest item in the budget.

I had never concealed my mistrust of stage actors, but during the transitional period the film-industry could think of nothing else. To me their style of acting seemed even less suited to the talking-pictures than to the silent. People imagine that in a talkie nothing matters except the actual dialogue. I, too, believe in dialogue, but to me it is only part of the sound-track: a sigh, the creak of a door, the sound of footsteps on the pavement, things such as these can say as much as the spoken word.

I saw the possibility of spellbinding situations between Catherine Hessling and Michel Simon in *La Chienne* – in particular a dramatic scene based on a popular song of which I was particularly fond, 'La Sérénade du Pavé'. I have often used this device to give shape to a situation in a film. The style of *La Grande Illusion* is partly due to 'Le Petit Navire', the song which Pierre Fresnay, in the part of a captain of Hussars, plays on a flute. The Piedmontese and Corsican songs in *Toni* had a lot to do with setting the tone of that film and 'Le Petit Cœur de Ninon' is of major importance in *La Bête Humaine*.

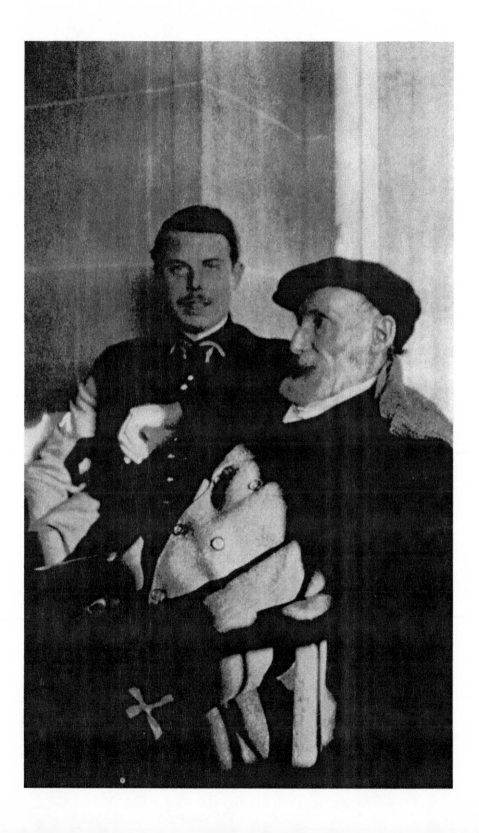

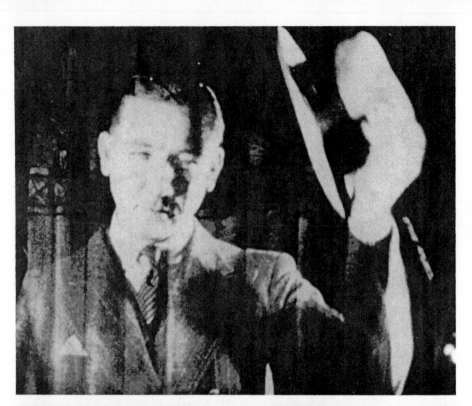

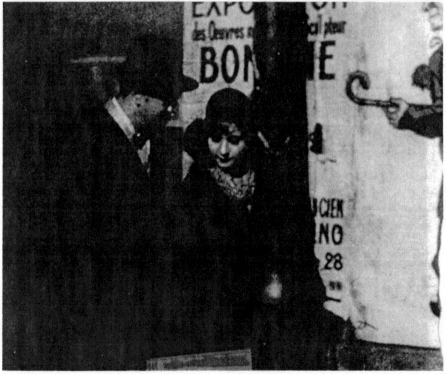

Opposite above: Georges Flamant as the
pimp in *La Chienne*, 1931
Opposite below: Michel Simon and Janie Marèse:
their first encounter in the street
Above: Michel Simon inspects a chamber-pot in
On Purge Bébé
Below: Fernandel's first screen appearance was
in this film

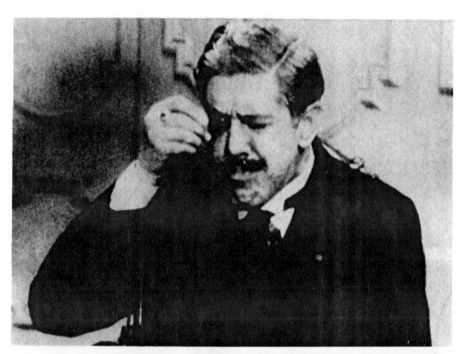

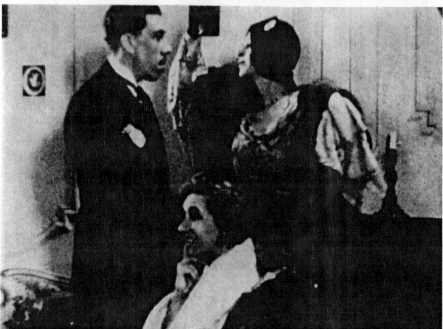

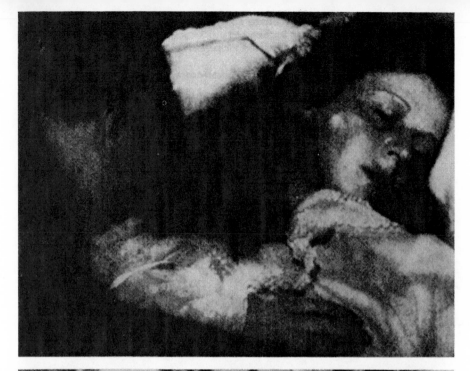

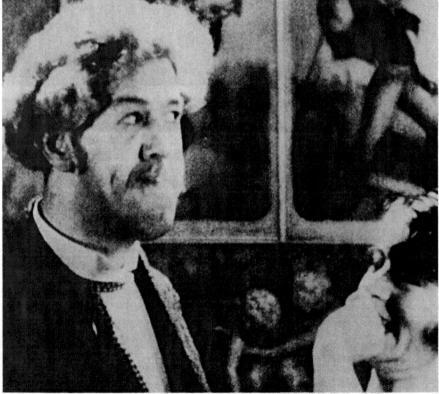

The happy event which led me to hope that I might be able to make *La Chienne* was the appointment of Pierre Braunberger to the post of co-director of the Billancourt Studios. I picked up the phone the moment I heard the news; but Braunberger explained that he had a partner, and that even with the latter's agreement he could not undertake such a big production without the consent of his backers. He assured me that he wanted me to make *La Chienne*. His sincerity was apparent, but at the same time he wanted to keep his job, and I don't blame him. His partner was Roger Richebé, the son of a big exhibitor. Richebé père owned a large number of cinemas, principally in and around Marseilles. He also owned a reel of film depicting a bullfight. When he felt that the feature film being shown was becoming tedious he would interpolate his spool. *Back Street* would suddenly become a bullfight, to the bewilderment of the audience. The association of Roger Richebé and Braunberger made the Billancourt Studios a large concern. The principal backer, brought in by Braunberger, was Monsieur Monteux, proprietor of the best known brand of shoes in France.

I must apologize for dwelling at such length upon the circumstances surrounding the making of *La Chienne*, but that film was to be a turning-point in my career. I believe that in it I came near to the style that I call poetic realism. Although it got off to a disastrous start, both public and critics recognized that I had sacrificed my earlier conviction on the altar of external truth, the more so since this external truth was seen to be a powerful aid to internal truth.

But before we come to the actual making of *La Chienne* I must say something about the obstacles I had to overcome. It began with a sort of summary examination intended to determine whether I was capable of directing a film with due regard to economy. It took the form of making a feature film taken from a Feydeau comedy, *On purge bébé*.

The man in charge of the sound was Joseph de Bretagne, who was to have a share in nearly all my future French productions and played a large part in my film education. He taught me his creed of authentic sound, and with him I really did use a minimum of trickery. Nor have I ever changed my mind about this. I regard dubbing, that is to say, the addition of sound after the picture has been shot, as an outrage. If we were living in the twelfth century, a period of lofty civilization, the practitioners of dubbing would be burnt in the market-place for heresy. Dubbing is equivalent to a belief in the duality of the soul.

There is not a yard of dubbed film in *La Chienne*. When shooting out of doors we sought to damp down background noise with hangings and mattresses. We tried the experiment of attaching a microphone to the projector. Hotchkiss, the manager of Western Electric, was passionately interested in these experiments. He took a hand in them, realizing that my achievement might extend the range of the talking film. At that time we had not thought of recording sound on location, particularly not in a town, where the street noises are so loud that they may swamp the dialogue. But on the other hand I did not want to shoot street scenes in the studio. I wanted the realism of genuine buildings, streets and traffic. I remember a gutter whose waters rippled in front of a house which was to serve as background for an important scene. The microphone made it sound like a torrent. It must be borne in mind that in those days we did not possess directional microphones. I solved the problem by taking a close-up of the gutter and thereby justifying the noise it made. Joseph de Bretagne was delighted to have a part in the experiment, even as an onlooker, and his enthusiasm gave me great pleasure. It was the beginning of a friendship that has lasted to this day.

I triumphantly passed the test of *On purge bébé*. With the help of my two assistants, Pierre Prévert and Claude Heyman, I wrote the script in a week, shot it in another week and completed the editing in a third. Three weeks after shooting began the film was shown at the Gaumont Palace and brought in a lot of money. Not only had I passed the test but I had acquired the reputation of an innovator. As the title indicates, the story has to do with a lavatory. The flush sounds several times in the course of the film, acquiring the significance of a musical accompaniment. In my concern for realism I used a real flush in one of the studio toilets. The result was a cataract of sound that delighted the producers and caused me to be regarded as a great man, which is one more proof that one must not attempt to order one's destiny – Providence knows more than we do.

I have spoken already of my pleasure in working with Michel Simon, and to this I must add the joy of discovering Fernandel. The studio did not think it possible to use that improbable face. They said he looked like a horse. It called for Braunberger's insistence to get him accepted.

Satisfied with the result of the test, my examiners agreed to produce *La Chienne*. This was in 1931. I learned later that the intervention of Monsieur Monteux, prompted by Braunberger, had decided the matter. But I was still not at the end of my troubles. The leading woman's part would have suited Catherine marvellously, but the actress Janie Marèse was under contract to Billancourt Studios and so it was natural

for her to be chosen. In any case, Catherine was precisely
the kind of actress likely to displease Richebé. So I gave up
Catherine and accepted Janie Marèse. This betrayal marked
the end of our life together. Catherine could not bear the
disappointment. I offered to sacrifice myself by giving up
La Chienne, and she refused the offer, hoping that I would
insist. But I did not insist; and this was the end of an
adventure which should have been pursued in happiness.
The cinema was for both of us a jealous god.

'La Chienne'

The leading players in *La Chienne* were Michel Simon, Janie Marèse and Georges Flamant. All were equally remarkable, and all pursued the cult of realism to the point of living in their private lives a situation not unlike that in the film. Since that heartrending story was based on a novel by a writer labelled a humorist, a great many people, and especially Roger Richebé, expected a comedy. They were disappointed. The story in a nutshell was about the downward drift of a clerk who robs his employer to satisfy the demands of a little tart. The clerk is an amateur painter whom the art-dealers find to have a certain amount of talent. He gives all the money to the girl, whose pimp is insatiable in his requirements. When he finds out about the pimp the clerk stabs the girl with a paper-knife. The pimp is arrested, convicted of the murder and guillotined. The real murderer becomes a beggar.

It happened that the three protagonists, carried away by the parts they were playing, ended up by sharing the sentiments of the three characters. Michel Simon, playing the clerk, fell genuinely in love with Janie Marèse, who fell for Flamant, playing the pimp. Flamant was a remarkable amateur actor whom I had chosen for the part because, having frequented the *milieu* – the criminal underworld – he had picked up their jargon and behaviour. I will not go so far as to say that Flamant 'pimped' Janie Marèse, far from it; but he got her away from a wealthy protector whose influence in the worlds of the cinema and the theatre would have greatly helped her in her career. Flamant kept his hold

on Janie by the use of methods that were in the best romantic tradition of the *milieu*. He would make her undress
and lie naked on a couch while he crouched at her feet. He
would stay like that for hours 'without touching her' . . .
'You see, mate, all I do is look at her. I look at her with
devotion, but I don't touch her. After an hour I can do
anything I like with her. Without touching her – that's
what's important.'

Janie Marèse, the daughter of respectable parents, had
been educated in a convent. I rehearsed her in her part
before shooting the film. There was only one thing against
her, and that was her over-refined accent. I made her
imitate Maurice Chevalier and it worked perfectly.

As for the murder, in the real-life story it was replaced by
an accident. Flamant, dazzled by the prospect of becoming
a star, bought himself a big American car. He scarcely knew
how to drive. When the shooting of the film was finished
he took Janie for a drive, crashed the car and she was killed
in the accident. Michel Simon was so heartbroken that he
fainted during the funeral and had to be supported while he
walked round the grave. In the course of my film career I
have encountered many actors who lived their parts, but
none of them followed Pirandello to this extent. Michel
Simon was no longer himself: he was Monsieur Legrand, a
clerk in an office. Only he could have undergone such a
transformation.

Even at the beginning of his career legends sprang up
around Michel Simon. He was reputed to be particularly
interested in unorthodox sexual practices. He did not deny
it, and indeed I think these rumours amused him. He was
exceptionally penetrating in his condemnation of the
stupidity and bad taste of our time. He was a believer in

health foods long before they became fashionable. I mentioned to him that nowadays fermented cheeses never had cheese mites. In my young days if one forgot to cover up a piece of Camembert one found it swarming with maggots the next day; but these have vanished since cheeses were protected by chemical products added to the milk. Michel Simon mourned for the days of mites – 'One had only to scratch the rind to get rid of them,' he said; and for him this was symbolic of our time, which sacrificed quality for convenience. If any mention was made of his so-called perversity he would reply, 'There's only one thing on earth that has a little life in it, and that's a woman's clitoris.' He loved animals, especially monkeys; he was even said to have had a love-affair with a she-monkey, but I personally doubt the truth of the tales that were told about him. In any case, where the she-monkey is concerned I can bear witness to the purity of their relationship. That charming animal had a real affection for him, a need for love that was touching and utterly chaste.

After the shooting, the editing of the film was accomplished without incident. Pierre Braunberger, who had closely followed the shooting, was delighted. Richebé, who had been away, had it run through for him. Since he had expected a comedy he was very much put out, but he thought that by editing he could make it into the kind of film he wanted. He asked another director, Fejos, to take charge of the operation; but when the latter heard that I did not agree he refused to do so. Richebé then passed the film over to an accommodating lady named Madame Batcheff. I protested, but in vain. 'It's for your own good,' people who witnessed this act of robbery told me. 'You've been living with the film for months. What it needs to make it really first-rate is a wider perspective – a fresh eye.' I have heard that talk about 'a fresh eye' many times; it is simply a euphemism designed to reconcile a film-maker to the theft of his work.

The day after my film had been taken away from me I went to the studio to try to rescue it. I found two men posted at the door who told me that they had been put there to prevent me from entering. I protested bitterly, calling for Braunberger and Richebé and all the big shots, but in vain. My cutting room was closed to me; my film had been handed over to a person who, although doubtless competent, understood nothing about it. For three days and nights I drifted from bar to bar in Montmartre, trying to drown my sorrows in drink. It was a young director, Yves Allegret, who saved me. He took me to Braunberger, who advised me to apply to Monsieur Monteux and made an appointment for me. Monteux received me at the home of his lady-friend, the enchanting Berthe de Longpré, famous throughout Paris for her flawless bosom. My story filled her with indignation and she insisted that Monsieur Monteux should at once order Richebé to let my film go out in the form I intended. I may mention in passing that I was to meet Monteux and this lady later on in very different circumstances. It was in Cannes, during the Second World War. Monteux, being a Jew, was in great danger. Berthe de Longpré was still with him, having refused to desert him.

The first showing of *La Chienne* was at the Palais Rochechouart. Jacques Becker, who was doing his military service, applied for special leave in order to be there. When the lights went up after the running of the film I found myself facing a non-commissioned officer in the Hussars whose tense expression suggested that he was in the throes of a nervous crisis. I recognized Jacques and asked Valentine Tessier to take care of him. She was sobbing unrestrainedly, equally moved by the film. 'Look after Jacques,' I said. 'He's got some sort of cramp in his face.' But Valentine kissed me again and again. Even my brother Pierre, generally so guarded in his language, said in a shaking voice: 'It is very good, Jean, very good.' Finally Jacques Becker recovered his self-control and said to me: 'I shall have finished my military service in two months. From that day on you'll find me on your doorstep, and I shall go on pestering you until you've taken me on as your assistant.'

My staff for the shooting of *La Chienne* was outstanding – Claude Heyman, Pierre Schwab and the delightful Pierre Prévert, who was like a character out of *A Midsummer Night's Dream*. His brother, Jacques, often came along to see me and helped to maintain the sardonic spirit which the film called for. It was the heyday of the 'October Group', and Surrealism was glittering with its early brilliance. We dreamed of founding a 'Société du Geste Gratuit' of which the aim would be to reward totally pointless actions. For example, anyone who set fire to the house of a neighbour who had done him no harm would be rewarded. Anyone who stopped the traffic to let an old woman cross the street would be condemned, whereas anyone who stopped the traffic for no reason at all would be rewarded. It was a theory that favoured universal peace. Crimes as a rule are committed for a purpose, wars are declared in the hope of conquest. By making these acts profitless we should have peace on earth except for a few madmen.

Despite the success of *La Chienne* at its preview, Richebé still had his doubts. He decided to try it out in the provinces and he selected the town of Nancy. Here it became involved in politics. Certain groups on the extreme right, among them the 'Croix de Feu', got it into their heads that it was a revolutionary film, I have no idea why. Perhaps they saw it as an insult to the judiciary. Anyway the showing in Nancy was greeted with roars of disapproval, whistles, hoots and the banging of seats, and finally a warning that this would happen again if the film was not withdrawn. It seemed to be the end of my hopes in the cinema. Once again I had to think about getting out. I had lost confidence in myself. After all, perhaps that audience and those critics were right. Perhaps it was silly of me to go on: but fortunately, as the poet Georges Fourest says, God has a finger, and his finger was there to confound my enemies.

I was friendly with a distributor named Siritzky, whom I had met at the house of Marcel Pagnol. He was a Russian Jew with a passion for the cinema, and a man of exceptional physical strength, which was what had first interested Marcel Pagnol. He could swing a smith's hammer and check it a few millimetres above a coin standing on edge. He had been a quartermaster in the Turkish Navy. Marcel Pagnol said of him: 'A man who has served in the Turkish Navy can't help knowing about films.' His life had been a succession of ups and downs, and the thought of another failure did not alarm him.

He had started in the film business by opening a small cinema in a remote suburb. Here he showed unusual films, the kind ordinary exhibitors fought shy of. His success had brought him financial support, and at the time of my troubles with *La Chienne* he was running half-a-dozen cinemas, including a very classy one in Biarritz. He asked to see my film and liked it very much. Accordingly he arranged with Richebé to show it in his Biarritz house. But

he presented it in an unusual way. By means of press in-
sertions and placards he advised families to stay away from
the film: it was so horrifying, he said, that it was not suited
to sensitive viewers – although, when one considers
current film-production, I was the most timid of pioneers.
The result was that on the first night people had to be turned
away. The film ran for several weeks, a thing that had never
before happened in Biarritz. This attracted the notice of the
management of the Colisée Cinema in Paris, and they
arranged to show the film. It was an immense success and
had a record run.

I imagined that after the success of *La Chienne* it would be
roses, roses all the way. But nothing of the kind. The uproar in Nancy had caused me to be regarded as a con-
troversial director. Moreover, I brought along ideas and
stories of my own, whereas the producers prefer to use
theirs. I have said that the money-men think they know
what the public wants, and I shall go on saying it. The truth
is that they know nothing about it, any more than I do. The
mistake lies in the fact that most people believe that what is
being sold is a story, whereas what is really being sold is a
number of personalities, those of the film-maker and the
actors. The film-maker is persuaded that a given story will
enable him to express himself, whereas the money-man, for
his part, believes that any story he likes will attract the
public. I am talking of honest film-makers and money-
men who are no less sincere in their beliefs. There is no way
of financing films except by falling in with the views of the
financier. If the director has sufficient strength of personality he will control the operation as a whole and make himself what he ought to be, the real author of the film.

I am reminded of an incident which, better than any dissertation, illustrates the belief of the money-men in their infallibility. I had an appointment to discuss a film project with an important producer of German origin. He was very fat, an elephant of a man, and he spoke French with a thick German accent. We settled down in his office and I started to outline my ideas; but I had scarcely begun when he cut me short. 'You have a reputation for wanting to make films for intellectuals,' he said. 'There's no money in that. We've got to please the midinettes if we want to make money.' And then, disposing his vast bulk more comfortably in his armchair, he smiled coyly and added: 'Me – midinette.'

I owed my next film to Michel Simon. We both thought that the Fauchois play, *Boudu sauvé des Eaux*, had the makings of a splendid film, above all because of the possibilities which the role of Boudu offered Simon. The part, which was that of a layabout incapable of adapting himself to life, might have been made for that brilliant actor. Thanks to Michel Simon's reputation, the financing of the film presented no problem. It succeeded beyond our hopes, the public reaction being a mixture of laughter and fury. Boudu foreshadowed the hippy movement long before it came into being – indeed, he was the perfect hippy. During one sequence in which he cleaned his shoes with a satin bedspread the audience, especially the women, cried out in horror; but they were soon won over by the outrageousness of the situation and the players.

As usual, I had made great changes in the original story. Fauchois, the author, took this in very bad part and threatened to have his name removed from the credits. Thirty years later, upon seeing the film again, he was astonished by its enthusiastic reception. He was brought on to the stage,

and the ovation he received caused him to forget my un-
faithfulness to his story.

After a period of involuntary unemployment, neither my
first nor my last, I again yielded to the temptation to produce a film of my own. The money came to me from private
sources, nothing to do with the film trade. The story was
based on a wonderful novel by my friend, Simenon, entitled *La Nuit du Carrefour*. Jacques Becker was production
manager, my nephew, Claude Renoir, was assistant cameraman; the script-girl was Mimi Champagne and Jo de
Bretagne was in charge of sound. All friends, in short, with
my brother Pierre playing the leading part. The supporting
cast were all amateurs except for a few professional actors
who were personal friends. The team also included the
musicologist, Jean Gehret, the painter, Dignimont, the
film-critic, Jean Mitry, and the dramatist, Michel Duran.
My aim was to convey by imagery the mystery of that
starkly mysterious tale, and I meant to subordinate the plot
to the atmosphere. Simenon's book wonderfully evoked
the dreariness of that crossroads situated fifty kilometres
from Paris. I do not believe there can be a more depressing
place anywhere on earth. The small cluster of houses, lost
in a sea of mist, rain and mud, are magnificently described
in the novel. They might have been painted by Vlaminck.

My enthusiasm for the atmosphere Simenon had evoked
caused me once again to discard my own views in the
matter of basing a film on a work of literature. We rented
one of the houses at the crossroads, which happened to be
empty, and there set up our quarters. A good many of the
team slept on the floor in the living-room. We had our
meals there. When the darkness was as mysterious as we
wished we aroused the sleepers and went to work. Within

fifty kilometres of Paris we led the life of explorers of a lost land. In the matter of mystery the result exceeded our expectations, particularly since, two reels having been lost, the story was pretty well incomprehensible, even to its author.

Marcel Lucien, the cameraman, achieved some remarkable fog effects, and the actors, both amateur and professional, were so influenced by that sinister crossroads that they became part of the background. They enacted mystery in a way they could never have done in the comfort of a studio. *La Nuit du Carrefour* remains a completely absurd experiment that I cannot think of without nostalgia. In these days, when everything is so well organized, one cannot work in that kind of way.

Thanks to my propensity for working with close friends, I have often made films in what amounted to a family circle. When we were making *Madame Bovary* in 1933, our life in the little Normandy town of Lyons-la-Forêt caused us to forget our everyday problems. The 'family' included Pierre, my real brother, and Valentine Tessier, who was like a sister to me. We foregathered in the evenings with Gaston Gallimard, one of the backers of the film. Jacques Becker and Le Vigan were also there. Our main diversion was a game called 'lefoutro' inspired by Courteline's *Gaîtés de l'Escadron*. A napkin folded in the shape of a male organ was placed in the middle of the dinner-table, and the rule was that it must be studiously ignored. Anyone who showed the slightest sign of being distracted by it was rapped three times over the knuckles with 'lefoutro' while the following sentence was pronounced: 'I saw you making advances to your neighbour. You insulted Monsieur Lefoutro. You are hereby punished and your fault is pardoned.' The guilty person could protest – 'How could I have insulted Monsieur Lefoutro when I was busy cutting up my chicken?' In this case a vote was taken and the penalty doubled if the sentence was confirmed. Harmless games of this kind did more to prepare us for the next day's work than tedious discourses.

Marcel Pagnol

There exist in this world rare human beings who are possessed of gifts both for commerce and for the art of entertainment. Charlie Chaplin is the outstanding example, and on a more modest financial level one may cite the Swedish director, Ingmar Bergman. The latter has contrived to make films of his own choosing and to survive, thanks to an organization that seems to me in all respects remarkable. He works in collaboration with the Royal Theatre in Stockholm, and in winter, when the weather is not suitable for outdoor photography, he works for the stage. With the return of summer weather he makes films. His actors are paid both by the theatre and by the films in which he casts them. This is a wonderfully economical system of production. Since they are in the Swedish language his films obviously have a limited distribution, which limits the actors' salaries. Only those who speak English can from time to time indulge in the luxury of an American engagement.

In France an author of genius managed to create a perfectly efficient organization for the distribution of his films. This was Marcel Pagnol. Not only did he restrict himself geographically, like Bergman, but he did so also in the historical sense. His company, 'Les Films Marcel Pagnol', operated like a medieval workshop. While I was working on my film *Toni*, I saw him constantly. He used my Vieux Colombier electrical equipment. He collected technicians, actors and workpeople in his country house like a fifteenth-century master-carpenter. I had rented a lodging not far away and I competed with his outfit in thrilling games of *pétanque* or *boules*. We exchanged professional services: I occasionally directed a scene for him and he helped me out with problems of dialogue. He had his own distributing organization and, after the appearance of *Marius* and *Fanny*, he even owned a cinema on the Canebière in Marseilles. The great reputation he had achieved allowed him this degree of independence. Pagnol's commercial success was based on his talent. It worked, and worked very well.

Marcel Pagnol considered that the only purpose of women was to bear children, and that this was approximately where their usefulness ceased. He had made up his mind to have a child, and a fair-haired one, and he was looking round for a blonde mother, whom he proposed to marry. His friend, Léon Voltera, proprietor of the Casino de Paris, the most fashionable post-war music-hall, and also of the Théâtre de Paris, which specialized in serious theatre, advised him to choose one of his English dancing-girls, and every night Pagnol and Voltera looked in at the Casino de Paris, where 'les girls' were performing and, discussed the merits of the unwitting candidates. Sometimes they preferred one and sometimes another, but in the end they made up their minds and Pagnol called upon the winner. She accepted on the spot, delighted at the idea of becoming Madame Marcel Pagnol. I met her a number of times. She was a charming girl, but she wanted more out of life than merely the function of bearing children. In an unconscious protest the child she bore her husband was dark-haired.

Léon Voltera adored Pagnol. It must be said that, thanks to *Marius* and *Fanny*, the Théâtre de Paris, which was only separated by a passageway from the Casino, was always filled. Voltera was also the owner of Luna Park, the amusement park by the Porte Maillot. He would invite freaks from

Luna Park to first nights at the Théâtre de Paris, and thus
one was liable to see Parisian celebrities seated next to the
'living skeleton' or the 'bearded lady'. His reason for
gathering together this mixed assemblage of people had
nothing to do with publicity. It was simply an act of friendliness towards the people who worked for him.

One cannot talk of Marcel Pagnol without conjuring up
the powerful figure of Raimu. Although Raimu was perhaps the greatest French actor of the century, he was completely ignorant of some things. All he knew about the
cinema was that a close-up showed the details of a face.
During shooting he would constantly say to the cameraman,
'Make me big.' I was very fond of him, and I think he had a
liking for me. Perhaps he felt that intelligence, that quality
so highly esteemed by the world, is often accompanied by a
painful lack of simplicity. He played the parts entrusted to
him by Pagnol without thinking about them, trusting to his
own instinct and the immense talent of the author.

There is a widespread belief in the stupidity of actors, but
it is without foundation. Intelligence is as well distributed
among actors as among other kinds of human being; but in
the case of an actor his talent, or genius, has nothing to do
with his intellect. I have known actors with brilliant minds
who were lamentable on the stage.

This was not the case with Jouvet, who was bursting
with both talent and intelligence. Jouvet analysed his parts
word by word. He knew how to extract the deepest sense
of a text. His rehearsals were a constant series of discoveries.
Giraudoux often re-wrote his own lines after Jouvet had
found a new meaning in them.

Pagnol believes in nothing but dialogue, and in his case
he is right, since this is the medium that serves him best.

My own conception is diametrically opposed to his. I believe in dialogue not as a means of explaining the situation but as an integral part of the scene. Let us suppose it is a love-scene. The actress is happy in her part; she is beautiful and talented. The young man is extremely handsome and, what is more, has a pleasing personality. One has to convey to the public their overwhelming emotion. In the theatre there is only one way of involving the audience, and that is by finding language worthy of the occasion. But in a film, thanks to the close-up, so much explicitness is unnecessary. The texture of the skin, the glow in the eyes, the moisture of the mouth – all these can say more than any number of words. Most film dialogue seems to have been interpolated for the sake of clarification. It is a false approach. Dialogue is a part of the theme and reveals character. For the real theme is the person, whom dialogue, picture, situation, setting, temperature and lighting all combine together to depict. The world is one whole.

The Popular Front

I was astonished, on the eve of the Second World War, by
the way Hitler was accepted by so many decent people who
were themselves incapable of hurting a fly. The fact is that
they were counting on Hitler to rid them of things which
irritated them, such as unpunctual trains and strikes in the
public services. 'In Germany,' they said, 'nobody goes on
strike and the trains all run on time.'

The separation of mankind into fascists and communists
is quite meaningless. Fascism, like communism, believes in
progress. The followers of both creeds look to a social order
based on technology. Technology is the ruling god, whether
in Moscow or New York. But in the last resort one has to
take up one's own stand. If I were forced to do so, with my
back to the wall, I would opt for communism because it
seems to me that those who believe in it have a truer conception of human dignity. But for me, as I have said again
and again and shall go on saying, the real enemy is progress,
not because it doesn't work but precisely because it does.
Aircraft are not dangerous because they occasionally crash,
but because they leave and land on time and carry their
passengers in comfort. Progress is dangerous because it is
based on perfect technology. It is its success which has distorted the normal values of life and compelled man to live
in a world for which he was not intended. If only it allowed
us time to adapt ourselves. But no. No sooner have we
achieved some degree of stability than a new invention
comes along to upset everything.

I had just finished shooting *Le Crime de Monsieur Lange*,

which was a great success. This film had placed me in the category of left-wing film-makers, no doubt because it had to do with a workers' co-operative, a system that is now accepted in even the most right-wing circles. In 1935 the Communist Party asked me to make a propaganda film, which I was delighted to do. I believed that every honest man owed it to himself to resist Nazism. I am a film-maker, and this was the only way in which I could play a part in the battle. But I over-estimated the power of the cinema. *La Grande Illusion*, for all its success, did not prevent the Second World War. I tell myself, however, that many 'great illusions', many newspaper articles, books and demonstrations, may yet have some effect.

The making of *La Vie est à Nous* put me in touch with people having a genuine love of the working class. I saw in the workers' possession of power a possible antidote to our destructive egotism. Today, in the hemisphere to which chance has brought me, that of the 'over-developed' nations, there is no longer a working class. Material prosperity has been accompanied by a diminished purity of spirit. One nail drives out another. The bourgeois way of life has made the worker himself into a bourgeois. A genuine proletariat is now only to be found in the under-developed countries. The Brazilian peon is a proletarian, but the worker for General Motors is not.

Left-wing militants at the time of *La Vie est à Nous* were truly disinterested. They were Frenchmen with all the defects and virtues of Frenchmen, wholly without Russian mysticism or Latin grandiloquence. They were warm-hearted realists. Their views might differ, but they were still Frenchmen. I felt at ease in their company, enjoying the same popular songs and the same red wine.

I found myself one day in the presence of two opposed groups.

This happened at Vincennes, on the occasion of a big anti-Hitler gathering. One of the two groups was composed of carpenters, men with big moustaches wearing for the occasion the traditional clothes of their craft. The other was composed of young women laboratory assistants. They were arguing about the aims of the revolution. 'As for me,' said one of the carpenters, 'I'd take advantage of the revolution to loot the cellars of the rich. They can keep their pictures and silver dishes. All I want is good red wine.' A girl from the other group said indignantly: 'What right have we got to take the place of the bourgeoisie if we're simply going to imitate their debauched way of living? I want the revolution to improve the human condition, to make a nobler and more generous kind of man than is possible in a reactionary society.'

La Vie est à Nous, which I supervised, was shot principally by my youthful assistants and technicians. I directed a few sequences but had nothing to do with the editing. Another film, *La Marseillaise*, gave me an opportunity to express my love of the French. It came about through a proceeding which could not have been more unorthodox. A subscription was opened, the purchasers of tickets having the right to see the film for nothing. This was how the film was financed, and it proves that films can be made by subscription – always provided one does not expect to make a fortune out of them.

La Marseillaise told of the march on Paris of the Marseilles volunteers and the capture of the Tuileries which overthrew the monarchy. Around this historic episode I depicted the daily lives of some of the protagonists. We went from Louis XVI to Roederer, from the Queen to a working girl, and from the palace to the streets.

Thanks to these two films I breathed the exalted air of the Popular Front. For a short time the French really believed that they could love one another. One felt oneself borne on a wave of warm-heartedness.

The Spirit and the Letter

Une Partie de Campagne and *Les Bas Fonds* (The Lower Depths), both made in 1936, illustrate what I mean when I think of the relationship between a film-script and the direction of the film. It is a relationship characterized by an apparent lack of fidelity. There is a world of difference between the original concept and the final result. Nevertheless my infidelity is really superficial, for I believe I have always been true to the general spirit of the work. To me a script is simply a vehicle to be modified as one draws nearer to the real intention, which must not change. The intention is something that the film-maker has at the back of his mind, often without knowing it, but if it is not there the end result is superficial. The film-maker establishes his characters by making them speak, and creates the general ambiance by building sets and choosing locations. His own inward conviction only gradually appears, and generally in collaboration with the artisans of the film – actors, technicians, natural settings or artificial sets. We are subject to the in-immutable law whereby the essence is only revealed when the object begins to exist.

The film-director is not a creator but a midwife. His business is to deliver the actor of a child that he did not know he had inside him. The implement which he uses for the purpose is simply his knowledge of the environment and acquiescence in its impact.

Every human being carries a conviction within him, as it were a religion, conceived naturally and unconsciously. Every piece of work each of us undertakes is to be valued according to how far we are able to realize this conviction. For some people it is an undiscovered treasure, buried in the mass of lies that constitute our lives. What is interesting is that this progress of the creator towards his own inner truth does not prevent his collaborators from discovering theirs. On the contrary, it helps them.

How often has it happened to me that, when about to shoot a scene in a given setting, I have found that the setting does not fit the situation! One's arrival on the set where one is about to shoot a new sequence may be accompanied by most painful discoveries. I may not have realized, when the set was being designed in the office, that one particular door would be of so much importance, or that the whole set was too large, so that the actors would take an unconscionably long time to walk across it; and then one has either to build a smaller set or else introduce dialogue or business to render the crossing less tedious. The trouble is that the dialogue or gestures have to have dramatic value and fit in with the piece as a whole. In many cases adjustments such as this turn out to be fruitful, causing the film-maker to see possibilities that he had not envisaged.

I had undertaken to make a film of Maupassant's story, *Une Partie de Campagne*. It was intended to be a 'short', and in fact ran for fifty minutes. But the theme is so important that it could very well have been a full-length film. A tale of disappointed love, followed by a ruined life could furnish matter for a long novel. But Maupassant gives us the essentials in a few pages, and it was the transposition to the screen of these bare bones of a big story that attracted me.

We selected a site only a few miles from Marlotte, where I had made *La Fille de l'Eau*. My script was designed for fine weather, and I wrote it with scenes of brilliant sunshine in mind, although there were one or two cloud effects. But the wind changed and a large part of the film was shot in pouring rain. Either we had to give up or the script had to be altered. I liked the story too much to give it up, so I adapted the script. This turned out to be all to the good. The threat of a storm added a new dimension to the drama. When the shooting was over, Braunberger, who was producing, was so pleased with it that he proposed that I should turn it into a full-length film. But I could not agree. To do so would have been contrary to Maupassant's intention and to the intention of my own script. Jacques Prévert, who was consulted, agreed with me. In any case, I had to give it up in order to make *Les Bas Fonds*. I left the film in the hands of Marguerite, my friend and film-editor. Then the war broke out and I went to America. Marguerite did the editing on her own. Braunberger brought out the film after an interval of ten years. As I had foreseen, they had found it impossible to make it into a full-length film.

I made *Les Bas Fonds* for the Albatros Film Company, directed by Alexander Kamenka. It meant a lot to me, for I greatly admired that company's silent films. They had been defeated by the coming of sound. Either the Russian actors did not speak French, or else they did so with an impossibly bad accent. They lived in a community, outside the run of French life, and had had no chance to learn French. Their leading actor-director was Mosjukin, who had been brilliant in *Le Brasier Ardent* and *Kean*.

At the time of making *Les Bas Fonds* the original organization had been turned into an ordinary film-producing company. Owing to lack of money, Kamenka had been unable to preserve the co-operative nature of the company, which was one of the few that could be compared to the

Pagnol and Bergman organizations. Like his French and German colleagues, he had to work with the support of the banks; but he had lost none of his love of the cinema and showed himself to be a first-rate producer.

He had already had a script of *Les Bas Fonds* prepared by Zamiatin and Companeez, but I am incapable of working to anyone else's prescription. I am prepared to accept all manner of ideas and suggestions provided they arise out of working in collaboration. I told Kamenka this, but he was doubtful of my ability as a script-writer, although I had written the scripts of my previous films, some of which had been successful. But I was labelled a director, and this seemed to be an insuperable obstacle: a director does not write scripts. I suggested to Kamenka that I should join forces with Charles Spaak, author of *La Kermesse Héroïque*, with whom in any case I wanted to work. Kamenka agreed to this. The script which Spaak and I produced differed considerably from Maxim Gorki's story, so we submitted it to Gorki for his approval. His reply was a letter to Kamenka in which he declared himself in favour of free adaptation and said that he entirely approved of what we had done.

My discovery of new actors, while we were engaged in shooting the film, led to further changes. I discovered Jean Gabin, who was already a star, and, believe me, that was no small discovery. I cannot be said to have discovered Jouvet, having already seen him on the stage. He discovered me and helped me in that constant unfolding of the theme which I would call my method if I did not detest all methods. Gabin was at his most expressive when he did not have to raise his voice. Magnificent actor that he was, he got his greatest effects with the smallest means. I devised scenes for his benefit which could be spoken in a murmur. We had no idea that this style of acting was to be adopted all over the world, and that the number of murmuring actors was to be legion. It is a style that does not always produce the happiest results. Gabin could express the most violent emotion with a mere quiver of his impassive face where another man had to shout to get the same effect. 'Le Jean', as Gabrielle called him, could overwhelm the audience with a mere flicker of his eyelids.

Whenever possible I conducted rehearsals in the Italian fashion, to which Michel Simon and Louis Jouvet had converted me. It consists in seating the actors round a table and getting them to read their lines without any expression whatever – the text should be read as tonelessly as if it were the telephone directory. What happens is that the actor learns his part in this way, denying himself all reaction until he has explored all the possibilities of every phrase, every word and every gesture. Actors who try to interpret their role from the outset are very apt to fall into the commonplace. Every part of a stage-play or film should be an original creation, and hasty work does not permit one to escape the well-trodden paths. For example, when an actress is playing the part of a mother confronted by the dead body of her son, there is a very good chance that she will convey her distress in a manner based on performances that she has previously seen. Her sobs and tears will be the same as those she has used before, or will be like those of other actresses. So we get together, actors and director, and we go through the text two or three or even twenty times. And suddenly, in this lifeless reading of the lines, the director discovers a tiny spark. That's it! Starting from there the actor has a chance to achieve an original interpretation of the role. It is a magical procedure, and it seldom fails. In short, this is another instance of the influence of attendant circumstances upon the performer. In this case the attendant circumstance is the text; but in other cases it may be the make-up, the setting or the costume. In a word, I believe that artistic creation must be centripetal before it becomes centrifugal. Only when the artist has mastered the elements of his problem can he bring himself into it.

As Werner Krauss said to me, a clever actor using clichés can be sure of a superficial success, considering the public's fondness for finding itself on familiar ground. In my view, originality and success are strangers to one another; but I also hold that originality, despite appearances, will end by making itself felt, and that easy success is soon forgotten. People today have heard of Sarah Bernhardt only because there is a theatre named after her: my father thought she acted like a goat. Who in these days remembers Luc Olivier Merson, a painter who in his own time was showered with honours? One of the reasons for believing in immortality is that Van Gogh did not sell a single canvas during his lifetime. Public recognition and the rating of an artist at his true level often takes time. Real fame is generally posthumous.

In every successful film there is one scene to which its success may be attributed; but it is impossible to tell in advance which scene this will be. It is a sort of key that opens a locked door. The key itself may be rusty or badly finished, but no matter; for me it opens that particular door. Without the film-maker realizing it, the scene puts the audience in touch with every character in the film, and thanks to it they come to life and become recognizable people. Their words and gestures, from being matters of indifference, become passionately interesting and the audience wants to know more about them.

In *Les Bas Fonds* the scene in question, the key scene, was the one which I called the 'snail scene'. It takes the form of an avowal made by the Baron, Louis Jouvet, to Pepel, played by Jean Gabin. The latter, who is in love, talks of his longing to escape from the lowest depths and bring the woman he loves with him. He is resolved to give up his present way of life, that of a thief. 'My father was a thief and I was born a thief,' he says. The Baron replies by telling the story of his life, depicting its various phases by changing his costume. He has been what the differing clothes he wore have made him. While he is talking he notices a small snail climbing up a blade of grass. He picks it up and sets it to climb up his finger. I have been present at numerous public showings of *Les Bas Fonds* and have never known that scene to fail. When the snail begins to climb Jouvet's finger the audience warms and one senses their passionate interest in the movements of the snail. The Baron becomes familiar to them and they identify themselves with Gabin in listening to his story.

The Actor and the Truth

My attitude to my films is the same as the Baron's attitude to the different costumes he has worn in his life. They are what I have made of them, and I am what they have made of me. *Les Bas Fonds* was my nineteenth film. After twelve years' experience, reverses and successes, I was beginning to feel that I knew something about my business. I had even appeared in a film directed by Pabst and played parts in Cavalcanti's *Little Red Ridinghood* and *La Petite Lili*. I had also played in my own films. I consider it essential for a director to make an occasional incursion to the other side of the camera, and I do not forget that some great directors started as actors. I had realized what my path must be – to let myself be absorbed by everything around me. Life itself is an infinitely more rewarding spectacle than all the inventions of the mind.

I had learnt that the only way to impose one's personality is to help one's collaborators to express their own. Many directors have a passion for peering through the camera and deciding the exact frame. Why should not the operator be allowed to use his own imagination? A director should know enough about his business to be able to determine the frame simply by knowing the number of the lens and the distance between the lens and the object. Our function is not to copy Rembrandt but to put our own impress on every aspect of the film.

I am opposed to the method of some directors who play a scene themselves and then say to the actor, 'Now do it like that.' If the actors do as they're told the result will be a film

Above: My brother Pierre as Louis XVI in *La Marseillaise,* 1937 *Below:* Marcel Pagnol

in which all the parts seem to have been rendered by the same interpreter. What could be more tedious? To say nothing of the nonsense of corpulent gentlemen, quite possibly without acting talent, miming a love-scene for the benefit of a girl of eighteen and saying, 'Do it like me.' Apart from which, this gives the actor no chance to express his own personality.

A device of mine has become famous among my generation of actors. When, during rehearsal, an actor gives me an interpretation which I think false I never say, 'That's bad,' or 'You're wrong'. I say: 'Splendid! You have an excellent idea of the part, but I would like you to run through the scene again just to check one or two details.' So he repeats the scene and I point out an obvious inconsistency or suggest to him that it will be more effective if he lays less emphasis on a particular point. Gradually, in the course of repetition, I break down the actor's resistance and obtain from him, not my own interpretation of the scene but the one which I think best suits himself. I know this result has been achieved when the actor thinks it is his own doing and says to his colleagues, 'I advised Renoir that this and that ought to be changed. He agreed and the scene was much improved.'

I may cite an opinion about myself, expressed by Lulu Wattier, the theatrical agent, which greatly pleased me. Someone recommended an actor to her, saying that he had played a part in one of my films. 'That doesn't mean a thing,' said Wattier. 'Renoir could make a wardrobe act.'

I have sometimes cast actors in roles quite outside their normal range. This generally ends in commercial failure, but from the artistic point of view I have known it to give excellent results. It delights me to use an actor in a style

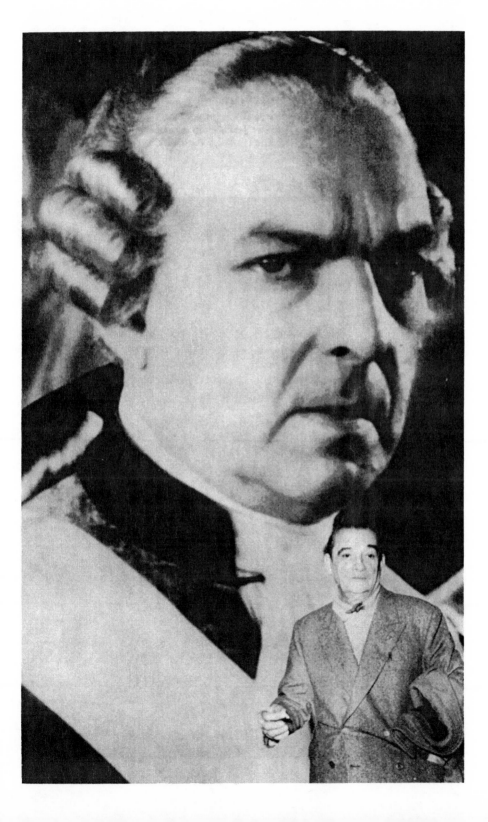

Background spread: Les Bas-Fonds, 1936: Louis
Jouvet as the Baron at the moment when he
loses all his money at the gaming tables
Above: Sylvia Bataille and Georges d'Arnoux in *La
Partie de Campagne*, 1936
Below: Jean Gabin and Louis Jouvet in the snail
scene from *Les Bas-Fonds*

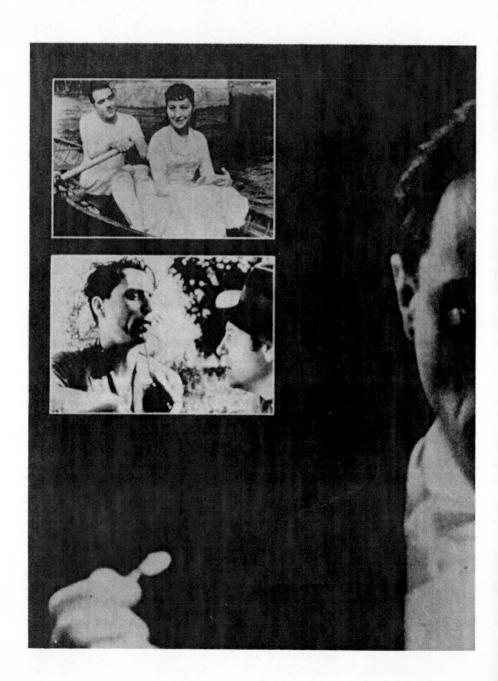

Above: La Bête Humaine, 1938: Jean Gabin and
Carette aboard the 'Lison', Jacques Lentier's
locomotive
Middle: Claude Renoir aboard the 'Lison' during
the shooting of the film
Below: The first meeting between Jacques Lentier
(Jean Gabin) and Séverine (Simone Simon)

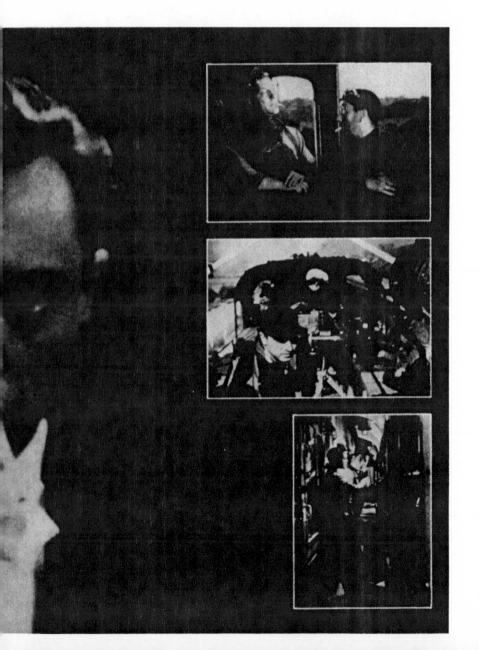

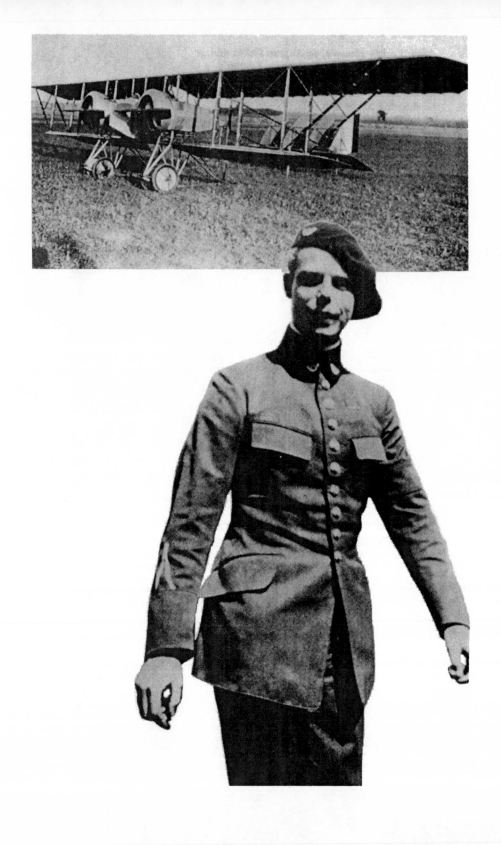

which is not his own; he is obliged to vary his acting in a
manner hitherto unknown to himself. He may even recover
some of the freshness which makes the acting of beginners
so attractive. I believe, indeed, that before casting a film
one should consider actors accustomed to playing other
kinds of part. This principle served me very well in *La
Bête Humaine*. The producers, in the name of orthodoxy,
wanted to cast Gina Manès, the great screen tragedienne,
in the role of Séverine. I argued that in this case the public
would know in advance that they were in for a terrific
drama. I proposed Simone Simon, who with her enchanting
pekinese profile causes one to expect all kinds of things, but
nothing in the field of tragedy. They allowed themselves to
be persuaded, and her Séverine was unforgettable.

As Pascal said, 'Only one thing interests Man and that is
Man.' Everything surrounding the actor should be sub-
ordinated to the aim of bringing the audience in touch with
a human being. The setting can make a large contribution,
not by the illusion it conveys to the beholder but by the
influence it can have on the actor. This is particularly true
in the case of outdoor shots. The audience only sees the
scene, but for the actor it is another matter. In *La Grande
Illusion* I set a scene in a hilly and muddy countryside. Jean
Gabin and Dalio were playing part of the escape sequence.
It was horribly cold and their clothes were caked with mud;
nothing could have been more uncomfortable. I was very
proud of the scene I had written; but alas, when we started
to rehearse the actors declared themselves incapable of
speaking their lines. We had to drop the scene to which I
attached so much importance. We took refuge in a house
buried in that dismal countryside and talked the matter
over. Presently one of us, I forget who it was, suggested

that my text should be replaced by the song, 'Le Petit Navire', sung with varying expressions. The song had furnished the sound-track of an earlier sequence and was symbolical of the escape. The result was splendid. In short, the setting had won. But in fact we had all won. In the cinema the finest setting, the most beautiful photography, the greatest acting, the most inspired directing, cannot exist separately. Everything is bound up with everything else.

In *La Bête Humaine* the close-ups of Gabin and Carette on a real locomotive were excellent, and during this sequence I only once made use of a mock-up. This was when Gabin commits suicide by flinging himself off the tender while the train is travelling at full speed. I could not ask Gabin to fling himself off a real tender. As he said when we were pre-paring the scene: 'Suppose the film fouls up in the camera during the shooting. I should then have to do the scene again, so it's really better for me to stay alive' – a very sensible remark. So he jumped off a bogus tender on to a thick pile of mattresses.

Those first-hand railway shots were in any case highly dangerous. The State Railways had lent us ten kilometres of track on which we could run and stop the train as we pleased. We hitched a platform truck, carrying the lighting generator, to the locomotive, and behind this an ordinary coach which served as a make-up and rest-room for the actors between scenes. When I decided to shoot with all these hindrances I encountered lively opposition. It was pointed out to me that mock-ups had been perfected to the point where it was impossible to tell them from first-hand shooting. But I was unshakable in my belief in the influence of the setting on the actors, and fortunately I won the day. Gabin and Carette could never have played so realistically in front of an artificial background, if only because the 'very noise forced them to communicate by means of gestures.

The cameramen were Curt Courant and my nephew, Claude Renoir. Curt Courant was a skinny little man, a real featherweight. He was always in danger of being carried off by the wind which blew like the devil through that rushing studio, and more than once I had to grab hold of him to prevent him being swept away. Claude had attached a small platform to the side of the locomotive which he occupied with his camera. The camera stuck out a little too far and was knocked off at the entrance to a tunnel; but Claude hung on and came through unscathed.

La Bête Humaine strengthened my longing to achieve poetic realism. The steel mass of the locomotive became in my imagination the flying carpet of oriental fable. Zola, from the depths of the grave, gave me powerful assistance. His novels are filled with wonderful passages of popular poetry. For example, Séverine and Jacques Lentier have arranged to meet in the Square des Batignolles. It is their first meeting. Jacques Lentier is so moved that he cannot utter a word. Séverine says with a faint smile, 'Don't look at me like that, you'll wear your eyes out.' A trifle, but it had to be thought of. The setting of locomotives, railroad sidings and puffs of steam had furnished me with that poetry, or rather had supplied it to the actors and enabled them to get into the skin of their parts better than any amount of direction.

Albert Pinkevitch

When I think of the fruitless struggle with which my life has been filled I am amazed at myself. So many humiliating concessions and wasted smiles; so many denials and, above all, so much lost time! I am a speedy director. If instead of exhausting myself with visits that led nowhere I had spent the time making films I should certainly have made a dozen more than I have. I am also an economical director – but that doesn't interest them. It is the banks who pay, and it is the public that keeps the banks in business. A word which in the producers' jargon has lost all meaning is the word 'commercial'. A given film is a masterpiece and has pleased audiences in minor cinemas; but it is ignored by the big distributors because it is not 'commercial'. This is not to say that it does not make money, but simply that it is a type of film that does not appeal to the money-men. Even after *La Grande Illusion* had made a fortune for its producer I had difficulty in raising money for my own projects. I was not, and still am not, 'commercial'.

A 'commercial' film should include a number of stars. Actors are chosen, not for their suitability for a part but simply for their box-office value. A shrimp of a man may be cast as an athlete simply because he has a 'name'. A 'commercial' film must be in colour and wide-screened. Above all, as I have said before, anything new must be introduced with the utmost caution. This is a rule that applies to other fields besides that of the cinema. The public is lazy; to indulge this laziness is to hold the key to success. Maurice Chevalier, a commercial artist if ever there was one, told me that he never opened his performance with a new song. He sandwiched it between established favourites. His public greeted the new song without much enthusiasm and only warmed to 'Valentine' or 'Louise' – songs he had been dishing up to them for years.

The golden rule with a 'commercial' film is that it must never surprise the public except physically. It may draw from the audience cries of terror at the accumulation of murders and disasters, but the audience must not be confronted by any kind of problem. 'Don't forget that the public is twelve years old,' a producer once said to me, and this is the honest opinion of most of them. Fortunately there are exceptions. Otherwise there would be no good films. Personally I have several times had the pleasure of collaborating with producers who brought me the fruits of genuine experience. I must mention David Loew, to whom I owe *The Southerner* and Alexander Kamenka to whom I owe *Les Bas Fonds*.

I believe that any spectacle, film or stage play can only reach a certain level if the author collaborates with the public. Every spectator must be able in his own fashion to interpret both the situations and the general sense of the piece. The spectator is a human being capable of reflection and therefore of imagination. Being human he is attracted by the least effort; but also, being human, he is devoured with curiosity. In my position as an author-director my approach to the spectator is the same as my approach to the actor. It is enough to leave a door open for him and to send him home with his personal interpretation of the situation and the feelings of the protagonists. If the situation in itself does not permit this multiplicity of interpretation, then the author may fall back on some device so simple that even the most dull-witted spectator realizes that it is an appeal to the imagination. Tartuffe is arrested by the King's officers, but few spectators believe that this is the end of the matter. Some believe that he will return in triumph to the home of his benefactor, and others that he will get out of prison and prey on another victim. Everybody has his own answer to the riddle of Tartuffe. As a rule, the ending of a play does not allow so much room for surmise. It is in the sentiments of the beings portrayed by the actors that the spectator may find food for his own imagination and thus become the collaborator of the author.

The story of our efforts to raise money for *La Grande Illusion* might itself be made the subject of a film. I touted the manuscript round for three years, visiting the offices of all the French and foreign producers, orthodox or avant-garde. Had it not been for Jean Gabin not one of them would have taken a chance on the film. He accompanied me on numerous occasions, and eventually found a financier who, impressed by his solid confidence in the film, agreed to produce it.

I can see us still, Gabin, Charles Spaak, my collaborator on the script, and myself, seated on a sofa of which the springs protruded through numerous rents in the up-holstery, while in a dusty ante-room we awaited the verdict of a producer whose voice reached us every time the padded door of his office opened. Albert Pinkevitch, my friend Albert, had steered us into that den. Without him there would have been no *Grande Illusion*. He bustled between the great man's office and our disreputable sofa trying to find compromises which would lead to an agreement. There was one scene, set in a château, of which the cost would be prohibitive – a farmhouse would do equally well. Having brought us this proposal Albert returned to the office to report our rejection of it. Finally we settled for a military encampment of the kind that was to be found behind both lines. Every time Albert came to see us he reported that the boss wanted to make sure that there would not be a château. After his last appearance Charles Spaak suggested an explanation of this childish insistence which we found so appropriate that we burst uncontrollably into laughter. In his solemn voice, and speaking with expressive deliberation, he said: 'You know, I don't think he likes that château.' He reminded me of Athos in *The Three Musketeers*. And when eventually we thought that we had won, a matter of a silver dinner-service threatened to ruin everything. I said that I would make do with plate.

Albert Pinkevitch was a born negotiator with a gift for making both sides feel that they had gained important concessions. In fact, the concessions he apparently gained were unimportant, while the real concessions were buried under trivialities.

Albert was a plump, dark-haired Jew with very expressive eyes which filled with tears when he was appealing to someone, so that it was almost impossible to resist him. He was the son of an engineer who had had a hand in developing the Rothschild oil wells in Roumania. Baron Rothschild, who had a high regard for Pinkevitch père, brought the youthful Albert to Paris and lodged him in his own mansion, intending to make a rabbi of him. But Albert did not go along with this. He was then aged about fifteen, and consumed with the desire to trade. One evening he climbed over the wall encircling the garden of the luxurious Rothschild mansion and set out to fend for himself. He went in for all kinds of street-trading – anything suited him provided it was out of doors. He sold shoe-laces outside the Gare du Nord and clockwork toys on the outer boulevards. But his studies of the Jewish religion had endowed him with real distinction of mind. His language was a wonderful mixture of slang and grammatical speech. He had a passion for puns and easy plays on words. He helped me in a great many ways with *La Grande Illusion* but above all in the jargon used by the character played by Carette.

'La Madelon'

La Grande Illusion, filmed during the winter of 1936, had the advantage that I had no need to trouble about the influence of a great work of literature. While we were working on it, it had not even a title. Only when the film had been shot, edited and sub-titled did it occur to me to call it *La Grande Illusion*. The producer was not enthusiastic but accepted this for want of anything better.

My story was a banal one of escape. I maintain that the more banal the subject of a film, the greater are the possibilities it offers to the film-maker. I do not use the word 'banal' in the sense in which it is understood by producers. To them it simply means 'nothing that shocks'. To me it means a simple canvas affording scope for the imagination.

One of my reasons for making the film was my exasperation at the way most war-themes were treated. Heroism, chivalry, *'le poilu'*, *'les Boches'*, the trenches – so many pretexts for the most dreary clichés. The Musketeer and the *'Soltat t'l'Empire'* came into their own and took advantage of conventional prejudice. Excepting *All Quiet on the Western Front*, I had not seen a single film giving a true picture of the men who did the fighting. Either the drama never got out of the mud, which was an exaggeration, or else the war was made into a kind of operetta with cardboard heroes – the gallant grocer, temporarily clad in a uniform he had never asked for, talking a language of crude heroism which was entirely the invention of writers behind the lines. Among the inventions which most aroused the derision of the troops were the entertainments served up to them.

I have elsewhere told the story of the opera star who sang 'La Madelon' in the costume of a musical comedy waitress. In conventional terms, the lady was admirable; nicely plump, with her bosom well propped up in a stiff corsage, she was greeted with cries of appreciation. Her *tricolor* skirt was short enough to reveal an admirable pair of thighs.

'La Madelon' was a triumph of 'behind the lines'. Despite its immense popularity, this patriotic song did not suit the troops, who greatly preferred the sentimental ballads of the turn of the century. One of these, 'C'est Quatre-Vingt-Treize à Paris' brought tears to every eye. It was the story of a young aristocrat who in 1793 comes to Paris to see the girl he loves, Lison, a simple working girl. He is arrested and sent to the guillotine, and the song ends with the following defiance:

> *I scorn the headsman, Sanson;*
> *His labour is half done:*
> *Through my great love for you, Lison,*
> *My head is not my own.*

That really mattered. The success of this tale of an aristocrat executed by the Jacobins was the more surprising since most of the soldiers in that division were anarchists. But the amateur performer who sang it was appealing to exalted sentiments, whereas the appeal of the opera-singer was of a very different order, being based entirely on sex, which in the France of those days was still a subject of ribaldry.

The opera-singer had a powerful voice. Smothering the hoots and jeers, she belted out the song with indomitable vigour. A voice from one of the back rows, even louder than her own, shouted '*Au claque!*' and the cry was taken up by the whole audience. What it meant, in the slang of the time, was 'To the brothel!' The singer later asked the colonel its meaning, and he replied imperturbably, 'It's the rallying cry of the regiment.' . . . 'How nice,' said the lady. 'I shall make it my own rallying cry.'

A story which delighted the behind-the-lines writers was the celebrated '*Debout les morts!*' incident – meaning, 'Rise up, the dead!' It was generally understood to refer to the heroic act of an officer who inspired his mortally wounded troops to a final charge against the German lines. The fact is that '*Debout les morts!*' was an old army joke dating from before the war, applied to men too lazy to get up in the morning. Its transformation into an act of heroism is typical of the spirit of make-believe that prevailed behind the lines.

If one is to put a label on them I would say that the fighting troops in the First World War were complete anarchists. They didn't give a damn for anything, least of all for noble sentiments. The destruction of cathedrals left them cold, and they did not believe that they were fighting a war for liberty. They cared nothing for death either, thinking that their present life was not worth living. They had touched the lees of existence. What is strange is that, despite this complete scepticism, they fought magnificently. They were caught in the machinery and had no way of getting out.

For *La Grande Illusion* I chose an exceptional case. The airmen slept in beds and ate at table; they were remote from the mud of the trenches and meals spattered by shell-bursts. They were fortunate and privileged men, and they knew it. They also knew that there was nothing they could do about it.

Then I took my characters into a POW camp, and this, too, was a special kind of life – a life of luxury compared with that of the infantryman in the trenches. I had no wish to depict the latter's sufferings. That was not the intention of the film. My chief aim was the one which I have been pursuing ever since I started to make films – to express the common humanity of men.

The Intoxicating Smell of Castor Oil

Everything was unorthodox about *La Grande Illusion* – to start with, the way in which the idea came to me. To explain this I must go back to the year 1915, when the wound I sustained while fighting as a Chasseur Alpin led me, after vicissitudes, to join flying-squadron C 64.

This squadron was sent out on a variety of missions. It was an army – that is to say, an all-purpose – squadron. We kept observation on the German lines in our sector, supplying the cartographic service with photographs of the enemy positions. We were also at the disposal of the gentlemen of the General Staff when they felt like enjoying the thrill of an incursion into enemy skies. The leader of our squadron was like a child lost in the wilderness. He invented missions which had not been ordered, and these attempts to escape from the boredom of our hutments, with their view of an interminable field of potatoes, did not always turn out happily.

I have a very clear recollection of the last of these excursions. We had been celebrating the birthday of one of the team and had drunk a good deal of the *champagne nature* which we got from the local wine-growers. It was a murky day, and somebody had the idea that by taking advantage of the low clouds and brighter patches we might upset German digestions with a little machine-gun fire without much risk to ourselves. We chose as our target a large French village occupied by a German brigade headquarters, passed the word to our mechanics, and within a short time half a dozen twin-engined Caudrons were ready to take the air. We set off to hunt Germans as light-heartedly as if we had been hunting rabbits: such was the effect of the war upon our minds that we took these shabby exploits for granted. The thought of them now turns my stomach: it is perhaps because I took part in them that I so detest them.

Finding a gap in the clouds, we swooped down on the village. But the Germans had installed some highly efficient AA defences; I was caught in a barrage and had only just time to seek cloud cover. I came out of it determined to give the staff scribblers, now running for shelter, a burst or two of machine-gun fire. We despised all desk-warriors, who lived such comfortable lives compared with the men in the front lines; but we had a certain affection for the German front-line troops, who suffered as much as our own. They were men of our own kind, whereas the desk-warriors were scrimshankers.

Our captain's plane had been shot down and lay burning. I desisted and headed back home. That senseless operation cost us the lives not only of our commanding officer but of a young flight lieutenant whom we considered the best pilot in the squadron. It prompted the General Staff to put an end to that kind of skylarking, and it was also the end of the twin-engined Caudrons. They were wonderful machines, but they had had their day and the German Focke-Wulfs had no difficulty in avoiding their angle of fire and shooting them down.

I adored my old Caudron. Those were the last planes to be built entirely of wood. Banking was effected by torsion of the wings. They put me in mind of kites. There was also the intoxicating smell of castor oil which was used to lubricate rotary engines, still in use in the fighter Nieuports and the reconnaissance Caudrons. When we got out after a flight the oil was dripping from our overalls. For me those rotary engines – Gnôme-Rhône or Clerget-Blin – were a symbol of aviation. I was inclined to despise the aircraft with normal four-stroke engines – good enough for taxi-work, was what I thought of them. It must be said that the Farman-Renault pilots took the criticism in good part. They themselves called their planes 'hen-coops'. It was through my Caudron that I made the acquaintance of the man destined to become the hero of *La Grande Illusion*, Major Pinsard.

I was summoned one morning to the head office and introduced to a staff-officer acting upon an assignment the nature of which he did not condescend to explain. He was a captain of Hussars, reflecting in his whole person that *je ne sais quoi* which makes cavalry officers a race apart.

We got into the plane. I had to make a second take-off, having been put off the first time by a flight of partridges. My passenger had supplied me with the necessary detail regarding the place he wanted to observe. All went well until a Focke-Wulf fighter appeared on the scene. I signalled to my passenger that I was going to turn back, but he took no notice. Pilot and observer in my old Caudron were seated one behind the other, so that it was almost impossible for them to communicate. The Focke overhauled us and gave us a burst of tracer bullets. I looked round at my passenger and asked him, with gestures, if he was not now convinced. But not a bit of it. He was quite undisturbed. I banked and, getting the Focke in my sights for a few seconds, fired at him but missed.

The Focke seemed to be playing with us. He swept over us, passed us and returned to the attack. It was like a swallow attacking an elephant. I swore to myself that if I got out of this alive I would ask to be transferred to a fighter-squadron – this business of being hunted instead of huntsman seemed to me wholly lacking in charm. But at this moment a third protagonist came swooping out of the sky. I saw that it was one of the French fighter squadron operating in our sector. This was a squadron of what we called 'show dancers', by which we meant pilots who were absolutely fearless. Their Rhône-engined Nieuports had been replaced by the latest Hispano-Suiza Spads.

It was soon over. The Spad got on the tail of the Focke, gave it a burst and then climbed to repeat the attack. That vertical climb left me breathless with admiration. Meanwhile the Focke was belching black smoke. It went into a spin and crashed on a small hill, on top of which there was a chapel. I have to mention the chapel because of my feeling that we owed the timely appearance of our rescuer to the intervention of some saint.

His victory was celebrated by a champagne dinner in our mess. It was not the first exploit of Major Pinsard, who was one of the most brilliant of French fighter pilots. I admired him enormously. Apart from the fact that he had saved my life, he represented in my eyes the perfect type of pre-1914 Dragoon '*sous-off*' (or NCO). Moreover, he remained faithful to pre-war uniform. It was a pleasure to me to look at him in his tight black tunic and red breeches. Pinsard and I became good friends. I spent hours listening to him talk about horses he had trained. But one day my squadron was transferred elsewhere and Pinsard vanished from my horizon.

I was to meet him again in 1934 in Les Martigues where I had gone to shoot *Toni*. Not far from Les Martigues there was a huge flying field which was both a school and a testing ground. The pilots working there had spotted our small party of actors and when we were shooting out of doors, which was nearly always, they performed aerobatics over our heads. Their interest in us interfered with my insistence upon authentic sound. Pierre Gaut, the producer of the film, suggested that we should call on the senior officer and ask him to send his planes elsewhere. The duty-officer passed us on to a captain who showed us into the office of the General Officer in Command. Directly I set eyes on this important personage I had a feeling that I had seen him before.

It was Sergeant-Major Pinsard. He had won a general's star and lost his moustache. General Pinsard took the necessary steps to enable me to shoot *Toni* without the company being deafened by the noise of his aircraft, and we got into the habit of dining together whenever we were free. He told me about his wartime adventures. He had been shot down seven times by the Germans and every time had managed to land safely. Also, on all seven occasions he had escaped from imprisonment. The story of his escapes seemed to me a good basis for an adventure-film, and with this in mind I made notes of what seemed to me the most typical details and filed them away.

Later I talked to Charles Spaak, who was enthusiastic about the idea and helped me to make a first sketch of what was destined, after many changes, to become *La Grande Illusion*. Most of the changes were due to the arrival of a heavy-weight in the scales – Erich von Stroheim.

Making Part of a Whole

Toni has often been described as the forerunner of the Italian neo-realist films. I do not think that is quite correct. The Italian films are magnificent dramatic productions, whereas in *Toni* I was at pains to avoid the dramatic. I attached as much importance to the countrywoman surprised while doing the washing as to the hero of the story. I had various thoughts in mind. For one thing, a number of carefully selected close-ups seemed to me a way of depicting my characters that was abstract and even stark; and also the use of natural backgrounds enabled me to achieve a realism that was as little distorted as possible.

Now, after a lapse of time, when I can see things a little more clearly, I think I may say that what characterized *Toni* is the absence of any dominating element, whether star performer, setting or situation. My aim was to give the impression that I was carrying a camera and microphone in my pocket and recording whatever came my way, regardless of its comparative importance. Nevertheless, I had given myself a framework. *Toni* is not a documentary; it is a news item, a love-story that really happened in Les Martigues and was told to me by my friend Jacques Mortier, who at the time was Chief of Police in that small town. I scarcely needed to adapt it for the screen.

Another way in which it differed from Italian neo-realism was in my use of sound. I am a passionate believer in authentic sound. I prefer sound that is technically bad, but has been recorded at the same time as the picture to sound that is perfect but has been dubbed. The Italians have no regard for sound, they dub everything. I remember visiting Rossellini when he was shooting *Paisa*. The actor in the scene he was directing asked to be given some lines. 'Say whatever you like,' said Rossellini. 'I shall alter the dialogue anyway in the editing.' This was a joke, but it was symptomatic. The difference of approach does not prevent me from being a profound admirer of Italian films. Although Rossellini and De Sica use artificial sound, the feeling conveyed by their films is none the less profoundly real. In *Toni* the sound of the train arriving at Les Martigues station is not merely the real sound of a train but that of the one which one sees on the screen. On the other hand, the entirely artificial sound-track of *Rome – Open City* is nothing but a sort of accompaniment to one of the most masterly productions in the history of the cinema.

Toni, made on a small budget, signalled the accomplishment of my dream of uncompromising realism. I saw in it the final defeat of the Musketeers and all heroes of melodrama. How wrong I was! While I imagined I was filming a squalid episode based on real life, I was recounting, almost despite myself, a heart-rending and poetic love-story.

Every scene in the film was shot either out of doors or else in a genuine interior. The actors, although they were not all amateurs, all came from the Midi, and their local accent was as genuine as the countryside of Les Martigues, which provided the background for the film. For the first time in my life, it seemed to me that I had written a script in which the elements completed one another, not so much through the plot as by a sort of natural equilibrium.

Toni was to speed up my separation from the notion of the predominance of the individual. I could no longer be satisfied with a world which was nothing but the dwelling-place of persons having no link between them. The problem of life is not one of isolation for fear of having to share that treasure, the self, the absolute self, but of integrating with others. In the film I began to feel the importance of unity. I had always liked the close-up and I still do. As I have said, the close-ups of the beautiful Hollywood actresses had had a lot to do with driving me into the cinema. But too many close-ups of faces entirely filling the screen express the isolation of the individual. One reason for this is that these close-ups are generally photographed at different times. Take, for example, a passionate love-scene between a man and woman. On the screen, and by the use of editing, they are physically together, but for technical reasons – lighting, sound, camera-angles – the woman has not been photographed at the same time as the man. This can be seen and, even more, it can be felt. To my mind, a love-scene, like any other, should be shot with the protagonists together. They have to forget the existence of the camera, the director, the microphone and the lighting equipment. In *Toni* I made a point of using panning shots which clearly linked the characters with one another and with their environment.

This caused me to try out a variety of lenses, and I came to the conclusion that optically one must not expect miracles. Either one uses a wide lens which gives greater luminosity at the expense of the background, which becomes hazy, or else the lens one uses gives the details of the background but is less luminous and therefore requires additional lighting. From the moment when I realized the importance of unity I tried never to shoot a scene without some background movement more or less related to the action. It may seem surprising that I never used changes of focus. I do not care for this device. Those variations of the distance between foreground and background seem to me artificial.

Another of my preoccupations was, and still is, to avoid fragmentation, and by means of longer-playing shots to give the actor a chance to develop his own rhythm in the speaking of his lines. To me this is the only way of getting sincere acting. There are two methods of obtaining these longer sequences. One can leave out close-ups altogether and use as many middle-distance shots as possible, including general shots; but in this case the audience is too far away from the actors to be able to see their expressions. The other method, which I think better, is to shoot the actors in close-up and then follow their movements. This calls for great skill on the part of the operator, but the effect is sometimes remarkable. For myself, this pursuit of the subject by the camera has brought me some of my most thrilling moments, both in my own films and in those of other directors.

La Grande Illusion is perhaps the film in which I used the second method most satisfactorily. Needless to say, if the technique is to be perfect it must be imperceptible – as is true of all techniques. The audience must not notice that the camera is positively dancing a ballet, subtly passing from one actor to another. A sequence of this kind, if it is to succeed, must be like an act in itself, and this without forgetting the background, which is particularly difficult to cover because the ground is littered with lighting material.

I may mention two sequences in *La Grande Illusion* based on this principle. The first is the meal in the first POW camp where the camera moves over the details of the scene without ceasing to link up the whole until the sequence is ended. The other is the singing of the 'Marseillaise' in the prisoners' theatre. This sequence opens with Gabin standing on the small stage and ends with the audience, having gathered up all the ingredients in a panorama extending through 180 degrees. The operator to whom I owe those sequences is my nephew, Claude Renoir. He was supple as an eel and shrank from no acrobatics.

Realism in 'La Grande Illusion'

I often make use of the following example to explain my approach to the basic question of interior as opposed to exterior truth. An actor is cast in the role of a fisherman. In his concern for realism he decides to use no make-up. He pays a visit to a small Brittany port and takes part in fishing trips out to sea. He has procured the worn clothes of a real fisherman, and he acquires a genuine sun-tan; passing him in the street one may detect no difference between him and the genuine article. After this meticulous preparation he plays the part, some of the sequences being shot on a real Brittany fishing-boat. The director does not even use a stand-in for a scene of real storm. And the end of it all is that our actor, unless he is a genius, looks like a ham. Indeed, the real scene surrounding him seems to have the effect of emphasizing his own lack of reality.

But now let us suppose that Charlie Chaplin is playing the sailor. The sequence will be shot in the studio, against a painted backcloth. Chaplin will not even trouble to wear a genuine sailor's get-up. We shall see him in his usual tail-coat, complete with bowler-hat, enormous boots and cane, but after a few minutes we shall accept the eccentricity of his attire and believe we are watching a real sailor.

This question of exterior and interior truth is at the heart of the acting profession. In the nineteenth century the bourgeois intellectual drama reached its peak. We are now in process of emerging from that trend and the *commedia dell' arte* is coming back with a rush.

At the beginning of my career in films I was only inter-

Above: La Grande Illusion, 1937: Jean Gabin
as the working man Maréchal and Pierre Fresnay
as the aristocrat Boieldieu
Below: Erich von Stroheim – great, genial and
indescribable
Inset: During the shooting: my nephew Claude
Renoir is on my left, and Jacques Becker on the
extreme right

ested in artificiality. Then, as I have said when talking
about my use of panchromatic film, I went through a period
of total realism. I now believe that it is impossible to separate realism from transposition, whether on the stage or
screen. In *Nana* I was able to indulge my penchant for
fantasy that breaks the bounds of realism. The wildness of
the reality is beyond the imaginative scope of even the
best designer. Catherine Hessling studied the fashion
journals of the period at the Musée des Arts Décoratifs.
Lestringuez and I were soon persuaded that, for all his
talent, Claude Autant-Lara was far from conjuring up the
exuberant fantasy of the real dresses of the period. But here,
too, I was wrong: the dresses in *Nana* dismayed audiences
nearly as much as the personality of the actress. In this field,
as in all others, the public demands transposition. Reality
can be too shocking. I must confess that I have never completely learnt the lesson of *Nana*.

In *La Grande Illusion* I was still very much concerned with
realism – to the point, indeed, that I asked Gabin to wear my
old pilot's tunic, which I had kept after being demobilized.
At the same time I did not hesitate to add fanciful touches
to certain details in order to heighten the effect – for example in von Stroheim's uniform. His part, which at first
was a very minor one, had been greatly enlarged because I
was afraid that, confronted by the weighty personalities of
Gabin and Fresnay, he would look like a lightweight. In
art, as in life, it is all a question of balance; and the problem
is to keep both sides of the scales level. That is why I took
liberties with von Stroheim's uniform, which was quite out
of keeping with my realistic principles at that time. His
uniform is authentic, but with a flamboyance quite unsuited
to the commander of a POW camp in the First War. I

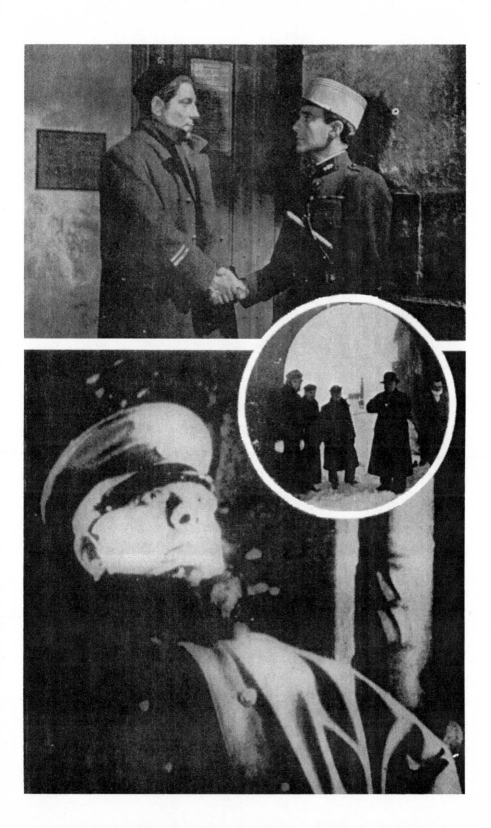

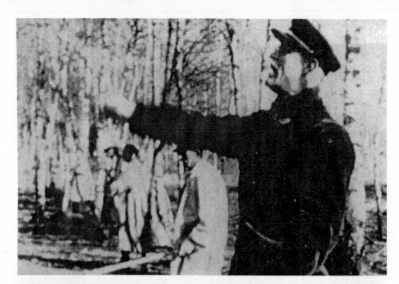

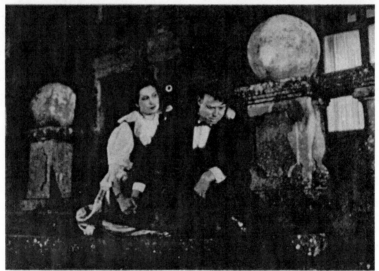

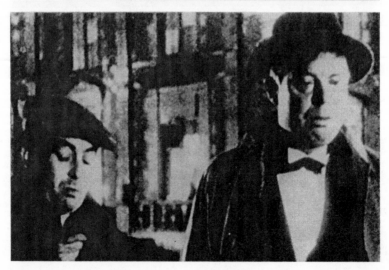

Above: La Règle du Jeu, 1939: Gaston Modot as 161
the gamekeeper Schumacher accompanying the
shooting party
Middle: Octave (Jean Renoir) and the Marquise
(Nora Grégor)
Below: Octave and the poacher Marceau (Carette)
leaving the château at the end

needed this theatrical façade to counterbalance the impressive simplicity of the Frenchmen. There are instances of stylization in *La Grande Illusion*, despite its strictly realistic appearance, which take us into the realm of fantasy, and these breaks into illusion I owe largely to Stroheim. I am profoundly grateful to him. I am incapable of doing good work unless it contains an element of the fairy-tale.

The recollection of that film takes me back to a particularly happy period in my life. I had been able to engage my friend, Carl Koch, to check the authenticity of the German scenes. Koch was married to Lotte Reiniger, who was the creator of some wonderful shadow-show films. Catherine Hessling and I made their acquaintance when her masterpiece, *Le Prince Achmed*, was being shown in Paris. We became great friends and worked together on a number of film projects.

Carl Koch had been a German army captain of artillery in the First War. In 1916 he was in command of an anti-aircraft battery in the Rheims sector. 'It was a good sector,' he told me. 'Nothing against it except the incessant attack of the French squadron opposite us.' As it happens, in 1916 I was flying in a reconnaissance squadron in the same sector, and we were the main target of a German battery which gave us a lot of trouble. Koch and I concluded that this was his battery: so we had made war together. These things form a bond. The fact that we had been on opposite sides was the merest detail. Indeed, as I come to think of it, it was even better – a further instance of my theory of the division of the world by horizontal frontiers, and not into compartments enclosed in vertical frontiers.

'La Grande Illusion' — Minor Quarrels

Carl Koch's real profession was philosophy, and because of it he was a perpetual student. There was nothing about what is called film-technique that he did not know. He had himself designed Lotte Reiniger's studio, where that mistress of shadow-show made the very complicated takes of her films.

But the subject which most interested Koch was romanesque art, and it was his ambition to visit all the romanesque chapels in the Saintonge region, which was, it seems, one of the most important centres of the religious art of the tenth and eleventh centuries. Those small churches and village chapels are very pure specimens of the period, but they have to be discovered. It was after this period that the population, migrating towards the cathedrals in the big cities, began the steady exodus from country to town; and those modest sanctuaries, bereft of their intended function, were used as barns and stables.

Koch and I drove back from the south through the lovely Beaujolais country. He asked me to make a detour to look at a statue in a Roman church. We pulled up outside a dreary little chapel freshly re-roofed with the glaring red of mass-produced tiles. Koch was thinking of nothing but his statue. He marched in, and finding his way amid pews and pulpit went unhesitatingly up to a statue of St Joseph carrying a lamb in his arms. I was then treated to the lecture I had been hoping for. It was altogether fascinating, and for more than an hour I lived in the shadow of Anne de Beaujeu. But what had most impressed me was the certainty with which

Koch had found the statue, which he had never before set eyes on.

For a brief period in his life, Koch had been principal of a nursery school. To see that respectable gentleman down on his knees, helping his young pupils to build a clay fortress, was a surprising sight. He maintained that this game was more stimulating to the mind of a five-year-old child than any amount of manufactured toys. He explained the use of the moats and towers, and then, lying on his stomach, he launched an attack of toy soldiers. When the attack was defeated by rain he took advantage of the circumstance to declare his belief in the influence of weather on earthly affairs.

On another occasion I watched him explaining the formation of valleys in mountainous country with the help of watering-cans of which the contents were poured over a heap of sand. That sand-heap played a large part in his method of teaching. Koch was a universal spirit, something like the eighteenth-century philosophers. He was a friend of Bertold Brecht, and it was through him that I had the privilege of knowing that remarkable poet, artist in logic and masterly organizer. The *Dreigrösschen Oper* had just opened with great success in Berlin.

My meetings with Brecht often took place in my home in Meudon, which provided him with a perfect setting. The house had been built on the remains of a convent destroyed during the Revolution. Brecht would come accompanied by his secretary, a young Berlin woman who brought with her, not a typewriter but one of those small hexagonal accordions that are, I think, called concertinas. Hanns Eisler, Kurt Weill and Lotte Lenya would also come along. Brecht would ask me to sing old French songs. I sing very badly and have no voice. This did not worry Brecht in the least. The secretary picked up the tune on her concertina. That was the origin of certain songs that became world successes.

There was a certain affinity between Brecht and Koch. Both had the same love of paradox. Physically they were at opposite poles. Brecht was a lean German with an ascetic tendency. Koch was a plump German who enjoyed his comforts, a gourmand as well as a gourmet (he taught me how to roast beef over an open fire), cultured to his finger-tips, unconcerned with politics but capable of doing battle for a symphony or a fine painting. Koch, the pacifist, could explode in furious rages. Brecht was proud of having been born in Augsburg, a town which he claimed was of Celtic origin. Koch was a Rhinelander, that is to say, pure German. They both agreed in denouncing the Prussians. According to them it was those northerners, those impenitent mytho-maniacs, who were plunging the world into disaster.

During the shooting of *La Grande Illusion* the team was lodged in an inn near the castle. The inn-keeper, who was also a wine-grower, slaked our thirsts with a particularly attractive but highly treacherous white wine. Koch had a dispute with Stroheim about the over-elaborate clothing of the actress playing the part of his hospital nurse. The argument became heated, with Stroheim defending the artist's right to transpose and Koch replying that he had not fought in the war and should therefore keep his mouth shut. Stroheim's answer was to call Koch a petty-bourgeois, an unjust accusation, for Koch was an aristocrat in spirit. He stood up, intending to go for Stroheim, but the latter checked him with the lordly gesture of one of his own characters and stalked out. Koch, in a fury, flung his glass at him, but it arrived just too late and smashed against the door as Stroheim closed it behind him. Almost immediately afterwards the door was reopened to reveal Stroheim smiling at the joke and holding out another glass which he offered the dumbfounded Koch. Koch then went out to cool off. He was greatly upset by the episode, which emphasized the stylishness of Stroheim's world – the more so since Stroheim was his god.

We found Koch a little while later. He had fallen into a ditch and was groping for his spectacles on all fours in the snow. The adversaries were reconciled over glasses of white wine, and the underlying reason for their quarrel was buried. This was Stroheim's refusal to see the world as other than made in his own image: his godlike stance made it difficult for him to come to terms with people.

To complete the portrait of Erich von Stroheim I am bound to lay stress upon his ingenuousness. The ideal he sought to live up to might have been the invention of a twelve-year-old boy: it was an impressive reincarnation of the Musketeer, but this would not have satisfied him. He wanted to resemble the Marquis de Sade. He had dreams of boundless luxury, perverse women, flagellation, sexual exploits, bacchanalia and drinking bouts. One evening when he came to dine with us in Hollywood during the last war my wife, Dido, offered him a glass of Scotch. He checked her, saying, 'No, please, the bottle.' Dido put the bottle down beside him and turned to attend to D. W. Griffith, who was seated at the other end of the table. I had hoped to listen to an absorbing conversation between those two masters of the cinema, the more so since Stroheim had worked for Griffith – as an actor, according to some people, or as an assistant according to others. But they ignored each other and the whole subject of films. Suddenly Dido noticed that Stroheim was turning green. This was the effect of the whisky, which he did not stand at all well, despite his notion of himself as a heavy drinker. She had just time to show him to the lavatory. An amusing detail is that Stroheim spoke scarcely any German. He had to study his lines like a schoolboy learning a foreign language. But in the eyes of the world he remains the perfect prototype of the German officer: his genius triumphed over the literal imitation of reality.

At the beginning of the shooting of *La Grande Illusion* Stroheim behaved intolerably. We had an argument about the opening scene in the German living-quarters. He refused to understand why I had not brought some prostitutes of an obviously Viennese type into the scene. I was shattered. My intense admiration for the great man put me in an impossible position. It was partly because of my enthusiasm for his work that I was in film-business at all. *Greed* was for me the banner of my profession. And now here he was, my idol, acting in my film, and instead of the figure of truth that I had looked for I found a being steeped in childish clichés. I was well aware that those same clichés, in his hands, became strokes of genius. Bad taste is often a source of inspiration to the greatest artists. Neither Cézanne nor Van Gogh had good taste.

This dispute with Stroheim so distressed me that I burst into tears, which so affected him that there were tears in his own eyes. We fell into each other's arms, damping his German army-officer's tunic. I said that I had so much respect for his talent that rather than quarrel with him I would give up directing the film. This led to further effusions and Stroheim promised that henceforth he would follow my instructions with a slavish docility. And he kept his word.

This is what I know about the beginning of Erich von Stroheim. The source of my information is Carl Laemmle, Jr, the son of the founder of Universal Studios. He was twenty when his father decided to retire and leave him in charge of that huge concern. Young Carl produced a number of screen masterpieces, among them *All Quiet on the Western Front* and *Back Street*.

From his first days in Hollywood, when he was still quite unknown, Stroheim wanted to make films. Meanwhile he earned his living by working as an actor, playing bit parts when he could get them.

He resolved to tell Carl Laemmle, Sr, of his ambitions, and not finding him in his office in the San Fernando Valley studios, he went to his house. Laemmle was then living in Sycamore Avenue, at least ten miles from the studios. Since he could not afford the bus fare, Stroheim went on foot, and the door was opened to him by Carl Laemmle, Jr, then aged twelve. Stroheim was very thirsty and young Carl gave him a Coke. The old man appeared and Stroheim told him that he wanted to make a film both as actor and director. So impressive were his eloquence and determination that, against all reason since he was quite unknown, Laemmle signed him up. *Blind Husbands* was the first film directed by Stroheim and luckily it was a success, because it cost 100,000 dollars, whereas the original budget had been 25,000. From the first Stroheim showed himself to be extravagant, dictatorial and a genius. His third film, *Foolish Wives*, cost so much that Laemmle decided to use its wild expense as an advertising gimmick, and an electric sign, in New York's Times Square, chalked up the expenditure from hour to hour. But the film made money, and

Stroheim's reputation became fabulous. Nevertheless, *Merry-Go-Round*, his fourth film, was arbitrarily taken away from him after a few weeks' shooting – money again.

Stroheim died in 1957 in his country house near Paris. Hollywood had closed its doors to him, obviously because of the enormous cost of his films, but also because he was a genius and could not be fitted into the mediocrity of bureaucratic film-making. He ended his life acting in French films. A few days before his death the French Government gave him something which he had long coveted – the *légion d'honneur*. His funeral was exactly suited to his extravagant tastes. The carved wood coffin was so big that the path leading to the little chapel had to be widened. The funeral procession, composed of French film celebrities, was preceded by a Tzigane orchestra from a night-club playing Viennese waltzes. Jacques Becker followed the coffin, carrying the dead man's *légion d'honneur* on a white silk cushion. The cows in a neighbouring field, surprised by the unusual spectacle, came crowding up to the fence – occupying front-row seats, as one might say. Jacques Becker had wanted to make a speech but was too moved to do so, his words being stifled by sobs. I was unable to accompany Erich von Stroheim, my master, to his last resting-place. I was kept in America by the shooting of a film. It was a reason which Stroheim would have perfectly understood.

'La Règle du Jeu' — 1939

You spend an evening listening to records and the result is a film. I cannot say that it was French baroque music that inspired me to make *La Règle du Jeu*, but certainly it played a part in making me wish to film the sort of people who danced to that music. I based my thought on it only at the beginning. It does not accompany the film except generically. I was entering a period of my life when my daily companions were Couperin, Rameau and every composer from Lulli to Grétry. By degrees my idea took shape and the subject became simplified, and after a few days, while I lived to baroque rhythms, it became more and more clearly defined.

I thought of certain of my friends whose amorous intrigues seemed to be their only object in life. As Lestringuez said: 'If you want to write the truth you must get it well into your head that the world is one large knocking-shop. Men only think of one thing, and that is laying women; and the ones who think of anything else are played out – drowned in the muddy waters of sentimentality.' Lestringuez was, of course, speaking for himself, but his words impressed me and I decided to transpose the characters, enacting that hitherto non-existent theme into our own period. Then I began to see the outline of the story, but not to the point where I had decided on any definite style.

I needed a background: it was the Sologne which provided me with the setting in which the actors were to discover the truth about the characters they were playing. Its mists took me back to the happy days of my childhood when Gabrielle and I went to the Théâtre Montmartre to be enthralled by *Jack Sheppard, ou les Chevaliers du Brouillard*. Nothing is more mysterious than a countryside emerging from fog. In that cotton-wool atmosphere the sound of gunshots is deadened. It is a perfect setting for a tale by Andersen. One expects to see will-o'-the-wisps emerging from every pool, or even the King of the Marshes himself. The Sologne is a region of marshes entirely devoted to hunting, a sport which I detest. I consider it an abominable exercise in cruelty. By situating my story amid those vapours I gave myself the chance to depict a shooting-party. These various elements crowded through my mind, compelling me to find a story in which they could be used.

My first idea was to produce an up-to-date version of *Les Caprices de Marianne*. This is the tale of a tragic mis-understanding: Marianne's lover is mistaken for someone else and killed in an ambush. I need not go into details; I introduced so much else into it that the story itself was reduced to a thread. An important element is the emotional honesty of Christine, the heroine. Since the authors of films and books are generally men, they tell stories about men. I like to describe women. Another important element is the purity of Jurieu, the victim, who, trying to fit into a world to which he does not belong, fails to respect the rules of the game. During the shooting of the film I was torn between my desire to make a comedy of it and the wish to tell a tragic story. The result of this ambivalence was the film as it is. I had moments of profound discouragement; but then, when I saw the way the actors were interpreting my ideas, I became wildly enthusiastic. My uncertainties are apparent in the development of the story and the acting of its pro-tagonists. I recall the hesitations of Christine. The part was played by Nora Grégor, who was none other than Princess Stahremberg. Her husband, Prince Stahremberg, was an Austrian landowner who had founded an anti-Hitler peasant party. In his own domain the peasants voted for him, but the wave of Hitlerism was to sweep them aside.

I had got to know him shortly before La Règle du Jeu. He and his wife were in a state of great disarray. Everything they believed in was collapsing. One could write a novel about the state of mind of those exiles. But I was content to use the appearance of Nora Grégor, her look of 'bird-like' sincerity, to shape the character of Christine. Once again I started from externals to arrive at the creation of a character or a plot. I must ask forgiveness for dwelling upon this point, but, having reached the time of life when I must face the fact that I shall make no more films, I am more than ever attached to that principle. One starts with the environment to arrive at the self. I respect and admire artists who proceed in the opposite direction. Abstract art corresponds to the necessities of our time. But personally I remain a man of the nineteenth-century and I need observation as a point of departure. My father, who mistrusted imagination, said: 'If you paint the leaf on a tree without using a model you risk becoming stereotyped, because your imagination will only supply you with a few leaves whereas Nature offers you millions, all on the same tree. No two leaves are exactly the same. The artist who paints only what is in his mind must very soon repeat himself.'

One does not really know what a film is until it has been edited. The first showings of La Règle du Jeu filled me with misgiving. It is a war film, and yet there is no reference to he war. Beneath its seemingly innocuous appearance the tory attacks the very structure of our society. Yet all I thought about at the beginning was nothing avant-garde but a good little orthodox film. People go to the cinema in the hope of forgetting their everyday problems, and it was precisely their own worries that I plunged them into. The imminence of war made them even more thin-skinned. I depicted pleasant, sympathetic characters, but showed them in a society in process of disintegration, so that they were defeated at the outset, like Stahremberg and his peasants. The audience recognized this. The truth is that they recognized themselves. People who commit suicide do not care to do it in front of witnesses.

I was utterly dumbfounded when it became apparent that the film, which I wanted to be a pleasant one, rubbed most people up the wrong way. It was a resounding flop, to which the reaction was a kind of loathing. Despite a few favourable notices, the public as a whole regarded it as a personal insult. There was no question of contrivance; my enemies had nothing to do with its failure. At every session I attended I could feel the unanimous disapproval of the audience. I tried to save the film by shortening it, and to start with I cut the scenes in which I myself played too large a part, as though I were ashamed, after this rebuff, of showing myself on the screen. But it was useless. The film was dropped, having been judged to be 'too demoralizing'.

Many explanations of this attitude have been propounded. For my own part, I think the audience's reaction was due to my candour. The film had been shaped in response to influences in my personal life, the most powerful being those of my childhood. But that part of my life had been lived with my parents and Gabrielle, people incapable of not perceiving the truth behind the mask. To use a word that crops up frequently in the modern vocabulary, life with my family had been a 'de-mystification'. We are all 'mystified' – that is to say, fooled, duped, treated as of no account. I had the good fortune to have been taught to see through the trickery in my youth. In *La Règle du Jeu*, I passed on what I knew to the public. But this is something that people do not like; the truth makes them feel uncomfortable. A quarter of a century later I gave a lecture at Harvard University. *La Règle du Jeu* was showing at a nearby cinema. There was a burst of cheering when I appeared on the platform. The students were applauding the film. Since then its reputation has steadily grown. What seemed an insult to society in 1939 has become clear-sightedness.

But the fact remains that the failure of *La Règle du Jeu* so depressed me that I resolved either to give up the cinema or to leave France.

Them and their Ceilings

Providence, in the shape of the 1939 war, settled the matter in favour of the latter course. The war was another step towards the final collapse. Upon mobilization I regained my lieutenant's stripes and was posted to the Army film-service. During the phoney war I photographed soldiers yawning with boredom. I can recall only one incident in all that period that did something to relieve the monotony.

My team consisted of a cameraman with his assistant, and an engineer, also with an assistant. They travelled in a specially equipped van and I led the way in a small car. Our equipment was all visible; we were quite obviously 'cinema'. I was ordered one day to go and photograph the school-children in a front-line village. I went to the wrong village and found myself suddenly surrounded by Germans: the front was not clearly established in that sector, and without realizing it I had driven into the enemy lines. A German NCO came up to us, looking puzzled and amused. I saluted him and he returned the salute. The rest of the Germans, who seemed to be as bored in that village as we were in our own quarters, had the fatuous grin which people can never restrain at the sight of a film-team. Some of them, carrying tradition even further, went through the motions of turning a handle. I again saluted the German officer, turned round and drove quietly back to the French lines.

An incidental advantage of that period of idleness was that it enabled me to discover Strasbourg Cathedral. All my life I have been an anti-tourist, and a building has only to be listed in the guide books as of 'great interest' for me to refuse to go near it. My friend Lestringuez summed up this attitude of mind pretty well when he said of Versailles in autumn, its avenues covered with dead leaves, 'The thought of all the thousands of half-wits who have been thrilled to death by the sight makes it intolerable to me.' – Another case of *hostellerie*.

While I was shooting *The River* in India some members of the party arranged an excursion to the Taj Mahal. It was the period of full moon, the time when one 'absolutely must' see the Taj Mahal. I refused to go and spent the evening in an Italian bistro in New Delhi, the consequence of which is that I have never seen the Taj Mahal.

As for Strasbourg Cathedral, you may perhaps remember my friend Pierre Champagne's passion for Bugatti cars. We frequently went to the Bugatti works at Molsheim in Alsace, about ten kilometres from Strasbourg. While our car was being overhauled we would spend the day in a café drinking beer laced with small glasses of *prunelle*. It never occurred to us to visit the cathedral. But when the war broke out my team and I were sent to photograph it. I was seized with admiration and began to question the snobbishness in reverse which was, and sometimes still is, one of my rules of conduct.

The Italians had not yet entered the war, and the French Government, ready to do anything to ensure their continued neutrality, was showing them every possible favour. It happened that Mussolini had seen *La Grande Illusion* and he asked for the author of the film to be sent to Italy to give a course of lectures on film-direction at the Centro Sperimentale in Rome. The French Government promptly agreed, and, being in uniform, I had no option but to obey. I did not know Italy. My wife, Dido, at that time my secretary, chose to go with me. This presented no problem since she was a Brazilian and therefore a neutral. Koch also came along.

That stay in Rome was a revelation. Even today, despite the tourists, the town remains an overwhelming spectacle. I began teaching at the Centro Sperimentale and filming *Tosca*. The phoney war, still continuing in France, had no effect on our life in Rome. But the dream was rudely shattered. It was Michel Simon, playing the role of Scarpia in *Tosca*, who brought us a hint that some serious event was on the way. Michel Simon's two passions in Rome were for the ceiling paintings in the palaces and the settees in the brothels. He visited one of these establishments every evening and had long conversations with the ladies, showing them photographs he had taken of the ceilings. But one evening he found his usual settee in one of the houses occupied by men in civilian clothes talking German. He complained to the Madame, but she was too frightened to do anything. Simon went home in disgust and the next morning told me what had happened, concluding in typically Michel Simon fashion, 'They make me vomit, them and their ceilings.'

The Germans, meanwhile, were setting about the conquest of the Eternal City. Their method was simple. The only Italian newspaper favouring France was that of the Vatican, the *Osservatore Romano*. The Nazis hired a gang of local thugs – pimps, pickpockets, stick-up men and so on – and posted them at all the newspaper kiosks selling the paper. Prospective purchasers were beaten up. Within twenty-four hours even neutral papers had become pro-German. I myself was one of the sufferers. I asked for the *Osservatore Romano* in a restaurant and was duly set upon.

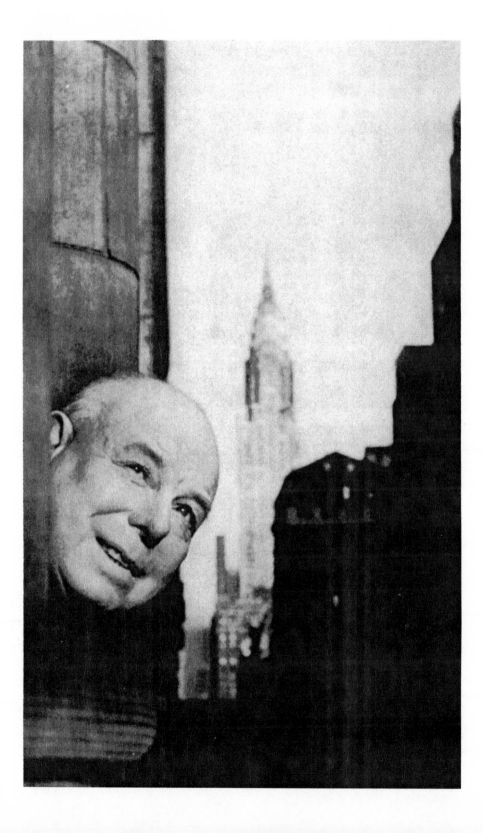

Left: On my first arrival in New York I was warmly welcomed by Robert Flaherty
Right: Dido and I
Below: I began to look more and more American. Here, during the shooting of *Swamp Water* in Georgia, 1941

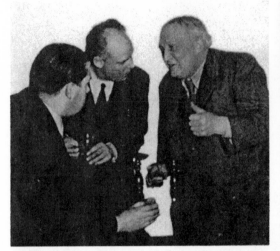

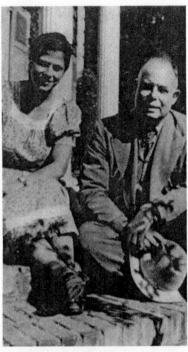

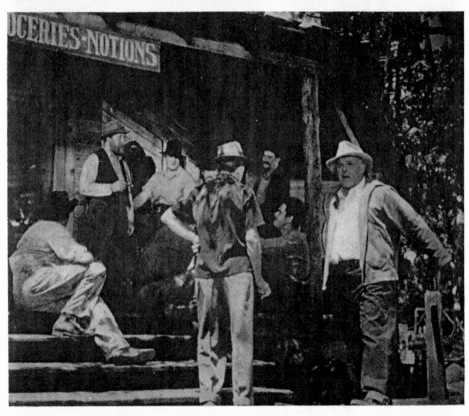

Things would have gone badly with me if I had not invoked the name of Mussolini, who was, after all, responsible for my being there. The French ambassador, to whom I reported the incident, advised me to leave by the next train. Dido stayed a few days longer, being protected by her Brazilian passport. She wanted to retrieve a copy of *La Grande Illusion* and also to deposit certain papers at the Brazilian Embassy.

The chauffeur who drove her to the Embassy was performing a courageous act. A recent decree had forbidden women to use motor-cars. The car was stopped by a dense crowd of enthusiastic citizens who were awaiting the appearance of Mussolini on the balcony of the Palazzo Veneto. They would have dragged Dido out of the car if the Duce himself had not appeared in time to save her. He was there to announce to the citizens of Rome that Italy was henceforth to fight at the side of Germany. He began his speech with an expansive gesture and the words: '*A chi – il mondo?*' . . . '*A noi, a noi!*' bellowed the delirious crowd. Dido can now laugh at that incident, which was in the best tradition of the Italian theatre, but she did not find it funny at the time.

Exodus

Koch and Michel Simon stayed on in Rome after my departure to complete the filming of *Tosca*. Simon had a Swiss passport and Koch, being a German subject, had nothing to fear except recall to his own country. My farewells to my collaborators were sad occasions, and I particularly regretted parting from Luchino Visconti because of all the things we might have done together but did not do. He had worked with me on a number of films, among them *La Partie de Campagne*. I was never to see Luchino again, despite the great friendship between us. Such is life.

Apart from the political situation, what distressed me was that I had scarcely begun filming *Tosca*. At my request Koch, who had worked with me on the script and knew my methods as a director, took my place. I gather that *Tosca* is an excellent film, but it is Koch's work, not mine. I have never seen it. Fortunately, as you know, I find my happiness in 'doing'.

After the filming Koch returned to Berlin, where he remained until the final collapse. Every man capable of bearing arms was mobilized for the defence of the city against the Russians. Koch, who was nearly fifty, was drafted into a regiment armed with bazookas – a strange weapon which he was no more capable of using than were his comrades. They were dressed in National Guard uniform dating from 1870 and sent to defend a small birch wood on the outskirts of the town. A captain of territorials was in command. He posted his men behind the trees with the encouraging words: 'Hang on till the last of you is killed. The Russians must not pass.' Despite this stirring exhortation, those amateur soldiers, having consulted together, decided to make a bolt for it.

Koch fetched up in a village which was almost immediately occupied by the Russians, who rounded up everyone of military appearance in the market-place. Koch found an NCO who spoke German and did his best to persuade him that the uniform he was wearing, although out-of-date, was none the less military, and that he was entitled to the soldier's chief privilege – namely, not to be shot. The discussion was cut short by the arrival of a car containing a woman in officer's uniform who seemed to be the Russian commander. Koch rushed towards her, his face glowing with happy astonishment. 'We met in Paris, don't you remember?' The lady was no less astonished, never having set eyes on him before. She asked in perfect German: 'Who introduced us?' After a bare moment's hesitation Koch came out with the name which seemed to him the most improbable in Russian ears. 'Lestringuez,' he said. The lady's expression relaxed. She gave an order and Koch was released. Well done, Lestringuez!

Dido was able to catch the last train from Italy to France. It was empty and was only running because no one had remembered to cancel it: the phenomenon known as 'momentum'. The presence of this solitary passenger intrigued the Italians, and at Vintimiglia, the frontier station, the staff came to gaze at the intrepid lady who was forsaking the peace of Italy to plunge into the inferno of war. 'You'll find the Tedeschi (Germans) in Paris.' When Dido pointed out that the Tedeschi were already swarming all over Italy they merely shrugged their shoulders. The Italians, in their two thousand years of history, have got into the habit of being invaded. To them it is unimportant, and anyway they always end by defeating the invaders. Politically submitting to her conquerors, Italy in practice converts them to her own way of life. Her artists and architects, her builders and cabinet-makers invade the conqueror's territory not with cannon-fire but with works of art and daily use.

Dido had some difficulty in tearing herself away from the sympathetic Italians. 'Don't go!' they besought her. 'You can still choose. Once you've crossed the frontier it will be too late.' In fact, the only invader Dido found in Paris was myself. I was trying to hire a car in order to join my son, Alain, who belonged to a regiment under orders to stop the Germans at the gates of Paris – nothing less than that! To my great surprise, I had no trouble in hiring a car at the Peugeot works. The clerk with whom I dealt probably considered the war a trifle compared with the proper functioning of a great business enterprise. Another case of the world being divided into horizontal compartments.

I found in my apartment a letter which Alain had sent me by way of a civilian who had a motor-cycle, and following his instructions I ran my son to earth in a suburb, one of a party of fifty horsemen without horses, but who possessed a large lorry. He was only an NCO, but since the officers had all disappeared the responsibility of feeding those fifty men devolved upon him. Dido had come with me. We lunched out of tins, seated on a bench in a square that might have been painted by Utrillo. Suddenly a staff-officer appeared with orders for the party to regroup farther to the rear. Alain became busy with the details of the operation, and, with Dido's approval, I decided that we would seek shelter with the Cézannes at Marlotte.

We found them trying to organize their own flight to the south, and joined forces with them. We put Paul, the son of the painter, and Renée Cézanne in the three-seater Peugeot which I had hired; I drove, and Dido, Jean-Pierre Cézanne and his wife Marjorie rode behind us on bicycles. Jean-Pierre had recently married Marjorie because she was Jewish and the word had got round that Jewish women married to Gentiles would not be sent to a concentration camp. Our small caravan had an odd appearance owing to the pictures which Paul Cézanne had tied on to the back of the Peugeot. People could not understand why anyone should take so much trouble to save windbreaks.

Thus we reached La Creuse, without having suffered anything worse than a few light bomb attacks by Italian planes. It occurred to us that the Germans would probably occupy Bordeaux and we decided to stop at a hamlet in the centre of France, off the main road. The villagers welcomed us with open arms, proud to have 'their' refugees. Our presence lent them prestige and aroused the jealousy of the neighbouring villages.

Dido and I often think of our sojourn on the farm of Père Antoine, where we lived a life of almost perfect happiness. We went off on bicycles to buy food during the day. Père Antoine allowed us to use a big barn filled with straw and hay as our living-quarters, and we hung its walls with Cézanne's paintings – an astonishing sight. Paul Cézanne was delighted. The rough stone of the walls, the racks containing the remains of the farmer's donkey's meal, and the agricultural implements, made a perfect background for them. Never had Cézanne's paintings been so appropriately hung. My very dear friend, Paul Cézanne, was able by a freak of international politics to give his father's work a setting

which the latter would certainly have relished. At night in
that barn we fell asleep amid the great peace that emanates
from masterpieces. Our oil-lamps provided an ideal light.
Their flames, flickering in the draught, gave us the impression that the persons in the pictures were alive and about to
speak to us.

Our host's she-donkey occupied a stall next door. When
we asked Père Antoine what he called her he replied,
'When she's good I call her Mignonne, but when she isn't
I call her a mule.'

Great disasters are slow in showing their destructive
effects. Despite the invasion and the fact that France was cut
in halves, the post and telegraph services were functioning
almost normally – another example of the power of momentum. I could send a telegram to a friend in Paris telling
him where I was. The reply was a letter from America –
from my friend Robert Flaherty, who made the film *Nanook
of the North*, urging me to go to the American Consulate in
Nice, where a visa for the United States awaited me. He had
guessed that I was in danger because of my anti-Hitler
attitude. Films such as *Le Crime de Monsieur Lange*, *La
Marseillaise* and *La Vie est à Nous*, together with numerous
newspaper articles, if they had not moved the masses had at
least caused a lot of ink to flow. I had to wait some months
before the French authorities let me have an exit visa. I
spent the time with my brother, Claude, in the property of
Les Collettes which he had inherited.

What had persuaded me to accept the American offer
were the visits to Les Collettes of two Frenchmen representing Nazi cultural institutions. They wanted me to work
within the framework of the New France, saying that I
would be given all possible assistance in making any films I

chose. They were often accompanied by a handsome Russian lady who looked like a thriller-type adventuress. She worshipped Hitler as though he were a god, and went into ecstasies whenever she spoke of him. Lestringuez, who had joined us, responded to these lucubrations with aggressively earthy good sense. 'Hitler,' he said, 'has pissed on the leg of mutton. There was a leg of mutton before he came, although it was not perfectly cooked or fairly divided. Some got solid slices out of the middle, and others had to put up with the scrag-end. But at least it was there. Well, it's still there, but now it's uneatable.' And he repeated, pulling a face, 'Hitler has pissed on the leg of mutton.'

It was time to clear out. Dido and I travelled by sea from Marseilles to Algeria, Morocco and Lisbon. I need not dwell on the long periods of waiting at every stage of the voyage. At Lisbon we got places on an American ship, and I was delighted to find myself sharing a cabin with none other than the writer Saint-Exupéry. We began a series of absorbing discussions on the subject of my old hobby-horse, the influence of the environment. Saint-Exupéry believed in this and did his utmost to escape from it. He even went so far as to refuse to learn English, saying that he had had quite enough trouble learning French. I did not speak any English myself at the time, and Saint-Exupéry made the most of the interpreter with whom good fortune had provided us. Dido could not move a foot without one or other of us calling her back. Saint-Exupéry, to Dido: 'Would you mind ordering some tea for me?' . . . 'Can't you order it for yourself? All you have to say is "tea".' . . . Saint-Exupéry: 'I don't want to.' And, pouting like a child: 'I'd sooner go without tea.'

Robert Flaherty was awaiting us on the dockside in New

York, and Dido flung herself into his arms. She has always adored him. Then he embraced me with all the warmth of his friendship, and to be embraced by Bob Flaherty was quite something. He was a man made of love. That is why he had so much feeling for the characters in his films. He loved them, that is all. He loved Dido and he loved me. When we were with him we seemed to be living in an immaterial world, a world in which the cares of everyday life, colds in the head, money troubles, no longer existed – the loving world of Robert Flaherty. He suddenly noticed the felt hat I was wearing. At that time French hats were narrow-brimmed, whereas those of the Americans, or anyway Bob Flaherty's, were broad-brimmed. Bob roared with laughter, grabbed my hat and flung it into the water. Then he took off his own hat and planted it on my head.

On the day after our arrival he took us to breakfast at the Hotel La Fayette, which was famous for its breakfasts. It was a meal worthy of Pantagruel, with salads followed by a variety of smoked fish and these in turn followed by enormous steaks washed down by a bottle of French wine. The debauch ended with a trolley of sweets. The Hotel La Fayette dated from the eighteenth century. It no longer exists, having been condemned as a fire risk. Its very age made it attractive. I was later to lodge there myself, perferring it, ant-ridden though it was, to the more efficient splendour of newer hotels. Bob had a passion for old hotels. He himself had an apartment at the Chelsea Hotel, where Mark Twain had lived.

We got the impression, during our first days in America, that the Americans lived in the past, a recent past but one whose rites were lovingly preserved. The Royalton Hotel, where our friend Rochemont had found rooms for us, was about half a century old and lived on its regular customers. The decrepit lift-boy chatted on familiar terms with George Jean Nathan and Sherwood Anderson. The latter, whose works I had read in French translation, and whom I greatly admired, sent me a friendly note of greeting. He would have liked to welcome us in person, but had been obliged to leave New York on the day we arrived. He hoped, as I did, that our meeting was only postponed; but we never got the chance.

Bob insisted on taking us to Washington before we left the East for Hollywood – or, according to the New Yorkers, before we left civilization for barbarism. He took along every close or distant friend who wanted to come and gave us all a tremendous meal at a Washington restaurant – over twenty of us altogether. When it came to paying the bill he found that he had not enough money on him. No matter; he signed with a flourish and was bowed out by an obsequious *maître d'hôtel*. We were given a typical glimpse of the Flaherty life-style and a foretaste of American open-handedness.

First Days with the Redskins

Dido and I had arrived in New York on 31 December, 1940, and the sight of the streets on that New Year's Eve was enough to amaze any newly arrived Frenchman. The brilliant lighting in Times Square was in itself bewildering after the black-out in European towns, to say nothing of the streets teeming with cars and pedestrians, compared with the empty streets of towns under curfew law. We walked on a sea of paper, and it was explained to us that New York office staffs are accustomed to celebrate the New Year by tearing up calendars and flinging the sheets out of the windows of the skyscrapers. Loud-speakers in front of the theatres were bellowing to attract custom.

We resolved to explore the extraordinary city. A few days after our arrival we hailed a taxi and Dido ordered the driver to take us 'anywhere'. He demurred, speaking with a strong Irish accent. 'You're French,' he said. 'You can't have that much money. It's my day off tomorrow. I'll pick you up at your hotel, but on foot, and we'll do a trip on the elevated railway. It's wonderful. You see the people in their homes, cooking, shaving, dressing. They don't take any notice of the elevated. It's as though you didn't exist and you see into their lives without their knowing.' We accepted the kind offer and got a zooming view of New York. When the trip was over he insisted on our coming home with him to eat the Irish stew his wife was cooking. Dido asked him why he was being so good to us, and he said: 'It's the way you talk. You're French and I'm Irish. We're all Catholics, and Catholics have to stand by one another.'

Thus no sooner had we landed than we came up against a fact that even the Americans are slow to recognize – namely that there is not one America but as many Americas as there are racial groups. These groups, scattered all over the country, nevertheless remain homogenous, lending substance to my theory of the horizontal division of the world into cultural, religious, economic and other entities, but not into geographical entities. The United States are, or rather were, a society of European malcontents. It is not long since, if you asked a citizen of the US his nationality, he would be more likely than not to tell you that he was Irish, Sicilian or Jewish. But wars, alas, have given rise to a national – that is to say, vertical – outlook.

On the plane to Hollywood, our final destination, my wife and I tried to picture what was in store for us. I dreamed of myself installed in that paradise, with Griffith, Charlie Chaplin, Lubitsch and all the other great figures in the world-cult of the cinema. Needless to say, the Hollywood of our imaginings was the old Hollywood, and I was greatly moved by the thought that I was to meet in the flesh the shadowy figures peopling the old-time cinema which I had so loved, as I still do, although I knew that it belonged to the world of ghosts. I saw myself meeting the actress who perhaps had influenced Catherine Hessling more than any other – Mae Murray, the satin doll. Her cameraman had used the softest of gauze screens for her enchanting face. He must have revelled in all the experiments needed to produce that triumph of sensual fluffiness, shadow and radiance. Nothing seemed real about that adorably artificial creature, with her floating walk and her flutter of false eyelashes bordering on bad taste. She was a representation of idealized womanhood, queen of a world in which corns on the toes were unknown. The public in these days would not accept that kind of make-believe: the taste for realism has killed the taste for fairy-tales. Modern cinema, in order to survive, has had to steep itself in the truth of appearances, and that is a pity. Besides, under a different exterior the child-woman still exists. Instead of emerging from a froth of lace she shows herself riding a surf-board in a bikini. I prefer the former. Both men and women are losing a great deal by taking the wraps off everything. A little mystery in the cinema, or in life for that matter, does no harm.

Another heroine whom I hoped to meet was Gloria Swanson, to me the embodiment of American womanhood, magnificently expressing the luxury which Europeans suppose to be part and parcel of every American. Watching *The Mark of Zorro*, I never doubted that all the people performing around Douglas Fairbanks owned three cars, a Hollywood villa with all mod. cons. and a country cottage. I did not know that Hollywood was the back of beyond. Other visions helped Dido and me to relieve the monotony of the air-passage from New York to Los Angeles, which in those days seemed interminable: Lilian Gish, the pathetic victim of villainy (for it was impossible to go to Hollywood without remembering *Broken Blossoms*), and Mary Pickford with her childish guile.

But we were getting near, and the expectation of reality swept away memories. Despite the darkness, we could see through the porthole that we were flying over a mountain. The irony of it is that although I was to live in the same part of Hollywood as Mae Murray and Gloria Swanson, I never met either. Perhaps it was from fear of not finding the reality equal to the legend, perhaps from fear of not under-

standing them. I knew very little English, and my conversation must have been lacking in sparkle. We did, however, get to know Lilian Gish. She was a woman of in-
comparable youth and charm, but she belonged to another
age. She was no longer given interesting roles. We bought
a plot of land alongside the house where she lived, hoping
to derive great pleasure from her proximity. Alas, she had
to go back East, and we never saw her again. Later on we
were to meet other stars who had sunk to playing minor
parts, among them Charles Ray and Mae Marsh.

The plane was still flying over mountains. The only signs
of life in the darkness were occasional specks of light,
doubtless indicating the existence of houses. But suddenly
we were dazzled by a profusion of light. We had reached
the suburbs of the town, and it was as though a river of
diamonds were flowing beneath us. In these days nearly
every town presents a similar spectacle, but in those days
it was still fairly uncommon. It looked like a symbol of
triumphant Hollywood. The plane landed. A limousine was
awaiting us.

We were wildly anxious to see the centre of the town, and
we strained our eyes looking for anything which would give
us some idea of the place we were going to live in. What had
looked from the air like a river of diamonds turned out to
be nothing but an outer boulevard full of petrol pumps and
super-markets. Other streets were like rows of bathing huts.
A stand selling orange-juice was shaped like an enormous
orange.

Next day we set out to explore. The Chinese Theatre was
unexciting; but we continued perseveringly to search for
something that would please us in that disappointing town.
We were hungry and found a hot-dog stall which sought to

attrack the public by disguising itself as a huge sandwich, the sausage being a dog of some kind, its head and tail protruding from the cardboard roll of bread.

I had signed a contract with Fox. Dazed by my salary, and never doubting, in my innocence, that I should receive it regularly for the rest of my life, I had not hesitated to rent a very nice house, large enough for us to entertain our friends. These were the fixed points in the sea of confusion into which I had been plunged by the New World, so open in appearance but in reality as mysterious as a tribe of Sioux Indians.

Saint-Exupéry, who lived with us, was working on his *Night Flight*. When we came down to breakfast in the morning we would find him eating his dinner! He worked at night. When by chance we came together at a normal hour he would entertain us with card-tricks, in which he possessed the skill of a professional. The trick which most impressed me was as follows: he would hand the whole pack to someone and ask them to shuffle it thoroughly; then he would shuffle it himself and ask someone else to cut it. He would hand it back to one of us and go into the next room, and from this distance ask for the pack to be cut again and announce the card that came to light.

He wrote his book with the help of a typist whom he never saw. He talked it into a dictaphone, tape being not yet in use. To the typist, this employer who slept while she was awake had all the glamour of a mystery man. She did her utmost to come face to face with him, and curiosity turned to love. We would come upon her wandering through the passages like a family ghost. Now and then she had an attack of nerves, which gave her a certain amount of reality.

A project which Saint-Exupéry and I cherished was the filming of *Wind, Sand, Stars*. It never came off, but it led to the discovery that we had been born to be something more than friends, namely accomplices. We had an interview with one of the big Hollywood agents, who would, we hoped, handle our project. He received us in his almost genuine Georgian office and offered us cigars. In the tradition of the great men of this world he made himself comfortable with his feet on the desk, and with condescending affability said to Saint-Exupéry, 'So you're a writer?' . . . 'I wonder,' said Saint-Exupéry. 'My real job is piloting an aeroplane.' The agent thought we were fooling. He rebuked me amiably, saying that he had no time to waste. But in the act of asking his secretary to show us out he was seized with remorse in case he had offended us, and he offered us a drink. The cocktail cabinet, with an impressive array of bottles, was concealed behind mock bookshelves. 'What do you think of that?' he asked proudly. 'The guy who designed it was a European – Italian, or maybe Portuguese.' Saint-Exupéry let fall a terse comment as we went down in the lift. 'What a creep!' he said.

While I was in Georgia, doing the location shots of *Swamp Water*, Bob Flaherty, having business in Hollywood, occupied our home with his brother, David. He kept open house, of which I heartily approved. Later on I met Orson Welles at a party. To my surprise he gave me a detailed description of the house, having been often invited there by Bob. I had just seen *Citizen Kane* and was flattered by this indirect link between us. Joris Ivens was also my guest, his wife being Flaherty's film editor. David Flaherty helped me with my English correspondence. Every evening, when he sat down to dinner, he made the same joke: 'We are now going to dine at Ciro's.' Ciro's was the fashionable night-club. Harry and Grace, our black servants, tried in vain to protect our cellar, defending my interests with a devotion that was the more praiseworthy in that they did not drink themselves. Harry possessed a brand-new car which I greatly admired; to us it seemed the embodiment of the efficiency of American democracy. We overlooked the catastrophic situation of the masses as a whole, and the fact that Harry and Grace were in no way typical of the American prolet-ariat. A part of the American way of life consists in maintaining this façade. The rich quarters are more prosper-ous than ever, a cunning mask over the wretchedness of the poor quarters; just as the cover-girls on American magazines cause one to forget the faces of the women who are not singled out.

'Swamp Water'

Fox Films welcomed me with open arms. I was particularly pleased by the friendliness of John Ford, being an enthusiastic admirer of his work. He took me aside in the studios and said to me in French: 'Dear Jean, don't ever forget what I'm going to tell you. Actors are crap.' Of course he only meant bad actors.

I was quick to realize that what Fox expected of me was not that I should bring in my own methods but that I would adopt those of Hollywood. I argued endlessly with Darryl Zanuck, the big chief, that if all he wanted was the sort of film he was in the habit of making he should not apply to me. Hollywood was bursting with talent. Why should he ask me to take the place of someone who would automatically supply him with the kind of merchandise he was used to? In that field I should be nothing but an imitator, whereas in my own field I might come up with something new.

His reply was that he proposed to get me to film French stories, which was the very last thing I wanted. I shuddered at the idea of directing sequences with moustached policemen and gentlemen in velvet jackets and imperial beards parading against a bogus-Montmartre, bogus-café background.

I talked one day to René Clair, who was in the same position as I was. He described the top film executives as 'redskins', saying that all they lacked was the feathered headgear. The comment carried particular weight, coming from that cultivated representative of the French *grande bourgeoisie*.

With some difficulty I persuaded Zanuck to let me try a purely American story. This was *Swamp Water* in 1941. The script, adapted from a novel by Vereen Bell, was by Dudley Nichols, the fine script-writer who had written John Ford's *The Informer*. It was the story of a man unjustly accused of murder who takes refuge in the marshland of Okefenokee and contrives to live there for several years. His whereabouts are known, but no one dares seek him out in that hostile countryside. By chance his daughter's lover comes upon him when searching for a lost dog. Eventually his innocence is established. The interest of the story depended largely on the characters, and I was fascinated by these primitive people.

The element of reality in *Swamp Water* was so powerful that it would have been madness to neglect it. This reality was the Okefenokee swamp, straddling the borders of Florida and Georgia. To attempt a studio imitation was absurd: no designer could reproduce the real thing in the way that Nature herself did. But Zanuck could not see why it should be shot on location. One of his assistants said to me: 'I don't know why you're being so obstinate about it. I've shown you round the studios and you've seen the kind of set we're capable of building. We've made films set in Paris and Vienna, and in small American towns, and no one has ever questioned the accuracy of the background. Do you think we've gone to all that expense just to go and shoot in a Georgia village?' . . . I went so far as to predict to Zanuck that a day would come when Hollywood teams would travel all over the world in search of authenticity. He let himself be persuaded and sent me to Georgia to do the outdoor shots of *Swamp Water*. That is how we came to visit the Deep South. I spoke English very little better than Saint-Exupéry. Dido acted as my interpreter.

We settled in a charming small town called Waycross, where the people showed us the utmost kindness. The filming proceeded without incident. The only member of the cast to come with us was Dana Andrews. Instead of engaging stars Zanuck had accepted two unknown actors, Dana Andrews and Ann Baxter, for the leading parts. Stand-ins had to be found locally. My accent and faulty English greatly amused the party. One day I was giving instructions to the local girl who was standing in for Ann Baxter. She was on the other side of an arm of the river and had to get into a boat. Rehearsing the episode, she was over-excited and too hurried. I shouted across to her: 'Miss, wait a little,' pronouncing the word as though it were 'wet'. The girl looked in consternation at Dana Andrews. 'Does he really want me to . . .?' 'These foreign directors sometimes have strange ideas,' Dana said wickedly.

We needed a bear for the film, and I heard that a store-keeper in a neighbouring village owned a tame one. The story of that bear is worth telling. A few years previously the storekeeper's wife had given birth to a beautiful little girl, who was, however, subject to epileptic fits. After consulting all the local doctors the father turned to the last Indian medicine-man in the district. His remedy was as follows: 'Get hold of a bear cub and bring it up with your child and the epilepsy will go away.' There were still bears in the Okefenokee swamp. The medicine-man's treatment was followed and the epilepsy went away. That particular bear was still living with the family. It was remarkably greedy. We drove it about in a van, and whenever we passed a shop selling ice-cream it roared, so that we had to stop and buy some. To its owner's great disappointment the bear never appeared in the film. On the day before it should have done so, the owner, wanting it to look at its best, took it to the barber and had its fur stylishly trimmed. The result was that it looked like a poodle and we had to do without it.

In those days the Okefenokee region was a sanctuary of very interesting wild animals. You must picture a sort of forest growing in black water and smothered in a lacework of Spanish moss. We travelled in canoes among the trunks of enormous trees, accompanied by crocodiles and giant tortoises, with the screeching of strange birds to supply background music. One small crocodile was extremely inquisitive. At first all one saw of it was a single eye peeping out above the surface of the water. As it grew used to us its whole head emerged, but if anyone made a movement it promptly dived; then the eye would reappear on the other side of the canoe. We saw a brown bear on a huge fallen tree-trunk, and by exercising caution we could get near to tufted water-birds. It seems that there were even black panthers.

The people of the district lived by selling the skins of the marsh animals, which was why the rarer species were dying out. The American Government had declared the region an animal sanctuary and, very wisely, had appointed a well-known local poacher to the post of warden. He had been completely converted to the idea of animal preservation and was a great deal more efficient than any ordinary State official. It was this friendly and cultivated man who introduced Dido and me to Bourbon, which is the national drink of the South. One evening after we had talked for some time about the difference between commercial whisky and the illicit article we asked him how we could get hold of some of the latter. He said he had no idea; the owners of illicit

stills took immense pains to avoid discovery. Then the
conversation turned to a remarkable woman who had become known as the Queen of Okefenokee and had for a long
time kept animal-hunting in the marshlands under control.
Suddenly the warden got up and signed to us to follow him.
He led us to a barn with a padlocked door which he opened.
The smell of spirit nearly knocked us off our feet.

I shall never forget a visit we paid to a house in the perfect
Southern style situated on the edge of the marsh. A lane
running between dwarf palms led to it. A little barefoot girl,
clad in a torn cotton dress, was playing at the entrance to
the lane. She was fair-haired, and the skin of her half-
naked body was as pink as a Georgia peach. At the sight of
us she ran towards the house. We thought it prudent to
wait. In a short time she came back, followed by two other
girls, older than herself but equally ragged. We said we
wanted to look at the house. One of the girls said that she
thought we might do so because I spoke with a French
accent and was not one of the city louts who chase after
girls and then desert them. She went back to the house and
we waited under the interested gaze of the two other girls,
who giggled while they stared at us.

The girl came back and asked us to wait a little longer
while Grandma got dressed in order to receive us. We
waited a good half-hour and then yet another girl appeared
at the end of the lane and announced that Grandma was now
ready. The house was surrounded by a verandah decorated
with dried rattle-snake skins. I trembled at the thought of
those barefoot children running about that perilous countryside. One of them guessed what I was thinking and said:
'That's not what's wrong with this place. We don't worry
about them, any more than we do about the crocodiles.' I

was about to say something when the old lady appeared. The sight of her took my breath away. She was thin as a skeleton, clad in a black evening dress, spangled and cut very low; but none of us was disposed to laugh. The old lady bore herself like a queen. She made us a curtsey. One of the girls brought a jug of whisky. I said something about the beauty of the place, and I meant it.

The house and everything inside it was made entirely of wood. Even the chimneys were wooden, plastered with clay on the inside to prevent them catching fire. The well was of wood, as were all its accessories. Dishes, furniture, cooking utensils, all were of wood and made by hand. I noted that the lighting was by oil-lamps. The old lady refused to leave her home and had never seen electric light.

I was fascinated, not only by the strangeness of the place but by the woman herself, surrounded by a cluster of beautiful girls like a queen by her maids of honour. We stayed the better part of an hour and then took our leave. I remarked to the mistress of the house that there was one room which we had not visited. She replied: 'It's my brother's bedroom. He's in bed. He's been in bed over thirty years. His heart was broken. The girl he was in love with went to Atlanta and became a whore. My brother wanted to kill the man who took her away, but our parents stopped him. So he went to bed and he's never got up since.'

Plus ça change

When the shooting of *Swamp Water* was completed I was made to realize that the film was no longer mine. I had already had a warning of this in connection with a scene which I had shot in a way to which Hollywood producers were unaccustomed. This had displeased the High Council presided over by Zanuck, which inspected the rushes every evening. The scene was a dispute between a father and his son, and I had treated it as a single, mobile whole, following my principle of bringing together all the elements of a situation in a single take. Orson Welles had done the same in his magnificent *Citizen Kane*, but Welles was far from being regarded as a trend-setter. It took twenty years for dismay at his films to be transformed into admiration. As I was not disposed to insist on my version of that family quarrel I agreed to re-shoot the scene in several takes. This was my first surrender to Hollywood.

That same evening I was informed that I was not to continue shooting *Swamp Water* and that the film was to be directed by someone else. To my great surprise the reason was not the scene over which we had differed. An assistant in the production department told me that my slowness was the reason: I had overshot the budget. He was genuinely upset. He proposed to talk to the Big Chief and blame my chief cameraman for the delay. Although, as I have so often stressed, I am no hero, this get-out annoyed me. I took a high line and replied that I was a slow worker and the slowness was my own responsibility. This was by no means what I really thought. I have good reason for considering myself a speedy director. I shot *Les Bas Fonds* and *Le Crime de Monsieur Lange* each in twenty-five days. But this harsh rebuff opened my eyes to the real system prevailing in the studios, which was simply dictatorship. I realized that I had landed not in the land of Mae Murray but in that of Alfred Jarry's farcical monarch, Père Ubu.

This happened in the evening. I said goodbye to the technicians and actors who were still on the set and went home. I was in despair. But in the middle of the night the telephone rang. It was Zanuck. He had watched several sequences from *Swamp Water* and reckoned that I had done 'a pretty good job'. So I was to carry on directing the film. Père Ubu had let me off the hook ... My rehabilitation was as rapid as my disgrace. At exactly nine o'clock next morning I walked on to the set. My team were all there, with about fifty extras. But their behaviour was odd. Instead of the usual buzz of conversation there was dead silence. I went towards my cameraman intending to ask him the reason for this, but suddenly, and spontaneously, there was a burst of heart-warming applause.

One of Hollywood's most dangerous enemies is the passion for red tape. I well remember the meetings devoted to the budget of *Swamp Water*. Here again we were in the kingdom of Père Ubu. The head office representative responsible for the finance of the film was obviously doing his utmost to cut costs. He kept coming back to the number of vehicles, tools, animals, etc. He turned to me and said: 'There's got to be some poultry on this farm of yours. How many hens do you want?' I thought for a moment and said, 'One.' He was so in the habit of bargaining that he thought I had misunderstood. 'I asked you how many hens you wanted on the farm.' . . . 'And I told you–

one.' . . . 'But that's impossible. You can't have a farm with only one hen.' I stuck to my guns. My farm needed only one hen, and there was no reason why I should be given two or ten or twenty. The man thought I was joking. He ordered five hens and the meeting went on.

My differences with the management were the delight of the entire studio, the more so since my faulty English led to my saying the strangest things. When a public relations man asked me how I liked working for the company I replied, quite seriously, that I was delighted to be working for 15th-Century Fox. This slip of mine went the rounds and I got the reputation for being a merry wag. What most annoyed me was to find that I was not in charge of the editing of my films. I was allowed into the cutting-room, but only just. The final editing was done by Zanuck himself or one of his assistants. It must be said that it was excellent, perhaps more skilful than I could have managed myself, but it was not my editing. And this process in the making of a film is, from the point of view of the director, one of the most effective means of putting his own stamp on his work. But since the death of Lubitsch the idea of the film-maker, as such, has vanished from Hollywood. It happens all too often that the post of director consists of little more than a folding chair with his name on it. The actors have rehearsed the scene with a dramatic coach, the chief cameraman has arranged the lighting, and the designer has done the sets. The director's responsibility is sometimes limited to saying 'Action' to start the cameras rolling, and 'Stop' to turn them off.

Among the assistants with whom Zanuck loved to surround himself there was an actor who had been a star in the silent days. He unfortunately suffered from chronic laryngitis, which ruled him out when the talkies came along. At the time when I was making *Swamp Water* a friend of mine was shooting a Biblical film on another set. Zanuck was away, and the ex-actor took his place at the showing of the rushes of the films in current production. This innocent-seeming procedure was a trial which could decide the fate of a director. About twenty judges were present on this occasion. Among the day's rushes on that night of Zanuck's absence there was a sequence to which the director, who was a friend of mine, attached particular importance. When the lights went up everyone was wildly enthusiastic, shaking the director by the hand, slapping him on the back and predicting that the film would be a tremendous success. The ex-actor, who came of a circus family and sometimes used circus jargon, embraced him with tears in his eyes, saying that his sequence was 'boum-boum'. It was an expression used by the clown Medrano which had come to be universally adopted, and it meant that a thing was good or bad, mediocre or magnificent – in short, anything you liked. But the next day Zanuck came back and saw the sequence for himself. He was silent for a while and finally passed judgement: 'Terrible. It'll have to be re-shot.' Yesterday's admirers edged away from the director. Zanuck turned to the ex-actor and asked: 'Well, what do you think of it?' . . . 'Me?' said the latter, 'I think it's . . .' and he came out with the most gloomy 'boum-boum' in the whole range of the expression.

Zanuck is a genius in his way. He has contrived, while using industrial methods, to give his productions the undeniable stamp of quality. Certain of the films he produced are recognized as milestones in our profession. He is one of the few film magnates who have taken an active part in the business, and he has often saved indifferent films by his skill as an editor. My problem in Hollywood was and will always be the same, arising out of the fact that the calling I seek to practise has nothing to do with the film industry. I have never been able to come to terms with the purely industrial side of films. Hollywood's detractors suppose that the weakness of the industry lies in its anxiety to make money at all costs, and that by catering to the public taste it falls into mediocrity. There is some truth in this, but the desire for gain is not the worst thing about it.

The real danger, in my opinion, lies in a blind love of so-called perfection, to obtain which a multiplicity of talents is called upon. Such and such a film is based on a literary masterpiece, scripted and revised by half-a-dozen leading script-writers and entrusted to a director who is equally celebrated. The actors are all stars, and the editor is the best man in the business. With all these trumps in its hand the studio feels sure that it cannot fail. How can so many talented people possibly produce a flop? And yet this often happens. The warrant for the failures is that by the use of effective publicity they still make money. It can even happen that, by a fortunate chance, by the drawing-power of the cast or the topicality of the subject, some of these productions are genuinely good.

A big Hollywood film is dished up like a melon, in separate slices. This is at the opposite pole from my belief in unity. It is a process of dividing the work and collecting important names. The term 'star' is not confined to actors: there are star writers, star cameramen and star designers, and each works separately, without any real link between them. Isolated in their ivory towers, these stars have to defend themselves against the intrusion of the common enemy, the producer. Each of them, accordingly, plays the prima donna, especially the cameraman. These last are the spoilt children of Hollywood film production. They take advantage of the general ignorance in the matter of framing and lighting. The director is the scapegoat. He is the person held responsible for delays which are really due to the whimsicalities of the cameraman.

This mania for perfection extends to every field. The Industry dishes up perfect cars, perfect shoes, perfect cookery and perfect houses – the whole adding up to perfect monotony. Settings as a rule are so little varied that it is enough to make one scream with boredom. The architects and designers plead not guilty. The things they give us are varied enough, according to their notions. In any American street we can find, so it seems, everything that is needed to gratify our taste for fantasy. One house is in the French provincial style, the one next door is Mexican and the one over the way is New England. Few people realize that the monotony arises out of identity of detail and not out of the general conception. The window-frames are all the same, mass-produced by the same machines. Door-handles are the same, floors are made of the same kind of wood. The nails and screws that hold the building together are all exactly the same size, all perfect.

Progress has robbed us of the sometimes clumsy hallmark of the craftsman who made a particular door. In the old days when I went through that doorway I would have a word to say to that craftsman, but I can get no joy out of a chat with a mechanical saw. Machine-work dulls men's minds, whereas handicraft ennobles them. A craftsman's products enrich life. Everything made by hand is like a message from its maker, it contains life. What difference does it make if the design of a mass-produced plate is the work of a master? – the monotony of its mass-production induces a feeling of sadness, whereas the variety and imperfections of primitive utensils bring lightness of heart. I have no hesitation in attributing the wave of boredom sweeping over the modern world to the monotony of the background against which we live. The saving grace of the cinema is that with a little patience, and with love, by avoiding conventional make-up and taking liberties with orthodox lighting, we may arrive at that wonderfully complex creature which is called Man. My dream is of a craftsman's cinema in which the author can express himself as directly as the painter in his paintings or the writer in his books. Now and then this dream is realized. Certain film-makers leave this impress on their works.

The master of masters, the film-maker of film-makers, for me is still Charlie Chaplin. He has done everything in his films – script, direction, setting, production, performance and even the music. We are far removed from that sliced melon. His films are not only examples of perfect unity, but all his work is one. One may say indeed of Chaplin that he has made only one film and that every facet of that film is a different enactment of the same profession of faith. It is with him, taking our respective proportions into account, that I feel the closest affinity. Chaplin is the god of non-violence and I am one of his apostles. It would be hard to find a more biting critic of our society; yet he does not preach or wind up his stories with pistol shots. He gives us an underdog who survives only by a miracle and thanks to his unexcelled agility. I have repeated his single theme in my film *The River* – the crippled war veteran anxiously inquires of the half-caste, Melanie, how they are to escape from their false positions. She answers, 'By accepting.' Chaplin takes note of the egotism and absurdity of the world, and like the early Christians, he meekly accepts it. It is an acceptance that softens the public heart and turns it away from violent solutions. There is no bloodshed in his films. I am convinced that our present wave of violence is due in part to the fact that for twenty years people have been deprived of the films of Charlie Chaplin.

The Love of Disguise

In 1943 I worked on *This Land is Mine* for RKO in collaboration with Dudley Nichols. It was a story of France under the Occupation which dealt with the inner conflict of a schoolmaster who is terrified of the Germans but becomes a hero despite his determination not to get involved. Charles Laughton played the part magnificently.

Dudley Nichols and I had set an important scene between a German officer and the schoolmaster in the street of a small town. Both had to walk along a paved sidewalk, the sound of their footsteps on the paving stones reflecting the difference between the two characters. To my intense surprise I found that this sidewalk was only imitation stone, made of soft cardboard. My old friend Lourié, the designer, had fought hard to get real stone but the sound department had vetoed it. They were afraid that the sound of footsteps on a hard surface would interfere with the dialogue, and it was the rule that the dialogue must always come over clearly. I did my best to explain that the contrast between military jack-boots and soft-soled civilian shoes was an essential ingredient of the scene, and I insisted on one point, namely that the actors, having to speak their lines through this sound of footsteps, would do so differently than they would on a silent surface. But it was no use. I was told that by dubbing the sound of footsteps the noise could be kept down to the requisite level.

The incident enabled me to put my finger on the precise difference between French and American taste. The French have a passion for what is natural, while the Americans

Above: Gabrielle in Hollywood, with her husband Conrad Slater and son Jean
Below: This Land is Mine, 1943: l. to r. Maureen O'Hara, Dudley Nichols, myself and Charles Laughton

worship the artificial. Of course, it is not a complete distinction, for every great artist is both a realist and a poet. The Americans produced Faulkner; the French produced Jean Giraudoux.

The Americans invented that unreal creature, the cover-girl. They have developed the art of make-up to the utmost of unreality. Every human being is something of an actor. We all like to display to the world an improved version of ourselves. But with the Americans this natural impulse is carried to the point where it becomes camouflage. My wife and I, paying a weekend visit to a respectable middle-class hotel in Palm Springs, thought for a moment that we had come to the wrong place: we seemed to be surrounded by sheriffs and outlaws. Those excellent people greatly enjoyed dressing up. They might have been film extras – and we had come there to get away from films! In these days such things are not uncommon in Europe – there is no stopping 'progress'.

I have talked about the monotony of American streets despite the apparent variety of the buildings. The house looking like a fortress with impressively thick walls is in fact a sort of hollow-walled box, the tarred paper and wire-netting of which the walls are built being hidden beneath a thick coating of plaster. One half expects the inmates of that historic pile to dress up in medieval costume to eat their hamburgers. The removal of a house is an amazing spectacle to any European. The feudal manor or Spanish hacienda is literally sawn into two or three pieces and conveyed along the roads to its new site. It must be added that these huge match-boxes stand up to the treatment remarkably well and are reassembled intact. They shiver harmlessly in an earthquake and are easily modified.

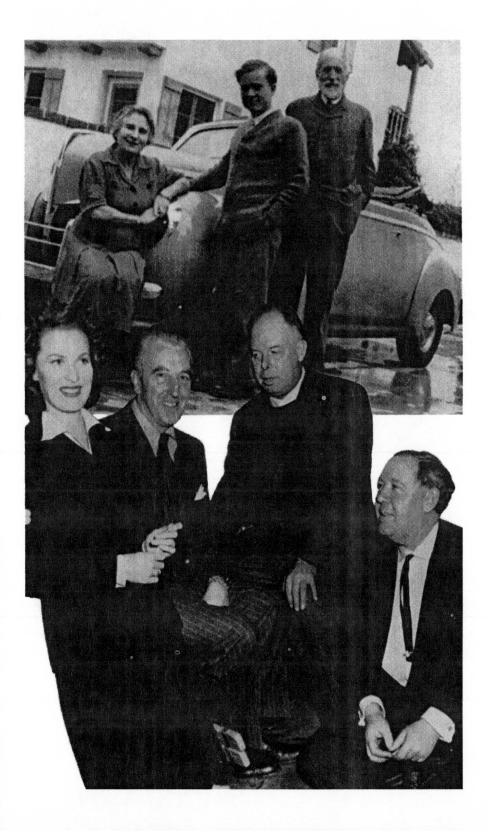

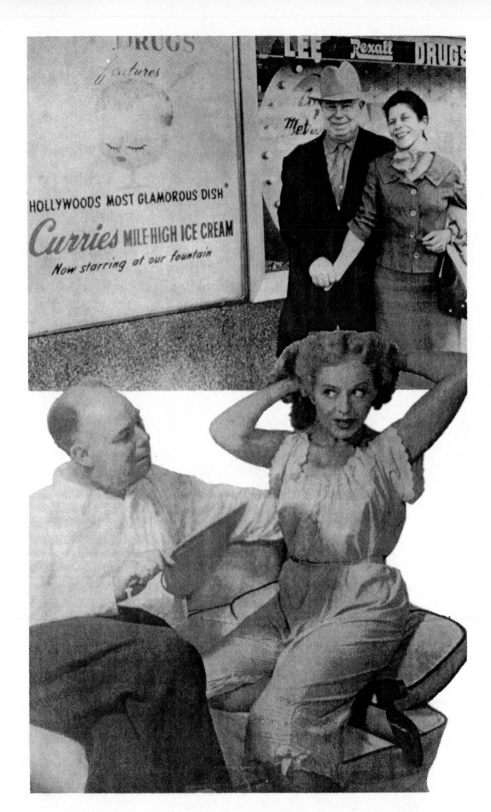

Above: Hollywood might not want me, but life still went on
Below: With Paulette Goddard during the shooting of *Le Journal d'une Femme de Chambre,* 1946

209

This fondness for disguise causes Americans to incline to the acting profession. They are born actors. Nothing is easier than to direct a crowd of American extras. They are not better than the French but they get into the act with disturbing rapidity. French actors and extras have more difficulty in divesting themselves of their own personality. They want to understand, and compel the director to explain exactly what he wants – which can be fatal, for who knows exactly what he wants?

I like actors. I regard them as the heroes and martyrs of their profession. The exercise of their calling makes it impossible for them to lead a normal life, especially the women. As evidence of this we have only to think of the number of actresses who commit suicide. If they were unsuccessful that would account for it, but the fact is that the female suicides are mostly successful stars. They have everything, fame, money, adulation, yet they are more unhappy than the little extra sighing for a credit. Possibly the reason is their sense of being treated not as a human being but as an object.

With men, a frequent cause of this kind of hypochondria is the feeling that 'it won't last'. Many male stars are terrified of the idea of having to play bit-parts after having seen their name up in lights for years. The person to whom this happens is afraid even to go to his usual barber. The barber is very important in American theatrical life, a kind of hallmark of success.

This sense of insecurity sometimes makes the stars odious, so that directors tremble before them and assistants are afraid to speak to them. They spend the time between shots resting in their caravans, playing cards or doing crossword puzzles. They don't trouble to pose while the chief cameraman fixes the lighting: a stand-in does this for them. Not until the last moment, when the set is in complete readiness, does the director venture to ask them to play their part. The star then takes up the required position, yawning and cursing, and leaning heavily on the director's arm as he descends the steps of his caravan. The sight of the jaded creature makes one think that he has come out of an operating theatre. Clifford Odets called the stars 'the invalids'. I would advise every apprentice director to spend some time as an actor. It will enable him to understand that behind this intolerable behaviour there lurks a tragic distress. Confrontation, whether with the public or with all the machinery of filming, is a stern ordeal. Above all, there is the camera, that all-seeing lens that is like an eye devoid of humanity. It is not surprising that when the trial is over the actor is impossible to deal with.

Swamp Water was my first encounter with American actors and actresses. It was the beginning of an idyll which caused me to recall my love-affair with French actors. I took a particular fancy, when the filming began, to Ann Baxter, whose acting and personality reminded me of Janie Marèse in *La Chienne*. There was no similarity between the two films but, in an entirely different role, she dominated the situation without seeming to do so. She tackled difficulties as they arose. It goes without saying that I had rehearsed in the Italian manner – readings round a table, the apparent uselessness of which had caused me to be accused of 'slowness' as a director. *Swamp Water* confirmed me in my belief in a horizontally divided world: like carpenters or veterinary surgeons, actors are the same the world over.

It pleased me to find in American studios habits which I had thought peculiar to the French. For example, the make-up girl's powder-puff. The scene is ready for shooting, the lighting arranged, the actor who is to be shot in close-up is in a state of utmost tension: nothing remains except for the director to pronounce the fateful word 'Action'. And at this moment the make-up girl dives into the magic circle and powders the actor's face. It tickles and makes him sneeze and the scene is ruined; he has lost the mood, and there is nothing for it but to start all over again. Then, slightly less exasperating, there is the case of the script-girl and the ties. I don't know why it is, but nearly all script-girls insist on straightening an actor's tie at the very moment when he is about to begin a scene. These habits which so annoyed me gave me the feeling that I was working in a French or Italian studio. And plain silliness is also inter-national. A custom which I believe to be peculiar to American studios was the suspending of operations while the star was having her period. The news being discreetly announced by an assistant director, everything stopped. I don't know if this tribute to the laws of nature is still practised. My stint with Fox happened thirty years ago.

Lucien Ballard, my cameraman for *Swamp Water*, was of Indian descent and wanted me to visit the country of his forebears. And so it happened that one fine morning we found ourselves outside a shanty with a sign proclaiming that it was a restaurant. We were received by a very dignified elderly gentleman. He stopped mending a tyre and went to fetch his wife. Ballard had promised me that we would get the best eggs and bacon in the world. The proprietor's wife appeared, and without waiting for our order started cooking them on a butane-gas stove. She was a delightful old lady who must once have been very beautiful, and the eggs and bacon were delicious. The old man said proudly: 'Nelly started life as a kitchen-maid in the London Savoy Hotel, and her eggs and bacon were so good that she was once allowed to prepare them for the Prince of Wales.'

On our way back Ballard told me about Nelly. She had met her husband in New York, when they were both working in the kitchen at the Waldorf Astoria. One of the things they had in common was their love of the open air, and one day, not being able to stand New York any longer, they had decided to go West. They bought a Ford and set off, taking only a few necessities. But in every town where they found work they came up against the same hard fact – that the towns were everywhere spreading over the countryside, so that before long there would be nothing but built-up areas. They tried working in second-rate hotels on the motor highways, but the reputation of Nelly's eggs and bacon spread around and new shanties sprang up. It was country no longer.

One day they stopped to fill the radiator in a place so deserted that they might have been on the moon. 'This'll do,' Nelly's husband said. He bought a plot of land with a few trees which denoted the presence of a spring; and here they built their restaurant, from the windows of which a virgin landscape was to be seen – literally nothing else. But Nelly's eggs and bacon attracted customers, and her husband had had the foresight to buy the surrounding land. They had paid a few dollars for it and could now have sold it for a fortune, but they held out and the place was still a desert.

I asked Ballard in astonishment why it was that they had such a love of solitude. 'It's quite simple,' he replied. 'They loved each other and still do, and if you're in love you get on better without company.'

Charles Laughton

Gabrielle had joined us in Hollywood with her husband, the American painter Conrad Slade, and their son Jean. We ourselves had left France after the signing of the armistice, but Slade could not make up his mind to go. As an American citizen his position for a time was tolerable, but events compelled him in the end to return to America. My last meeting with him on French soil had been in Cagnes. His love of Renoir amounted to a religion; and Slade, the eternal wanderer, had made this village into his true home.

As for Gabrielle, she could make herself at home anywhere. The natives of Cagnes, Gaudet the painter, Nicolai the grocer and Charles the eccentric, known as 'China', had considered her one of themselves. She kept open house and every lunch-time visitors walked in and sat down uninvited at her table. In the midst of a Europe dedicated to slaughter it was like an oasis. Not that the conversation was intellectual: on the contrary, the simpler it was the more readily was it accepted. There was an incident which delighted Gabrielle. Among her regular guests were two young men working on a new road. One of them had bought a pair of trousers at Conchon-Quinette, the local cheap emporium. The salesman who tried them on had been particularly interested in his sexual attributes, and the young man had put a stop to his investigations with a blunt, 'None of that.' The salesman had smiled disarmingly. 'I'm afraid I'm a big bad girl,' he said, blushing.

When Slade, Gabrielle and Jean arrived they moved into our handsome American-style house. I particularly wanted to live in an authentic setting. Since I was in America I wanted to live like an American. Slade, who came of an old New England family, was more out of his element than Gabrielle, whose talent for absorbing and being absorbed worked as well in California as anywhere else. She had very soon acquired a circle of admirers – neighbours, particularly young ones, delivery boys, men who came to see to the plumbing. They didn't speak French and Gabrielle didn't speak English, but still they listened to her with the greatest interest. The only expression she remembered was 'sit up', having noticed that this was said to dogs to make them sit on their tails. So she used it instead of saying, 'Please sit down', and when it was pointed out to her that it meant the exact opposite she replied that this did not matter in the least. And in fact people always knew what she meant. Mere contact with her enchanting personality was enough.

Among the customs she brought with her from France was the glass of wine for the postman. The first time Gabrielle poured him one he did not know what was expected of him. Slade, who himself never drank wine, explained the matter, and he readily fell into line. Gabrielle died in Hollywood. The Burgundy woman who brought Burgundy with her now lies in her husband's cemetery in Boston.

Despite her age, she possessed remarkable vitality, strong enough to face all vicissitudes. If there had been any malice in her she would have aroused passions. For her, as for the French before the era of romanticism, amorous adventures were primarily a subject of conversation; but if a flutter of this kind had interested her, it could have been with Charles Laughton, who frequently came to see us. She had christened him the 'big tabby', which pleased him, and he pretended to purr to suit the nickname. We were all close friends. Charles Laughton and Gabrielle were the witnesses at my marriage to Dido.

Charles Laughton in real life looked like a baby, but when called for, the baby could become an inspired scientist, as in *Galileo*. Without concealing his considerable stomach he nevertheless conveyed the impression of an ascetic prophet wholly intent upon the importance of his message. Second to his profession he loved flowers. He took the most tender care of the fuchsias in his garden.

We had much in common. A great lover of paintings, he possessed among others an admirable *Judgment of Paris* painted by my father, which he had bought from the New York dealer, George Keller. George himself told me how this had happened. Charles Laughton longed to possess a Renoir and asked George to show him a few. George started by showing him a very small one. The price was reasonable, but it was really too small. So then he got out the *Judgment of Paris*, a very big painting, almost too big for a private owner. The price was proportionate to the size, and it was too much for Laughton. But the next day, and on the following days, he went back to the gallery and asked Keller to let him view the painting again. He would sometimes lie on the floor in front of it and stay like that for an hour. And eventually he bought it. In the case of anyone else this would have sounded like play-acting, but not where Charles Laughton was concerned. He was genuinely in love with the painting.

He plunged wholeheartedly into the situations in the film he was acting in, to the point, indeed, that the least interruption upset him. Dido and I had two dogs, dachshunds, of which we were extremely fond. People were rude to them in the street, calling them Goering and Goebbels, one being fair-haired and fat and the other lean and dark. This annoyed Gabrielle, who thought it insulting to the dogs. Charles Laughton often dropped in on us to discuss some detail of the part he was playing, and sometimes he would be interrupted in mid-speech by the barking of the dogs. This caused him real suffering. He detested them. Among other instruments of torture in our house was a peasant clock which had the tiresome habit of striking loudly twice; and Laughton's visits were often round about mid-day.

Laughton had to play a scene in *This Land is Mine* in which, from behind prison bars, he watched the Germans rounding up hostages they were going to shoot. Among them was the headmaster of his old school, whose name was Sorel. All he had to do was to call out his name in the hope that his old friend would understand this word of farewell. We tried it a dozen times but it did not come right. We worked at it until the evening, and that prison sequence was the last that had to be shot on that set. Laughton kept saying: 'But I can't see Sorel. How can I call out to him?' I knew it was no use getting cross. 'What do you mean, you can't see him? He's there.' . . . 'Where?' . . . 'In your own mind.' . . . Laughton at once declared, to my great surprise, that he was ready to shoot. The result was wonderful.

We celebrated in his caravan, and while he sipped a small glass of Glenlivet malt whisky he told me something that had happened when he first went to London. He was playing the Emperor Nero in a big spectacular film, and he had to walk majestically down the steps of his palace. To get to the top of the stairway he had to climb up a ladder on to a small platform. At first he protested that he had no head for heights, which was true; and then he said that he did not feel 'in the mood'. The director had a chair taken up to the platform and advised him to rest for a few minutes. The next take didn't work. Meanwhile the whole company were kept waiting – actors, extras and technicians. Finally, after a dozen attempts, Laughton said in a voice worthy of Nero himself, 'I am in the mood.' 'No kidding!' said a little cockney electrician. That did it. The shot had to be postponed until next day.

Not only work on the film was interrupted by my tiresome dogs. Laughton had undertaken to teach me Shakespeare, of whose works I had only a superficial knowledge. This ignorance distressed him, and he felt that the gap must be filled: so, for my benefit and Dido's, he acted the plays we did not know, adopting a sweet voice for Ophelia, a sinister voice for Iago, and so on. I trust that in that actors' Paradise where he certainly dwells he will be reached by this token of my gratitude.

Dudley Nichols

Our first friend in Hollywood was Dudley Nichols, who wrote the script of *Swamp Water*. Dudley was a crusader; he could not stand injustice, and this was the cause of his frequent battles with the executives. I can see him now in the office of one of these great men, listening while we were showered with words of wisdom. 'What your script lacks,' the gentleman said, 'is a good old-fashioned love scene – the river bank, trees in blossom and the girl in her lover's arms – naturally, all bathed in romantic moonlight.' Dudley Nichols, during this exordium, had turned from pink to scarlet. He rose slowly to his feet, and turning his back on the speaker, said simply: 'The moon is rising.' Then he led me out of the room.

This Land is Mine was the second film on which I worked with Dudley. The story was intended to show that life for the citizen of a country occupied by an enemy Power was not as simple as Hollywood in the year 1943 seemed to think. The heroic utterances of French emigrés seemed to me in bad taste. The centre of the Hollywood Resistance Movement was the café known as 'The Players'. It belonged to Preston Sturges, the film-director, whose generosity was proverbial and who closed his eyes to unpaid bills. Wonderfully victorious attacks on Vichy were launched from that Sunset Strip café. It is not hard to be a hero when the enemy is 10,000 kilometres away. The leading character in *This Land is Mine*, played by Laughton, is a complete coward, terrified of the Germans, as he has good reason to be. Unlike the bold resisters in California, he does his best to go unnoticed; but he gets into trouble saving the life of a member of the Resistance Movement, and is shot, a hero despite himself. Real heroes are modest men.

The film had been shot in record time and had done well in the cinemas. I thought that its success would help us to get other stories accepted. One of our ideas was to make a film, *Sarn*, adapted from Mary Webb's novel, *Precious Bane*, with Ingrid Bergman. She herself loved the story, and with her in the lead any studio would have backed it; but she was under contract to David Selznick, who was anxious to make a new film of Joan of Arc. He thought of me as director. Selznick was a great producer and I should have been delighted to work with him, but not on Joan of Arc. I had a vivid recollection of Dreyer's splendid *Jeanne d'Arc* and lacked the courage to follow in the footsteps of my brilliant colleague. Selznick, on the other hand, did not wish to risk his star's reputation by letting her play the part of a girl with a hare-lip. So *Sarn* was never made, but it brought me something more precious than any film – the friendship of Ingrid Bergman and her excellent working-companion, Ruth Roberts. This enlargement of our family circle has proved unbreakable. It still lasts and will only come to an end when the family itself has ceased to be.

Dudley and I were also considering a new version of *Les Bas Fonds*. It was to be set in Los Angeles, based on the contrast between the modern buildings and the crumbling houses of the Victorian era. This, too, never saw the light of day. Dudley did not understand why. A warm friendship existed between us. We might have added a few good films to the list of Hollywood productions. What Dudley did not know about was my aptitude for being swept off my feet by stories which quite failed to interest the producers.

It had happened in France, and now it was happening again in the States. Projects failed to come off for what looked like practical reasons – the star we wanted was not free, or the distributors decided that the story was out of date. The early discussions were always favourable; generally speaking, the producers thought well of me. But on further thought they had their doubts, and finally, after a number of conferences, they told me that my idea was not 'commercial' – a song I knew by heart. There was nothing to be done about it: in spite of the money my films made I was not 'commercial'. It was worse than a label: it was like a tattoo mark on my forehead.

I did not want Dudley to waste his time working with someone who would be a hindrance to him, so I persuaded him that he should himself direct a film about Sister Kenny. It was an old project of his, backed by Rosalind Russell, who wanted to play the part. Sister Kenny was a picturesque character. She sailed through life like someone going into battle, wearing a huge feathered hat which recalled her Australian origin. Her treatment of polio, which consisted in wrapping the patient in warm, dry sheets, together with a few exercises, was regarded as quackery by the medical profession.

I went with Dudley to Minneapolis, where Sister Kenny had her clinic, to help him set up the film. We attended a meeting to which she had invited a hundred doctors, all her declared enemies. Questions were rained on her, and she answered them with great spirit. She brought the meeting to an end with the following demonstration. Enlarged photographs of the limbs of a boy suffering from polio were projected on to a screen, and she asked her audience if they thought it was possible for him to be cured. The unanimous answer was that it was impossible. Then a door opened and a hefty young man appeared who said that he had been the sick boy. Sister Kenny produced irrefutable proofs in response to the general incredulity. The young man answered every question that was put to him. One of the doctors asked him what he did for a living. He said that he was a truck-driver – and heavy ones at that.

Journey into Town

Every town and every geographical area has its characteristic colour. That of New York is now a light grey; before Pearl Harbor it was dark green. Passageways in houses, hotel bedrooms and shops tended to be in this colour, which contributed to the crushing effect of the great metropolis. Bright façades stood out in glaring contrast to this background. The back streets of New York are often miserable. Vacant lots are never cleaned up. Forty-seventh Street, for instance, where dusty jewellers' shops display in their windows diamonds worth thousands of dollars, is a striking example of New York style. And then there are the draughts. Like all American towns New York is divided into blocks, and at the resultant intersections a strong wind never stops blowing. It is quite common to see people dash into a drugstore to get a speck of dust taken out of their eye, for besides scattering the old newspapers that lie about everywhere the wind whips up the dust that accumulates in that immense garbage dump. There is also soot, the overflow from the surrounding factory chimneys. But I am leaving out the worst thing of all: we paid our last visit to New York before the days of smog.

And all this pollution conceals a brilliant intellectual life. New York is the world-capital of 'show business'. Go into any of the big buildings round Times Square, and on every floor, behind every door, you will find people concerned with show-business – agents, actors, theatre-managers, musicians, theatrical columnists. Broadway is the centre of show-business. Hollywood is no more than the product of

Broadway's success. The head offices of the big film companies are in New York. The denizens of Times Square have very often come from the Lower East Side, the Jewish quarter at the lower end of the town, where they started their careers in small music-halls catering for local audiences. They came from Berlin, Vienna, Bucharest or Warsaw with empty pockets but with heads well filled, and they brought with them a particular kind of humour, the product of their uprooting. The first target of their jesting was themselves. That is where Irving Berlin, George Gershwin, Danny Kaye, Clifford Odets and so many others came from, and it is from there that they set out upon the return journey and conquered the world. It may be said that Broadway, and by association the whole of show-business, was born in the minds of Central European Jews.

The speed of life in New York is very great, ideas pour out, currents change. Everybody walks fast, everybody is in a hurry. It is a competitive civilization: you have to get there before the next man, whatever your destination is. America is the land of output. Fortunately for the Americans there are loopholes in the system, one of which is the desire to talk about oneself. You go to buy a postage-stamp and the man behind the counter notes your foreign accent. 'What country do you come from?' . . . 'From France' . . . 'Say, my grandmother was French' . . . The temptation is too strong. He goes on to give you his whole family pedigree and in return questions you about your own. Meanwhile other customers are queuing up. The same thing happens with the tobacconist and the restaurant waiter.

Conversation with strangers is an American antidote to an over-regimented life. One thing is certain, that the most remarkable people I know adore New York. One of their most frequent remarks is: 'You live in California? But how can you bear it?' They forget that with its dirt and dust, and with the steam from the municipal heating spurting up in the middle of the streets as though there were a subterranean hell beneath them, New York is like a giant cook-pot on the verge of boiling over. To which unattractive picture one may add the growth of crime, hold-ups by day and by night, the increasing number of drug-addicts and racial disturbances. But in spite of it all New Yorkers persist in thinking that New York is the only place worth living in. All tastes are humanly possible, including masochism. We cannot exist without the insults and injuries the beloved inflicts upon us.

In 1944 the Office for War Information invited me to New York to help with the production of *Salute to France*, a film intended for the instruction of American troops being sent to France. The idea was to teach them that not all Frenchmen wear bérets and not all Frenchwomen are of easy virtue. So far as I know the film was never used, but it gave me the chance to meet the delightful Annabella again and to make the acquaintance of two remarkable theatre-animals, Garson Kanin and Ruth Gordon. Burgess Meredith was also around and I greatly enjoyed his company. He had married Charlie Chaplin's ex-wife, Paulette Goddard, and he opened the doors of the New York theatre world to Dido and me. Two years later I was to direct Burgess and Paulette in *The Diary of a Chambermaid*.

Paulette was still the waif of *Modern Times*, except that her rags had given place to clothes of the utmost elegance. Despite long interludes, our friendship still thrives. She is a beautiful woman with a lively mind; one can never be bored in her company. I asked her how Chaplin could have been

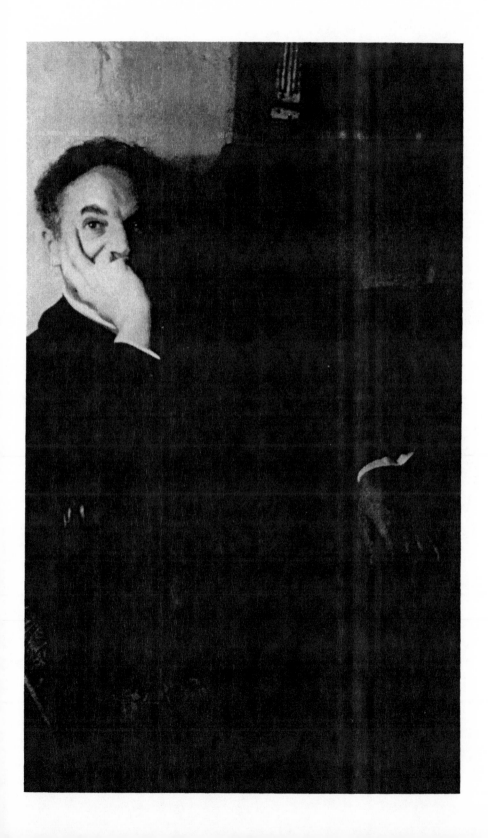

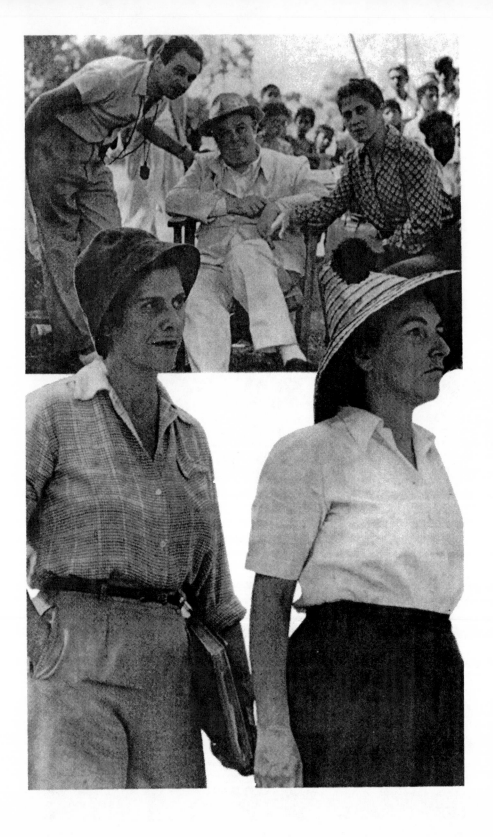

so mad as to break up their marriage, and she answered that
it was not he who had left her but she who had left him.
The reason was that he reserved all his comedy for his films.
In real life, according to her, he was not at all funny. Then
there was the huge house they lived in, a solemn, English-
style house, like a tomb, she said, without a single picture
in it, the only *objets d'art* being a collection of figurines in
English porcelain enclosed in a glass-fronted show-case.
But above all there was the fact that genius is hard to live
with. It is very exhausting to stay on the high mental level
of an exceptional person. One needs to sink back into good,
solid mediocrity in order to get one's breath. It is restful. It
was certainly not the quality of the mercurial Burgess
Meredith; but Paulette has an answer to this. She keeps
company only with remarkable men, but she changes them
often.

Paulette promptly took Dido under her wing, acting
somewhat as her sponsor in the American way of life.
'Have you any jewels?' she asked. Dido confessed that she
did not own a single one of any value. Paulette gently
rebuked her. Every woman ought to possess a store of
jewellery in case she should fall out with the man whom she
regards as the keystone of her life. Jewels are small, easy to
carry and easy to hide. You put them in your handbag, and
off you go. Dido listened gravely but did not seem convinced. To Paulette jewels were not only an insurance but
also a weapon. When someone accused her of being a
communist her reply was to threaten to fling her diamond
necklace in his face.

In the evening, we used to meet Marlene Dietrich and Jean
Gabin, who were living together. Marlene was singing French
patriotic songs in cabarets for the pleasure of doing so, and

she always ended with the *Marseillaise*. Gabin thought this ridiculous. He and Marlene had heated arguments. He called her 'my Prussian', and she would reply to this by tapping his forehead and saying in a languishing voice: 'That's what I like about you – it's quite empty. You haven't a single idea in your head, not one, and that's what I like.' The insult left this most subtle of actors quite unmoved.

Marlene was truly a super-star, not only on the stage but in life. At home she was the perfect housewife and an excellent cook, her best dish being *chou farci*. But outside this domesticity she adored the admiring tributes that were paid to her. One night, in a cabaret, she several times asked Dido to accompany her to the ladies' room. Dido was at first taken aback by the frequent request but soon realized that it was simply because Marlene wanted to show off her legs, and took Dido with her on the pretext that she needed to be protected against the women who assailed her. It was simply the enactment of a ritual. But it must be added that the worship of Marlene's legs was amply justified.

'Fidèle' — or, The Love of Art

The highlight of our trips to New York was the visit we paid to the Barnes Foundation in Philadelphia, an institution which displayed, for the benefit of a select public, one hundred and fifty Renoirs, chosen from among the most important.

Barnes was a person concerning whom there was much controversy, and my own account of him is based not on first-hand knowledge but simply on rumour. He was the inventor of the wonder-working antiseptic ointment known as Argyrol, and it was said that he had done so simply in order to cure himself of recurrent gonorrhœa. You may judge of the importance of his discovery in the 1914 war, when penicillin was still unknown. He had shared the work with two black doctors. The reason for his interest in painting and art in general was patriotism. He loved his country and considered that the one thing it lacked was artistic culture. He also considered that the two most important manifestations of contemporary civilization were the French school of painting and black American religious music.

He had built the Barnes Foundation, making of it a cultural centre to which only outstanding students were admitted. He believed that everything, even the art of the spectator, could be learnt. It helps to understand Mozart, he maintained, if one knows a little about the piano and can make some attempt to play his music, even if only with one finger; and to understand painting it helps to have attempted a few water-colours of one's own.

His collection was housed in a building constructed of
stone imported from France – 'the country of the re-birth
of the plastic arts'. No one was allowed to visit that remarkable exhibition except people who seemed to be prompted
by a genuine love of art and not by idle curiosity. It was
said that he himself studied all requests for permission to
view, but had them answered by his dog, Fidèle.

This is how Fidèle came to be his master's secretary.
Barnes was visiting Brittany, a part of the world which he
loved. A hungry dog in an impoverished fishing village
followed him to the inn where he had his lunch and seemed
greatly to enjoy the remains of the fish stew with which he
was rewarded. Barnes returned to the village a year later and
found the dog waiting for him near the same table. He was
touched by the thought of this dog who had remembered
him after a year's interval, and when he got back to New
York he wrote to George Keller, who was then in Paris,
asking him to find the dog and bring it over with him. The
fisherman to whom it belonged was happy to part with it for
a small sum. Keller had the dog washed and de-loused in
Paris, and it travelled to America in a first-class cabin.

The following are a few extracts from Fidèle's letters as
they were reported to me by someone who had no liking for
Barnes. I quote them because, although they come from a
malevolent source, they reflect something of the character
of the man who is associated in greatness with the great
Renaissance patrons of the arts.

Letter to Mrs X, of the family of bankers, shipowners and
railroad constructors.

Madame,
      I have received your letter of the —th, asking for leave

to visit my master's Foundation. Unhappily, being young and poor, my master was treated in a hospital founded by your family. As a result of intimate relations with one of the nurses he contracted a venereal disease. He has never forgotten this, and is therefore obliged to refuse your request.

Letter to Mr Y, a big publisher and newspaper owner.

Dear Sir,

I am honoured by your desire to visit my master's Foundation. Unfortunately, you have the reputation of being excessively interested in the young boys who operate your lifts. My master has nothing against homosexuality. Indeed, he considers it an absorbing pursuit which excludes other intellectual activities. In consequence, he is obliged to ask you to abandon the idea of your visit.

Dr Barnes had built his foundation on a piece of land which he acquired at Merion, a fashionable suburb of Philadelphia. He had divided it up into lots, reserving the best for himself. The purchasers of the other lots were all leading members of Philadelphia society. He had imposed conditions of sale which seem remarkably eccentric – for instance, no Christmas decorations, since he thought these horrible. Had they been painted by Matisse he would have been delighted to accept them. His neighbours, on the other hand, could not put up with his numerous black visitors and sent him a petition asking him to close the streets of that select residential area to black people. His reply was a threat to turn his Foundation into a black hospital. Now and then he gathered his black pupils together and got them to sing spirituals in front of Cézanne's *Card Players*.

I may add the disconcerting experience of a lady and gentleman of high social position who had been given permission to visit the Foundation. The door was opened to them by an attendant who was washing the tiled floor. Paying no attention to him, they candidly discussed the paintings, saying that they found Madame Cézanne ugly and the Renoir nudes too fleshy. Suddenly the floor-scrubber got to his feet, and shouting in a furious voice 'Get out!' drove them to the door. It was Barnes himself, who liked to know the views of his visitors.

The truth is that Dr Barnes was not as eccentric as he pretended. He was simply the High Priest of Art, to which his whole life was devoted, and any affront to art was an affront to his religion. I have a liking for Dr Barnes, and for a particular reason: he is the only person on earth who has collected my pottery.

'The Southerner'

Dido and I bought a house in what had once been a fashionable quarter. It was about fifty years old – prehistoric, in Hollywood terms. The garden was quite large and roses grew in abundance. The back of the house was shaded by a huge mulberry tree, of which the branches drooped like those of a weeping willow. At the far end of the garden there was a giant avocado, which, however, bore no fruit, all its sap being absorbed by its branches. And there was a small, comfortable apartment over the garage which we used as a guest-house.

A star of the silent screen, Agnes Ayres, had had the house built in the old American style, part timber and part stucco, in the days before she became a celebrity. It was an historic place. Rudolph Valentino, the idol of women all over the world, whose mistress she was, had come to visit her there, and their friend Roy d'Arcy occupied the garage apartment. I have these details from the film-director Robert Florey, who has covered the history of Hollywood from its beginnings. Today the memory of those romantic lovers has been almost effaced. A few old ladies come every year on the anniversary of Valentino's death and place flowers on his grave. And that is all. If you ask a fifteen-year-old boy who Valentino was, the chances are that he won't know. But only fifty years ago women by the million were ready to die for him. Screen fame is an ephemeral thing.

Gabrielle and her family came to live next door to us, in a house which made ours look like a futuristic monument.

Slade was delighted with it. There were things about it
which recalled the homes of his childhood – sash-windows,
a shingle roof, a porch, and above all the smell of wood. He
considered that the Americans were bad masons but excellent carpenters. The America of his childhood had lived
in wooden houses, and this type of building gave the
country an archaic style that is not without charm. When I
try to define my own feeling for those toy houses, the word
that comes to my mind is 'touching'.

I have a particular fondness for the Victorian houses,
with their lacework decoration, their towers, their capitals
and their purely ornamental balconies, on which it is un-
wise to tread lest you find yourself in the street. And
belonging to the same period – that is to say, the start of the
century – are the houses with Doric pillars, wooden, of
course. Those latter come from the South, but whatever
the style of traditional American buildings, they are a
symphony in wood. I remember a Los Angeles dance-hall
which was entirely surrounded by Greek pillars, like the
Church of La Madeleine in Paris. But whereas the Madeleine is heavy and blocks the horizon, American buildings
in the same style look as though they were made of paper.
Only one other country has done so much honour to
wood, and that is Russia.

The back-gardens of our two houses were only separated
by a light fence. We removed part of this, so that we shared
a single very large garden. Gabrielle and Dido were constantly crossing that national frontier, which made us think
of the frontier between France and Germany in the last act
of Giraudoux's *Siegfried*. I shall never forget Michel Simon
in the role of the customs official.

The life of émigrés was organized around small national

centres, the French around Charles Boyer and his wife, the Germans around Lion Feuchtwanger. The brothers Hakim were another centre round which the best elements in the European cinema clustered. I knew them well, having directed *La Bête Humaine* for them. They kept open house: one had only to ring the bell to be sure of a smiling welcome. René Clair and Julien Duvivier were often there, as was Jacques Deval, the author of *Tovarich*, and even Pierre Lazareff, when he happened to be in Hollywood. The producer Lukachevich and his wife Zita also went there when they were being unfaithful to their Russian circle. We drank French apéritifs and played French records, and games of *pelote* went on in the garden.

One morning of 1945 Robert Hakim came to see me with the proposal that I should direct a film based on George Session Perry's novel, *Hold Autumn in your Hand*. I was out of work again and with some eagerness asked to see a copy not only of the novel but also of the script which Hugo Butler had made from it. Hakim knew perfectly well that I would use this only as a springboard. Hugo Butler, to whom I had been mentioned as a possible director, liked *La Grande Illusion* and was ready to fall in with my ideas. That blessed *Grande Illusion*! I probably owe my reputation to it, and I also owe it a good many misunderstandings. If I had made a bogus *Grande Illusion* I should probably also have made a fortune.

The story of *The Southerner* (*Hold Autumn in your Hands*) in a nutshell is as follows. A young farm-hand, sick of working for other men, attempts to go it alone. He clears a patch of waste-land, having to fight against the malice of his neighbour, and his small son falls seriously ill. Finally he succeeds in growing a good crop of cotton, but it is ruined by a storm. He does not give in but tries to start again. This is only a vague outline of the story, the real theme of which is the malnutrition of the farm-workers. The little boy's disease is pellagra. To his parents' great surprise, the doctor cures him by making him eat vegetables and drink milk.

What attracted me in the story was precisely the fact that there was really no story, nothing but a series of strong impressions – the vast landscape, the simple aspiration of the hero, the heat and the hunger. Being forced to live a life restricted to their daily material needs, the characters attain a level of spirituality of which they themselves are unaware. Butler's script was excellent, but to my mind it failed to convey the calm grandeur of the theme. It laid too much stress on the leading character. But what I saw was a story in which all the characters were heroic, in which every element would brilliantly play its part, in which things and men, animals and Nature, all would come together in an immense act of homage to the divinity.

Hugo Butler was extremely generous. Touched by my enthusiasm for the subject, he suggested that he should withdraw and leave it entirely to me. It was now that I learned to esteem the producer, David Loew, whom Hakim had in mind. We were afraid that, without Butler's name and experience, he would refuse to finance the film. But I was captivated by him at our first meeting. We had a friend in common, and we talked about Albert Lewin and his attraction for the opposite sex. I suggested that, in order to avoid complications, I might give way to a more orthodox director. David Loew was moved by this; but he replied nevertheless that he liked my idea and wanted me to re-write the script in my own way. I went to work with the assistance of my secretary, Paula Salemson, and with the

counsel of Faulkner. The influence of that man of genius
had certainly a lot to do with the success of the film which,
made in 1945, is still shown in cinemas all over the world.
David Loew allowed me to have my old associate, Eugène
Lourié, as designer and Lucien Andriot as cameraman.

Lucien Andriot had come to the States in the following
circumstances. Before the 1914 War there was an immense
market for French films, and the episodic films – among
them *Protéa*, of which the star was a woman circus acrobat –
had been shown all over the world. A group of American
businessmen decided to bring the persons principally
responsible for the success of *Protéa* to New York to make
American serials. The best-known of these was the director,
Gasnier, to whom we owe *Mysteries of New York*. But
Protéa herself refused to come, and her place was taken by
Pearl White, whose name is still remembered by film-
lovers. Protéa asked the Americans to engage her younger
brother, Lucien Andriot, who was an assistant cameraman
and wanted to travel. He brought with him the canoe which
he had used on the Marne, but he had no chance to use it in
New York. Later on, having been signed up by Hollywood,
he again took his boat with him. After all, was there not a
Los Angeles river? – he had seen it marked on the map. He
had visions of little drinking-places like those on the banks
of the Marne, with tunes played on the accordion. But
when he came to look for it he found that it was dry –
nothing there but pebbles.

The Southerner offered me a second chance; my return to
the American film industry depended on it. As I have said,
Hollywood was very well disposed towards me; indeed, I
will go so far as to say that they were fond of me, and are
even fonder now that my health no longer permits me to

do any active work. They love me like a small girl loves her doll, provided she can change its clothes and, at a pinch, the colour of its hair. My ambition was to be accepted without having to throw my own ideas overboard. *The Southerner* might enable me to realize my chief aim, which was to run a small company specializing in low-budget, experimental films, with casts either of beginners or of actors who were down on their luck. I was confident that in doing so I would now and then unearth talents which would more than cover the modest cost of the films. The reason for my mistrust of stars is that they are like ducks: their plumage is waterproof. One may pour buckets of water over them and they come out perfectly dry.

After a good deal of hesitation Joel McCrea had more or less agreed to play the part of the Southerner, but before definitely committing himself he wanted to read the final version of the script. When he came to do so he did not like it at all, and he informed David Loew that he was dropping out. The film was to be distributed by United Artists, and, as in the case of all independent films, this was equivalent to financing it, since the distributor's guarantee meant that a large part of the budget could be borrowed from the bank. But United Artists were not particularly interested in *The Southerner*: what they wanted was the name of Joel McCrea up in lights. They told David Loew that they were letting the film go. Once again I proposed to Loew that I should withdraw. I was sincere in my anxiety not to make trouble for this man who had won my heart by the simplicity with which he approached the problems of the cinema. David never made fruitless gestures, preferring to reserve his strength for things that were worth while. He simply informed United Artists that he would take all his films away from them if they did not give The Southerner a fair distribution. They surrendered.

Another star was needed but they were all unapproachable. I asked David to forget about stars and look for a good actor, and to everyone's surprise I suggested Zachary Scott, who had hitherto specialized in polished gangster roles. He came from the South, so I could be sure his accent would be genuine; but another reason was one I have already referred to, my belief in getting actors to play parts outside their usual range. David agreed, and the filming of The Southerner began under the best possible conditions.

My first thought had been to shoot the film in Texas, where the novel had been written; but it was wartime, and transport was reserved for the army, which made it impossible for us to send down our equipment. Instead we chose a cotton-field not far from the small town of Madera on the bank of the San Joaquin river. The situation was ideal: all that was needed was for Lourié to build a tumbledown shack and for the shooting to take place while the cotton was in flower.

That part of California is the settlement of a large Russian colony, belonging, if I am not mistaken, to the Dukhobors, a religious sect which, being persecuted under the Czars, had emigrated to California long before the Anglo-Saxon influx. They were divided into two groups, ancient and modern. The Ancients refused to cut their hair or their beards or to allow any pictorial representation of the human person. Such was their authority that shaved faces were rare and cameras non-existent. A sight which gave me great amusement was that of those long-bearded citizens driving high-powered open cars with their beards fluttering like banners in the wind. The army needed cotton, so the

Dukhobors could afford Cadillacs. Those frolicsome beards would be less surprising in these days, but at that time they were startling.

The owner of the field we had rented was an 'Ancient'. Rather late in the day, after the signing of the agreement, he asked for further details and discovered that we intended to photograph actors. Being a strict observer of the rules of his sect, he wanted to cancel the agreement. But that particular field was the only one we had found which exactly suited our requirements. We refused to cancel, and the production manager threatened to claim heavy compensation. The matter was settled by our buying the field and promising to sell it back to the owner when we had done with it. While the film was being made we lived in a village of tents set up along the edge of our field. We worked hard, ate and slept well, and forgot about the war. In the evening we watched the rushes, and the local people came to look on, afterwards entertaining us with Russian folk-music and Mexican airs. David Loew presided over these rustic festivities. Our rather sombre story was shot in an atmosphere of serene gaiety.

To my great relief the film was a success. François Truffaut has recalled the manner in which the newspaper *Combat* described it on its first appearance in France, which was at the Biarritz festival. Henri Magnan reported on it over the telephone. It was a bad connection, and the sub-editor who took down his review called it *Le Souteneur* (*The Pimp*) instead of *The Southerner* and described it as '*un film de genre noir* (a sombre film) instead of '*un film de Jean Renoir*'.

Metro-Goldwyn-Mayer

Metro-Goldwyn-Mayer was a separate kingdom. People in the know asserted that its annual turnover was three times that of Portugal. But today the Metro-Goldwyn corridors are empty and its rotting sets scattered by the winds. Everything that could be carried away was disposed of at a fabulous auction sale. In its great days people joined at what would have been their age of military service in France and stayed with the corporation, passing through various stages of promotion, until they retired. They married and died with the corporation, and lived their lives in the comfortable certainty of belonging to an unshakable empire. The great conglomerate was one huge family, its members recruited from among the relatives, legitimate or otherwise, of the executives. I have nothing against keeping things in the family; on the contrary, that is what gives style to an enterprise. The Metro-Goldwyn style was due partly to the fact that they lived, as it were, in an ivory tower. Of course, there were exceptions, but the power of the organization was such that most people were quickly absorbed into it. That small world was the scene of numberless tragedies; suicide, nervous depression and death by alcoholism were of frequent occurrence.

Close by the entrance to the Metro-Goldwyn lot, its door on the same sidewalk, was a funeral parlour. In America these establishments take charge of the dead from the moment of their last breath, and this particular one brought a steady flow of black-clad mourners having little in common with the dream-factory next door. The Metro-

Goldwyn management found this exasperating, and vainly offered increasing sums to buy them out. The situation seems to me admirably symbolic of the world's greatest film organization. Fortunately or unfortunately for me, I never penetrated beyond its walls except as a visitor.

Albert Lewin was a Metro-Goldwyn executive, but spiritually as remote from that corporation – I should say, that empire – as he was from the High Court of China. His fellow citizens were over-awed by his string of university degrees. His first job had been as script-clerk in a King Vidor film, but he had soon crossed the enormous gap separating him from the post of producer. He was small, very small, and meticulously dressed. His suits, made by a Savile Row tailor, were of an English sobriety; only his arresting ties placed him in America, in Hollywood and in Metro-Goldwyn. His expression was one of unexpected malice. He was deaf, but got on excellently, even in the most difficult conversations, with the help of the small hearing-aid which he constantly readjusted. At managerial conferences he would switch it off entirely and hide himself behind a bland smile which everybody supposed to indicate entire agreement with what they were saying. He had escaped the general infection and ate nothing in the Metro-Goldwyn buttery except things that were genuinely edible. He was connected with films of undeniable beauty, of which the best known is still *The Good Earth*, with the astonishing Luise Rainer. He himself directed the spell-binding *Picture of Dorian Gray*. He adored the cinema and had a style peculiarly his own in which dialogue was of the first importance.

What most interested him was Surrealism. He paid frequent visits to Paris, where he consorted with Eluard,

Breton, the Prévert brothers, Paul Grimault and Duhamel. Max Ernst and Man Ray were frequent guests at his house in Hollywood. His wife, Millie, was a wonderful house-keeper. I have never tasted better roasts than those coming from her kitchen. The Lewins were collectors of pre-Colombian relics and, in general, everything having to do with primitive art. The talk at their evening parties was highly non-conformist – one could imagine oneself in the 'Closerie des Lilas'. When the conversation became too high-flown, Herbert Stothard, one of the authors of the musical, *Rose Marie*, would sit down at the piano and play extracts from it. The contrast was entirely in the surrealist tradition.

The ruler of the Lewin home was Aunt Yetta, Albert's mother, to whom he owed his position in life. She had arrived in New York fifty years previously, the daughter of impecunious Russian-Jewish immigrants, and had worked as a waitress in a Brooklyn café to provide for her two sons. Despite all hardships, she had managed to send them to college. Albert had gained a doctorate and the friendship of David Loew, his classmate, who had persuaded him to give up teaching and join Metro-Goldwyn. Aunt Yetta was by no means dazzled by her son's career, having re-mained immune to American notions of success. She ap-proved of his marriage to Millie, his cousin, and when necessary dragged him back into the path of marital fidelity as though he were a little boy. There was an aura of nobility about Aunt Yetta; Al Lewin's friends admired her and en-joyed listening to her stories. She made me think of a picture by Chagall.

Al Lewin missed New York, where he had grown up. He found Hollywood provincial. With all its wealth, he still thought of it as nothing but a spa, like Monte Carlo or Baden-Baden. So when he had earned enough by his labours with Metro-Goldwyn to ensure him a comfortable retirement he returned to New York, and when Dido and I were on our way to Paris we stopped off at New York simply to see the Lewins. We stayed in a hotel in the same block as their apartment and spent a week in absorbing conversation. But alas, Man proposes and God disposes. While Al Lewin was approaching the full enjoyment of his powers as a pure intellectual, Millie was beginning to suffer from the malady that carried her away. After her death Al did what he could to console himself. He invited hosts of friends, and made a show of being more absorbed than ever in abstract discussion, only interrupting this display to visit the cemetery, where he brooded in front of Millie's funeral urn. Then he too died, alone or nearly so. His solitude certainly did not surprise him: he had often said that the closest groups were nothing but solitudes brought together. We never again set foot in New York, after the deaths of Al and Millie Lewin.

'The Woman on the Beach'

In 1946 I had not given up the idea of making low-budget pictures which, however, would not be classed as 'B' pictures, the Hollywood rating for mass-produced films turned out in a few days. Those films had simple stories and did not call for meticulous preparation. The sets had often been used before in similar productions. They catered for the market in gangster films and westerns: in fact, they were the diminished successors of the films that had made the greatness of the American cinema. The Hollywood of the big 'A' pictures ignored them. They were a world apart, being shot in their own studios and dispensing with any kind of research which might waste time. In these days television has taken them over.

When I talked about low-budget production I meant films that would be as carefully made as any major film. The economy would be in the cost of the principals – producer, director, script-writer and leading performers – and in my method of cutting, whereby a number of takes were condensed into a single sequence, which made for much more rapid shooting. My idea had been taken up by Jack Gross, a remarkable producer who was under contract to RKO. We discussed my low-budget plans a number of times. But RKO wanted us for a major production which I was to direct. The star was to be Joan Bennett. I liked the story and the idea of making a film with that actress greatly appealed to me. It was agreed that Gross and I would collaborate on the script of the new film. But Gross died, and I had to take over the entire responsibility.

His death seemed to me a bad omen, nor was I mistaken.

I started out hopefully in the belief that the film presented no serious problems; but Mitchell Wilson's novel, *None Too Blind*, on which the script of *The Woman on the Beach* was based, was less simple than I had supposed. The theme was that of solitude, which is one of the great preoccupations of our time. Men sickened by our mass-produced civilization are struggling more and more to escape from the crowd. Solitude is the richer for the fact that it does not exist. The void is peopled with ghosts, and they are ghosts from our past. They are very strong; strong enough to shape the present in their image.

There is a race of genuine solitaries, but they are rare. Those born to be solitary contrive to isolate themselves in a world entirely of their own making. Most solitaries only appear to belong to this category, having been born to play a part in the world around them. It is only after what is as a rule a deeply hurtful event that they have become solitaries. If they fight against it, it is generally at the cost of fearful inward turmoil. This drama of isolation is for the artist an episode in the tragedy of which we are all actors and which ends only with our departure into eternity. The artist is simply a man endowed with the gift of making these inward conflicts visible. Art is the materialization of an interior and often unconscious dream.

The Woman on the Beach was a perfect theme for the treatment of this drama of isolation. Its simplicity made all kinds of development possible. The actions of the three principal characters were wholly without glamour; they occurred against empty backgrounds and in a perfectly abstract style. It was a story quite opposed to everything I had hitherto attempted. In all my previous films I had tried to depict the bonds uniting the individual to his background. The older I grew, the more I had proclaimed the consoling truth that the world is one; and now I was embarked on a study of persons whose sole idea was to close the door on the absolutely concrete phenomenon which we call life. It was a mistake on my part which I can explain only by the relative isolation enforced upon me by my limited knowledge of the language of the world in which I now lived.

The drama for me was that the elements which had hitherto constituted my life were changing, so that I was in danger of becoming as much of an outsider on the Place Pigalle as on Sunset Boulevard. I had discovered on my first trip to France after the war that the traditional French mistrust of all things foreign had been doubled by the German Occupation. I remember a typical episode. I had brought an English make of car over from England. Customs formalities had delayed me, so that I drove from Boulogne to Paris at night. French cars are fitted with amber headlights, whereas my own were white. Abuse was hurled at me at every crossing, and at one intersection three or four men got out of their cars and crowded round me in threatening attitudes. My wife tried to reason with them, but her Brazilian accent only made things worse. I finally gathered that the trouble was due to my white headlights, and I tried to explain that I had only just bought the car and would have the headlights changed directly I got to Paris. But what saved us was that I replied to a piece of particularly gross abuse from a lorry-driver with an even coarser bit of French army slang. This at once placated my assailants, and they went away.

But it was among my close friends that I found the

greatest change. Many of my film colleagues had worked under German supervision. Rightly or wrongly? They felt the need to justify themselves to me. But I don't like to pass judgment on other men or to have them pass judgment on me. Freedom of speech is an essential of any true dialogue. The French were still unaccustomed to not having their every word and gesture overseen. This surveillance had caused them to live in an atmosphere of constant mistrust. Although the outward appearance had not changed (laughter was perhaps a little more noisy), things were no longer the same. France was different and I myself was different. We were like an old married couple coming together after a long separation, still loving but each seeing faults in the other which at the start we had not seen.

It was natural that I should look for themes having nothing to do with a motherland who was no longer herself. I had a horror of sentimental images of pre-war France. Better a void than the pointed beard of the film Frenchman. But a void offers no solid foothold. Realizing the fragility of the thing I was making, I tried to change the story while the film was being shot. The result was a confused scenario leading to a final work which I consider interesting but which is too obscure for the general public. Nevertheless Joan Bennett is more beautiful than ever in her ghostlike part, Charles Bickford is moving in his efforts to conquer the void, and the admirable Robert Ryan subtly enabled us to share in his suffering. Hanns Eisler had written a musical score stressing the theme of solitude in which he played counterpoint with his customary talent. To conclude, *The Woman on the Beach* was the sort of avant-garde film which would have found its niche a quarter of a century earlier, between *Nosferatu the Vampire* and *Caligari*, but it had no success with American audiences. Worse still, it thoroughly displeased the RKO bosses.

I was under contract to make two films for that company. A few days after the première I had a visit from my agent, Ralph Blum, who reported that they were ready to buy me out for a fixed sum. I am no fighter; I accepted, and that was the end of it. But it was the end in the widest sense. The failure of *The Woman on the Beach* marked the finish of my Hollywood adventure. I never made another film in an American studio. It was not only that particular failure that was held against me. Darryl Zanuck, who knew something about directors, summed up my case to a group of film-people. 'Renoir,' he said, 'has a lot of talent, but he's not one of us.'

'The River'

One day, quite by chance, I read in the *New Yorker* a review of a book which sounded interesting. It was *The River* by the English writer Rumer Godden. The reviewer considered it one of the best novels published since the war. I read the book and was greatly impressed, not only by the charm of the writing, but by the fact that the story seemed to me to offer the basis of a film of high quality which would nevertheless be acceptable to the Hollywood film magnates – children in a romantic setting, the discovery of love by small girls, the death of a little boy who was too fond of snakes, the rather foolish dignity of an English family living on India like a plum on a peach-tree; above all, India itself with its exotic dances and garments, all this seemed to me to possess a reassuring neutrality.

Being convinced that I had found a story that would again open the doors of the Hollywood studios to me, I asked my agent to get an option on the film rights. He did his best to dissuade me. 'All I can see in India,' he said, 'is elephants and a tiger-hunt. Is there a tiger-hunt in the plot?' Despite the absence of this trump card, I asked him to offer *The River* to various studios and in any case to secure an option. He made me go the rounds of all the producers liable to be interested, but in every case the response was the same – India without elephants and tiger-hunts was just not India. I was on the verge of giving up when I was visited by a Beverly Hills shopkeeper who said he was interested in producing the film.

Kenneth McEldowney was a florist. He adored the

cinema and adored India, and served both his loves with wholehearted devotion. He had numerous cinema contacts through his wife, Melvina Pumphrey, who was PR representative to Esther Williams, the swimming star. During the Second World War, McEldowney had served in a US Air Force office in India. It was a position which had enabled him to be of service to certain prominent Indian citizens, and in return he had asked them to finance a film on India which he would produce. The proposal had advantages from their point of view. It was illegal for them to take their capital out of the country, but there was nothing to prevent them exporting a film which would earn foreign money.

The one thing lacking was a story. He was very keen on a hunt with elephants, but that in itself was not enough. One evening at a New York party he met a lady who was a close friend of Nehru, and told her of his difficulty. She advised him that a film about India would greatly please Nehru and other prominent Indians, but that he should avoid making it a purely Indian story, because the Indians did not believe that foreigners would know how to handle the problems of their country. She suggested that he should read *The River*, which was set in India but dealt with an English family. McEldowney did so, and although there was nothing about hunting with elephants he had hopes that this brilliant notion might somehow be fitted into Rumer Godden's tender and simple tale. He tried to buy an option, only to be told that this had already been acquired by a certain Jean Renoir. He got in touch with me and asked me to direct the film. I made four stipulations: first, that he should pay my expenses on a trip to India to see the country; second, that I should write the script in collaboration with the author of the novel; third, that there should be no elephant-hunt; and fourth, that I should have the last word in the matter of editing. McEldowney agreed. While we were making *The River* he did his best to film his beloved elephant-hunt, and when this failed he tried to replace it with a view of the Taj Mahal.

Dido and I made the acquaintance of Rumer Godden in a setting that could not have been less Indian. McEldowney, who in his enthusiasm had come over to set everything in motion, arranged for us to meet at a Thames-side inn, The Perfect Angler. From that day on Rumer, Dido and I became fast friends, and she came to stay with us in Hollywood while we worked on the first draft of the script. Then, after our first voyage to India, Dido and I went to England to work on the second draft, profiting by what we had learned. We had visited the scenes of Rumer Godden's childhood.

The most important thing I learnt on that first trip was the reason for the Indians' resentment against the British. It was not because they had conquered them, but because they ignored them. They treated them as though they weren't there. But the Indians have a longing for human contacts, a need for living warmth.

I loved the steps from the temples leading down to the river, and the graceful bearing of the women in their saris; and I was fascinated by what I learned of their music and dancing, and by their touching desire to make contact. But what particularly delighted me as a film-maker were the Indian colours, which afforded me a marvellous chance of putting my theories about the use of colour photography into practice. I had longed for years to make colour film, although I think that black-and-white has its own potency, in that it gives a film an abstract quality. It has the advantage that it can never be realistic, for whether we like it or not our external world is coloured.

The basic principle which was to govern my use of colour was to avoid laboratory effects. The problem is to put in front of the camera a landscape or set of the kind that best suits the scene that is being played. In other words, no special filters or re-touching. My second rule was to avoid landscapes with too delicate shades of colouring when shooting outdoors. Although our eyes are far superior to the most perfect manufactured lens, we still have difficulty in distinguishing all the shades that Nature offers us; and the artificial eye which is the camera can only work satis-factorily if we set it simple problems. The countryside of the Ile de France, for example, contains a myriad blended tints, of which the camera can bring us only a garbled representation. But tropical vegetation, on the other hand, offers us a limited range of colours: its greens are really green and its reds really red. That is why Bengal, like many tropical countries, is so suited to colour photography. The colours are neither too vivid nor mixed. Their lightness puts one in mind of Marie Laurencin, or Dufy, or, I venture to add, Matisse. The green and red of the Indian flag are different from the green and red on the flags of other nations.

While we were shooting *The River* we watched out for half-tints. Lourié went so far as to have the lawn in one of our scenes re-painted green. Nothing escaped our notice – house, curtains, furniture, clothing. In the case of the latter it was an easy task: the Indians have a fondness for white, that ideally simple colour. But the river itself, of course, was outside our control: we had to arrange the close-ups to suit the background.

The River is a sort of account of the life of an English family in Bengal, a story without beginning or end; indeed, it is as though one had taken an excerpt from the lives of a group of people without trying to make a story at all, and this framework limits the range of the subject. My principal problem was to make it authentic. I knew India through a few excellent books, in particular Forster's *A Passage to India*, but I had had no contact with the people themselves. Once again Providence came to my aid.

Directly we reached India my nephew, Claude, started harassing the producer on the subject of mobile electrical equipment, to begin with a generator and arc-light-projector. McEldowney decided to buy these in London, hoping to sell them when the film was finished. But the ship which had loaded the equipment was ordered to unload it in order to take on a cargo of arms for Indochina. This was at the time of the Franco-Indochinese war, and there was a steady flow of arms from London to Calcutta, where I ran into two young men from Cagnes, my own village, who had bought an aeroplane and were making a fortune out of this illicit trade. Their plane was not fitted with long-distance navigational equipment. 'But you can't go wrong,' they said. 'You've only got to follow the Himalayas until you come to the Ganges delta, and there you are.' I never discovered whether their weapons were intended for the French or the Indochinese.

It took McEldowney a good two months to find a ship willing to take on anything except machine-guns, and this gave me time to make a thorough survey, in company with Rumer Godden, of the countryside of *The River*. Another member of our party was her younger sister, Nancy, the wife of an Englishman who manufactured a remedy for

malaria. Nancy was a wonderful horsewoman, but unfortunately she could not resist the temptation to try higher
and higher jumps, in consequence of which she spent a lot
of her time in plaster. But she spoke perfect Bengali; she
listened to the tales the grooms told and passed them on to
us. Here is one which tells us a lot about the Hindu soul:
I must specify Hindu, because I do not think it would apply
to a Mohammedan. A Hindu servant was accused of stealing
a sweater which was found in the hut where he lived. He
denied having stolen it, and when his Memsahib refused to
believe him he said: 'If you continue to disbelieve me I shall
die in fourteen days.' And he did die, although no physical
cause of his death could be discovered.

There is a more cheerful tale which throws a different
light on the Hindus. Chandernagore, a little town on the
banks of the Hoogli river, almost a suburb of Calcutta, was
still a French possession and even had a right to its own
Governor. The Governor in question, a young diplomat
at the start of his career, told me that a few months previously he had had to deal with a revolt of 'untouchables'.
The reason was the installation in the Governor's mansion
of a modern water-closet. Until then an 'untouchable' had
had the job of emptying the chamber-pots, this being a
monopoly reserved for his caste. Hence the revolt, since
now the monopoly was abolished. The mansion was
besieged by an angry crowd threatening violence. But the
Governor had an inspiration: he promised that only an 'untouchable' would be authorized to pull the plug.

But it was the Indian members of my team who best
helped me to understand India, notably my assistant, Hari
Das Gupta, who introduced me to his family. They were a
model of the enlightened Indian middle class, and among

their number were professors, lawyers, doctors, Government officials and members of the liberal professions. Many of the girls had been to Shantinikitan University, a college founded by Tagore which taught the essentials of Western culture while at the same time preserving Indian customs. It was highly successful. The name of Rabindranath Tagore will always be associated with the intellectual growth of Bengal, which is indebted to him for its position as the cultural capital of India.

The name of Gupta is very common in India, particularly in the State of Bihar, north of Calcutta. It is that of a dynasty of emperors who bequeathed two treasures to the world – a remarkable collection of statues, to my mind the best of Indian sculpture, and the Lord Siddhartha Gautama, known as Buddha. This is how another Gupta, Ram Sen Gupta, no relation of Hari, became our operator. We were testing children who might be suitable for the film. The machinist operating the clapper showed himself to be extraordinarily quick on the uptake, guessing what Claude had in mind and positioning the lights before the electricians had read Claude's signals. We were attracted by his physical appearance: he was tall and thin and clad in an immaculate *dhoti*. When the tests were over we questioned him and learned that he was a skilled cameraman who had taken on the job of grip in order to bring himself to our notice. Claude at once gave him a test and engaged him as operator.

It was in the holy city of Benares that we made the acquaintance of Radha, the dancer. We had met her future husband, Raymond Burnier, at the home of Christine Bossennec, the French cultural attachée in Calcutta, who had asked me to give a lecture at the École Française. Raymond invited us to spend Christmas with him at his palatial residence in Benares. He had a passion for India, was thinking of being converted to Hinduism and wore his hair in a pigtail in the Hindu fashion. What caused him to hesitate was the fact that, not having been born of a high caste, he could be accepted only as an 'untouchable'. It was at his home that I met Alain Daniélou, the musicologist with such a wide knowledge of India.

Radha introduced me to the dance called 'Katakali' and in general to the music of the province of Madras, where she lived. Her father was president of the Theosophical Society. Claude and I were so charmed by her personality, after three or four days in her company, that we suggested she should play the part of Melanie. McEldowney at first took fright, thinking that the idea was madness: Radha's beauty is of a kind not easily intelligible to Western eyes. But we took him to a dance session which overcame his objections. These preliminaries were accomplished in Raymond Burnier's home under the friendly eye of an enormous bird, a crane named Syphon, which was extremely gluttonous.

We needed a small girl for the role of Harriet, the character on which the whole film depends. Since any Hollywood star was outside McEldowney's financial scope, he asked me to look for one among the local schoolgirls. He put an advertisement in the paper and there were over a hundred applicants. I followed my usual method of selection, which was to get them to read a few lines without attempting to act. A newspaper article serves the purpose better than a Shakespeare sonnet. The winner, after a number of eliminating rounds, was Patricia Walters, the daughter of a man on the staff of one of the local industrial concerns.

Above: Le Carrosse d'Or, 1952: with Anna Magnani
Below: Elena et les Hommes, 1956: with
Ingrid Bergman

Her general appearance, manners and speech were precisely those of a little English girl born and bred in India.
Physically she was ideal. The choice of an amateur actress
for the part was a sacrifice on the altar of what I call external
truth, and it also led to the choice of Tom Breen for the
part of Captain John. This character in the novel had lost a
leg in the war and could not resign himself to the resultant
physical disability. I tried several Hollywood actors but
found their limp exaggerated. I even talked to Marlon
Brando; but Brando was then reaching the height of his
powers and his very presence would have transformed the
film. With regret I dispensed with that great actor and
settled for Tom Breen, who really had lost a leg in the war.

It was taking a chance. The decision to have the part of
Harriet played by a small girl who resembled her in real life,
instead of working out the part with a young actress, made
The River an act of homage to external truth. Fortunately
external truth in India is anything but ordinary. It is as
though a designer of genius had conceived the setting of
everyday life. Of course one had to select, but Lourié knew
how to do this. He kept on presenting me with pictures
which, although absolutely natural, seemed to have been
composed.

The River, which looks like one of the most contrived of
all my films, is in fact the one nearest to Nature, which is
another instance of the fact that men's plans may lead to un-
foreseen results. If there were not a story based on the
immemorial themes of childhood, love and death, it would
be a documentary.

We set up house in a villa, on the bank of the river where
I shot nearly all the film, which belonged to the family of a
Maharajah who had vacated it when Queen Victoria trans-

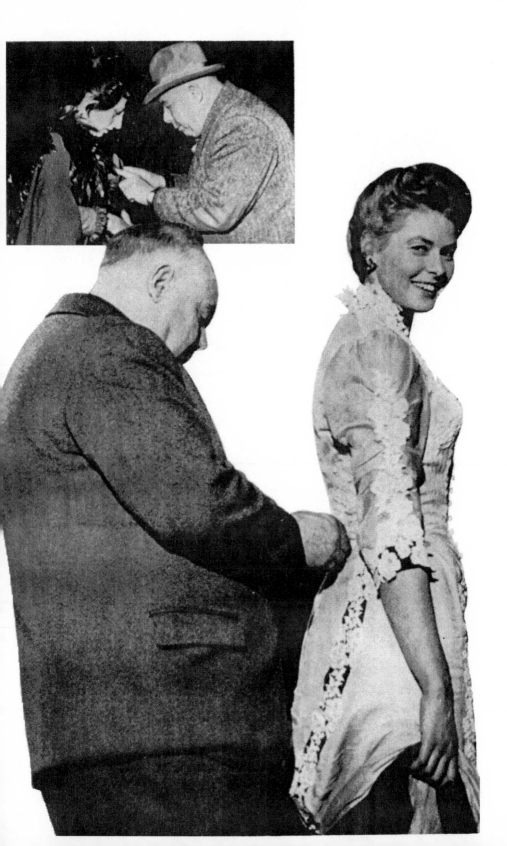

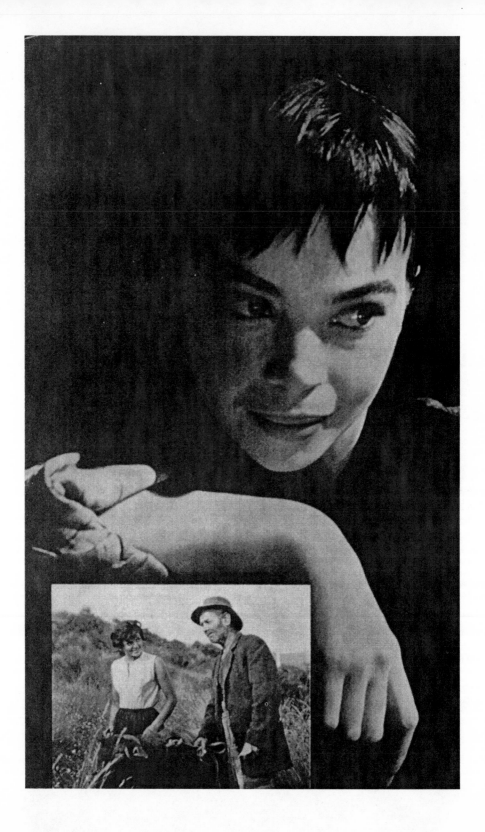

Leslie Caron in *Orvet*, 1955
Inset: Catherine Rouvel and Charles Blavette in
Le Déjeuner sur l'Herbe, 1959

257

ferred the seat of her Indian Empire from Calcutta to New Delhi. Rumer Godden sat in one room, digesting piece by piece the new elements introduced into the story and rendering them in her own elegant language. She also trained the youngsters playing the children's parts, getting them to dance and recite poetry. The results were excellent, they never seemed in the least affected.

This confirmed my theory concerning the use of amateur actors. If one is to succeed with them they need to be rehearsed, but never in the roles which they are going to play. One has to avoid the pitfalls of woodenness on the one hand and glibness on the other. It is simply a matter of getting them to read lines without stammering. When this stage has been passed one puts them to work on the script, but in the Italian fashion, without acting.

Another memory of India. The arc-lights which we had had sent from London caused painful injuries to the hands. The Indian electricians were not accustomed to these enormously heavy pieces of equipment and, when they moved them about, neglected to tighten the screws which kept them rigid. Some members of the team, a Brahmin among them, suggested that these mishaps were due to our neglect of the goddess Kali, who plays a highly important part in Hindu life, especially in Calcutta, which town she is supposed to have founded. She is the wife of Shiva, the second member of the Hindu trinity, personifying both creation and destruction, since for the Hindus one cannot exist without the other. Kali is depicted as being quite black and sticking out a scarlet tongue which reaches to her knees. The gesture is one of contrition; she is apologizing for having killed her husband. The members of the team advised that a small *puja* should be performed, a ceremony of propitiation to the goddess. It was enacted in the main drawing-room of the villa, where I filmed it.

A *puja* centres round a terracotta image of the goddess which for a few instants becomes the goddess herself. There are incantations accompanied by dances and the burning of incense. At dawn the image is flung into the river, clay returns to clay. The goddess was no doubt content with this ceremony, because there were no more injured hands.

Dido and I had great difficulty in getting back to normal when the shooting of *The River* was over. We were helped by Radha, who had become one of our best friends. We stayed with her at the headquarters of the Theosophical Society in Adyar, where we lived the life of Brahmins – no meat, tobacco or alcohol – which did us a great deal of good, although Dido cheated abominably, retiring to the lavatory to smoke cigarettes. Adyar left us with a wonderful picture of religious serenity.

We also brought back less monastic pictures of traditional spectacles. In Madras we witnessed a performance by a celebrated singer and composer. The crowded theatre was like a suburban cinema, and the curtain went up amid thunderous applause. The singer was sitting cross-legged in the middle of the stage against a backcloth representing a park like that of Versailles. The front of his head was shaved, and long hair grew on the back. But despite this hair-style, which looked so strange to Western eyes, we were struck by his beauty and nobility. Six supporting musicians were grouped around him, also sitting cross-legged. Now and then one of them struck a note against which the others tuned their instruments.

When the applause had died down the singer hummed a

few notes, but then he stopped and, addressing the audience, said simply, as Charles Laughton had done, 'I am not in the mood.' There was a murmur of disappointment, after which the audience went back to eating the small cakes which attendants were selling. The singer made three or four more attempts, but it didn't come right. He apologized and sipped tea and ate a few cakes with the members of his orchestra. I was told that this search for inspiration might go on for days and nights. Wealthy customers who had hired the musicians for a party were no better treated. If the singer did not feel in the mood no power on earth could make him perform. Fortunately in this case inspiration did not take a week and eventually he began to sing. It was wonderful. Although neither Dido nor I knew a word of Tamil we were deeply moved.

Clifford Odets

It cannot be said that Dido and I met Clifford Odets: he overwhelmed us. We knew him, of course, by reputation and one day he invited us to one of the parties he held for members of the Group Theatre who had left New York in the hope of finding work in Hollywood. The Group Theatre had revolutionized the American theatre by introducing a realism it had not hitherto known. Clifford Odets had done his share by writing *Waiting for Lefty*. His subsequent plays had been highly successful, and he was very much admired by people in any way connected with the theatre, less because of this immediate success than because it was realized that he had brought something new to the art of the dramatist. One met a great many New Yorkers at his parties. The expression 'one of the family' applied admirably to the relationship between Clifford and anyone who had had anything to do with the Theatre Group – the Strasbergs, the Adlers, John Garfield and so on. To these were added a very select group of people belonging to Hollywood, such as Charlie Chaplin, Hanns Eisler and Jascha Heifetz. His two greatest friends, apart from the Strasbergs, were Danny Kaye and Cary Grant.

My professional troubles made me reluctant to show myself in public and we refused Clifford's first invitation, saying that we were engaged. A week later he telephoned saying that he wanted us to meet the Chaplins. It was like inviting a devout Christian to meet God in person; but it happened that this time we really weren't free. Then he knocked on my door. I opened it and found myself confronting a man wearing a raincoat, although it wasn't raining, with tangled hair framing two large eyes that gazed at me with a malicious twinkle. 'I've got to you at last,' he said. 'You didn't want to see me, but I swore that I'd not only see you but that we'd become friends.' He had got to know me indirectly through the insane, being very much interested in a particular institute for the treatment of mental disorder where his plays and my films were put on for the benefit of the patients. I was, it seemed, a favourite of theirs.

Needless to say we accepted the Odets' next invitation and became excellent friends. But this was not enough for Clifford. He got me to read his plays, and it was a revelation. They are not documentaries – or, if they are, it is more like a protective skin. The precise delineation of character and the true ring of the dialogue are not what matters most. What matters is their bitter poetry, powerful, profound and despairing. I will pass over this side of Clifford's professional life. What I want to emphasize here is that this child of the theatre was also a brilliant film-director. His film, *None but the Lonely Heart*, with Cary Grant, is in my humble opinion a masterpiece. I will also pass over his political problems: like everyone representative of his period, he was a victim of the anti-communist obsession.

Our last evening with Clifford was particularly moving. His wife Betty, the mother of his two children, had vanished from his life. Clifford went on throwing parties, but the zest was gone. Time went by, filled with his efforts to set up a film about Mozart which I was to direct. Clifford adored music, above all that of Mozart. He had brought us together many times, Dido and me and a few other friends, for a barbecue in his garden. He told us one evening that he was going into hospital for a couple of days for 'a check-up'. His doctor thought it was a simple gastric disorder, but considered a thorough examination advisable. He was to go in a week's time, and on the evening before he went he asked Dido and me round for a last party in his garden.

He had invited no one else. It was a wonderful summer evening. Clifford had rigged up a special lighting system which made the garden look like the background of a fairy-tale. His daughter, Nora, aged fifteen, joined us, and his son Walt, a boy of twelve, waited at table. There was no one else there, only Mozart and ourselves, a party of friends gathered together on an occasion of unwitting solemnity. We did not know the reason. We talked very little, feeling that Mozart could say all that was needed. I have rarely felt so distinctly what one may call the waves of friendship, the obliteration of speech by the feeling itself. To say that people are united is not enough: it is more like the spiritual absorption of friend by friend.

We called Clifford up next morning to say we hoped his two days in hospital would not be too tedious, talking light-heartedly, but still feeling the kind of anguish that had gripped our throats while we listened to Mozart in the garden. The next day we went to see him, and he told us that the doctors considered an abdominal operation essential. What followed was what so often follows on these occasions. One enters the hospital still believing what the doctors say, and they, for their part, are honestly persuaded that an operation will make a new man of the patient – and so it may do, if a corpse can be said to be still a man.

Clifford, for his part, had no illusions. His friends, when

the news got round, all brought him tokens of affection, and in the corridor outside his room we talked about how well he was looking and how his temperature had gone down. It was after the second day that things began to go wrong. He had to have a second operation. Dido and I called to see him often during those last days of his life, and that silent conversation in the garden, ennobled by the music of Mozart, was continued between us. Clifford was less and less capable of speech: he had plastic tubes protruding from his mouth and nostrils. He was punctured all over with injections, but he kept his end up, knowing that it was all useless. Death is egalitarian, and at its approach we have to revise our priorities. The things we thought important are thrust back into the pit, and what we thought negligible comes into the stalls.

I am sure that the characters in Clifford's plays were gathered round his hospital bed to ensure his passage into immortality. Clifford loved wine, especially claret, and he asked us to take along some of the best bottles in his cellar. We did not do so: we wanted to avoid anything which looked like a parting gesture to the dying. He died in the certainty that we would taste the contents of those carefully selected bottles. On the last day he had a bottle of a great vintage brought to him. He asked for three glasses to be filled, and the tube to be removed from his mouth. He touched his glass with his lips. Dido and I drank the bottle to the last drop, and he smiled at us as we did so.

Artifice—or,
The Triumph of Internal Truth

As I said at the beginning of this book, I went into films with the firm intention of avoiding the adaptation of literary works to the screen. I had gone completely into reverse. After all, what is interesting about an adaptation is not its resemblance to the original work but the way in which the film-maker reacts to the original work, and if his reaction produces results seeming to have no connection with the original work, what does it matter? We don't admire a painting for its fidelity to the model: all we want is for the model to stimulate the painter's imagination. This summary statement is inadequate, because things become complicated if the painter is carried away by the sense of his own importance, in which case the final result is likely to be nothing but a monument to his own vanity. A real artist believes that his function is to follow the model. He is convinced, while he is working, that he is recreating the model, whether it be an object, a human being or a thought.

I had vowed, after *Nana*, never again to adapt a novel for the screen. With the same inconsistency, after being fanatically devoted to natural settings I became a worshipper of the artificial. I know the reason now that I am out of step. The fact is that I am an abominable tyrant. I have called myself a midwife. In reality I am ten or twenty midwives, as many midwives as there are aspects of the film. I wanted the actor, while thinking himself his own master, to be my unwitting slave. In return I got from him moments of brilliant acting: the new-born babe draws cries of admiration from its parents.

My tyranny extended into every field, from the setting to the most unimportant props, embracing the music, the pronunciation and the camera-angles. As with the actors, I insisted that the operator should do his own job. My business was to get him to do it in the way I wanted, but without specifically asking him, so that he remained convinced that he himself had decided the angles. In this state of guided liberty people give the best of themselves and the door remains open for discussion. I got nearer and nearer to the ideal method of directing, which consists in shooting a film as one writes a novel. The elements by which the author is surrounded inspire him. He absorbs them. This method enabled me to set actors, designers, cameramen, technicians in general and also craftsmen working to achieve the realization of ideas which meant little to them, but the execution of which became a passionate object in itself.

Coloured film presents fewer photographic problems than black-and-white. Panchromatic film had already done something to soften contrasts, and colour completed the process. With black-and-white and even with panchromatic one is liable to get plaster-white and black like boot-polish, but these extremes are easily avoided with colour. The problem is simply one of using the light necessary for the emulsion and selecting a scene so simple that it looks artificial; and the ideal answer to the problem of colour is to eschew Nature altogether, the external truth, and work entirely in artificial sets, as I was to do in my subsequent films. Inner truth is often concealed behind a purely artificial environment.

My characters in *Le Carrosse d'Or*, *Elena et les Hommes* and *French Cancan* are what it is customary to describe as unlifelike. But it is possible to be improbable and still true, and truth itself is generally improbable. You have only to sit outside a café; you will be amazed by the appearance of those 'real life' passers-by, faces such as no audience would put up with, a positive massacre. No artist would have the audacity to copy those faces without transposing them, and in doing so he makes them either more awful or more acceptable. Merely to photograph them does not express their reality.

In those films I used nothing but studio sets, but I included certain scenes of authentic detail – for example, the Viceroy's footbath during the morning audience in *Le Carrosse d'Or*, bringing the spectators back to the paradoxical truth.

So far as its outward appearance goes, *Elena et les Hommes*, filmed in 1956, is like a series of popular prints. The action of that seemingly artificial film is little suited to realistic settings. Reds and blues are opposed without transition. Claude Renoir shot some stormy landscape sequences which take us directly back to pictures designed for children. Ingrid Bergman, in the leading part, contrived with her usual genius to portray a character as unrealistic as the settings.

The story of *Le Carrosse d'Or* takes place in the eighteenth century, and centres round the coach which the Viceroy of Peru has had sent from Europe. His official mistress hopes that it will be among her perquisites, but the Viceroy has fallen for the star of a travelling *commedia dell'arte* company. He presents this lady, La Pericole, with the coach, and the result is a palace revolution; but she settles the matter by bestowing it on the Bishop of Lima. My principal collaborator on this film was the late Antonio Vivaldi. I wrote the script while listening to records of his music, and his wit and sense of drama led me on to developments in the best tradition of the Italian theatre.

The part of La Pericole was played by Anna Magnani, and many people were astonished that an actress famous for her portrayal of stormy emotion should have been used in a piece more suited to a Milanese puppet-show. If I had been dealing with a bourgeois type of actress, the film would have risked lapsing into affectation: the danger with Magnani was that it would go too far in the direction of what is called realism. Her dazzling interpretation forced me to treat the film as a light comedy. Another gift which she brought me was her natural nobility. Although she was accustomed to playing women of the people torn by passion, she was perfectly at her ease amid the subtleties of a court intrigue.

The studio's working hours were from midday until eight in the evening. At first Magnani never arrived before two. I explained to her that this added greatly to the cost of the production, but she was quite unmoved. I said that it was not a nice way to treat her fellow actors, who turned up on time and then had to wait. Finally I took her aside and declared that I would rather drop the film altogether than keep everyone hanging about. This really did shake her; she promised that from then on she would be punctual, and she kept her word.

Another problem with Magnani was to persuade her to spend the night in bed and not in night-clubs. She turned up worn out, with bags under her eyes and incapable of remembering any of her lines. My nephew, Claude, pulled a face at the thought of having to photograph her in that state. She would start by saying that she couldn't go on, that she looked foul, like an old beggar-woman; a string of excuses while she sat shivering in a huge mink cape chain-smoking cigarettes. I insisted on her letting herself be made up and then rehearsed her on the set. At the same time I asked Claude to switch on the lighting so that she could feel the warmth of the lights. Within five minutes the bags under her eyes had vanished, her voice had cleared and she looked ten years younger. She had become La Pericole.

A tiresome Italian habit from the point of view of work is the star's privilege of receiving visitors on the set while shooting is in progress. This clatter was intolerable to me, with my love of direct sound, and I said so to Magnani. It happened that on the same day a near-relation of the Pope came to see her, accompanied by her ladies-in-waiting. Directly I asked her to tell them to keep quiet she rounded on them in a fury. 'Out you go!' she shouted. 'Out you go, all you princesses!' The terrified ladies fled, and we went back to work in a silence hitherto unknown in a Roman studio.

I like *French Cancan* because it gave me another chance to work with Jean Gabin. It was a return to the past, to my companion in *Les Bas Fonds*, *La Grande Illusion* and *La Bête Humaine*, and I am grateful to the cinema for having given me this comradeship. I love Gabin and he loves me. But we do not know one another. He knows nothing of my private life and I know nothing of his. Our relationship is entirely professional, but I have a feeling that his tastes are pretty much the same as mine. We run across one another in the same restaurants. When we worked together we had no need of lengthy discussion to analyse the situation. We scarcely needed a script to know what we had in mind. Gabin was born to be an actor just as I was born to be a film-maker. Yet we differ in our approach. Gabin is forceful and asserts himself without effort. I am the opposite: I expound and seek to persuade by reason. As I said at the beginning of this book, I'm a born coward. I'm always afraid of putting my foot in it and causing the actor to despise me; but it is an obsession that does not trouble me when I am working with Gabin, for the simple reason that we think alike. If I were an actor I would want to play the parts he plays, and I am vain enough to think that I would not do it too badly. Now that the time is past when I enjoyed technical tricks and despised actors, an actor is one of the things I would most like to be. The gods, fortunately for me, have taken no note of this aspiration: actors, as a rule, are not happy people. The exception is Gabin. I am sure that he confronts the problems of life with the same calm certainty that he uses in getting into the skin of a part.

Jean Gabin is not one of those tormented actors of whom I spoke earlier. He has no need to withdraw to the silence of his dressing-room in between takes. He filled in the periods of waiting in *French Cancan* by giving Dido cooking recipes. 'Do you know how to make *lapin à la moutarde*? You take a spoonful of Dijon mustard . . .' He would break off for the next take, play it magnificently, and then, unaffected by the break, go on with the recipe where he had left off.

French Cancan was based on the life of Ziegler, the founder of the Moulin Rouge. Broadly speaking, the film is an act of homage to our calling, by which I mean show-business. Playing opposite the sober Gabin we had a fiery woman, the Mexican star, Maria Félix. With her tall stature she dominated the scene, and she especially dominated Françoise Arnoul, her rival for Gabin's affections. She comes of a tribe of American Indians renowned for their size and physical strength. When she shook you by the hand your arm was limp for the rest of the day. She ascribed her strength to her diet, which consisted largely of rare steak and raw carrots. Compared with her, Françoise Arnoul looked like a dragon-fly. There was a scene in which the rivals had to pull each other's hair, and Françoise Arnoul accidentally scratched Maria Félix with her bracelet. It then became a brawl in good earnest. Maria, in a fury, aimed a blow at Françoise which, if it had landed, would have taken her head off, and Françoise retaliated gamely with feet and fingernails. Maria lifted Françoise in the air, and it looked as though she might injure her severely. The cameras were all ready to film the scene, but I cut it short before we needed to send for an ambulance.

Limelight

There is a danger that the technical perfection of the cinema, and the fact that the director has so many elaborate effects at his disposal that he has no need to rack his brains to obtain them, may rob him of his creative impulse. It is a case of existing before thinking: one needs to have soiled one's hands with matter before entering the domain of the spirit. Technical knowledge has only one merit, that it prompts us to seek still further. I had an urge to enter a field that was quite new to me, that of the theatre.

In 1954 Philippe Dechartre and Jean Serge asked me to direct a live performance of Shakespeare's *Julius Caesar* in the amphitheatre at Arles, the occasion being the celebration of Caesar's founding of the town, two thousand years earlier. Unlike the Greek drama, Shakespeare's plays were performed in comparatively small theatres, and the use of the apron stage brought them out into the audience, all of which, together with the lack of echo, leads us to suppose that the players did not have to put much strain on their voices. We arranged with the Philips Company for them to install fifty microphones, so that no matter where an actor was standing his least sigh could be heard. This prompted me to take another decision, which was not to use actors accustomed to theatrical declamation but to rely on film actors who were used to microphones.

Paul Meurisse, who played Brutus, was the compère of the Tabarin revue. I had great faith in his versatility, and his profile was very much that of a Roman of the period. Moreover he had served in the horse-artillery and was an excellent rider. His entrance on horseback was loudly applauded by the large audience. I had enlisted the local townspeople for the crowd scenes: in the Midi of France they know what politics is all about. I explained the play to them and, full of enthusiasm, they did their stuff as though they were taking part in a local election.

On the evening of the performance the actors and I foregathered in the main lounge of our hotel while outside people were flocking into the amphitheatre. We were all in a state of panic, we hadn't even had time to hold a full rehearsal, and some of the players said they had entirely forgotten their lines. Parédès, playing Casca, said that he was in danger of tripping over his toga, which was too long. Then someone remarked that he envied the Orientals their serenity and someone else asked me if I had handled crowd scenes in India. This prompted me to a disquisition on the Hindu religion. I talked about Brahma, the master of the gods, of Shiva, the creator and destroyer, of Krishna, the preserver, and Radha, his beloved, the guardian of animals. As they listened to me their agitation subsided, and when the time came they were almost calm.

The sound system had gone wrong. The performance was to start with Beethoven's Fifth Symphony, the symphony of Destiny, in this case the Destiny of Brutus. But instead of Beethoven all we got was the clamour of the impatient audience. Eventually the sound system was put right and the Fifth Symphony entered upon a losing struggle against the general uproar. When it was time for the players to make their entrance I suggested to Parédès that he should trip over his toga, as he had done in the hotel. The procession moved into that hostile amphitheatre as though they were being thrown to the lions, and Parédès tripped on his toga and

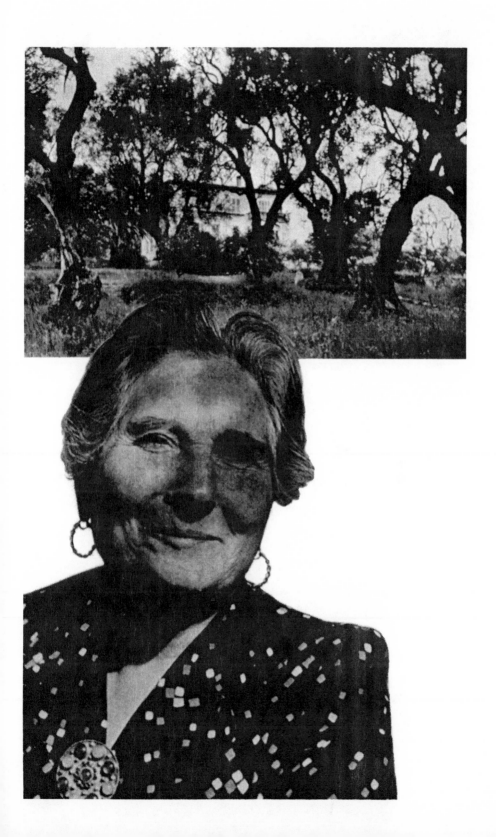

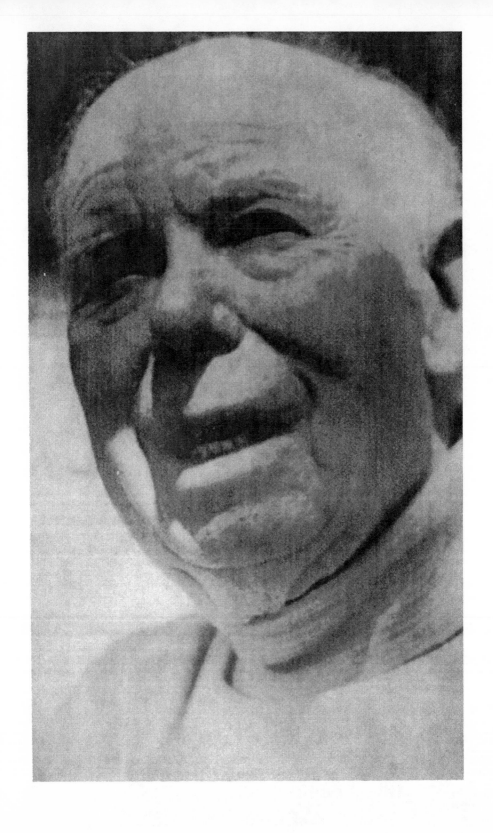

nearly fell flat on his face. This produced a brief silence followed by a huge burst of laughter. From then on the audience was on our side.

One of the merits of a Roman amphitheatre is that it is built of stone and not in danger of catching fire. We depicted the burning of Rome by getting lively young townsmen to light fires with kerosene in different parts of the arena, and at the close of the performance Roman cavalry formed up round Brutus's bier. This operation was carried out in darkness. The lights went up on the cattlemen of the Camargue dressed as Romans. The sight of them drawn up in perfect order aroused great enthusiasm. The applause was endless, and Paul Meurisse, by no means comfortable in his coffin, could not move until it was over. Whenever we meet in these days we recall that eventful evening in Arles.

My second theatrical venture was due to Leslie Caron. I had seen Leslie long before I came to know her. Our first encounter was on a platform at Victoria Station, London – an iron monument which aptly represents the monarch from whom it derives its name. Seated on a bench at the end of the platform were a lady and a young girl. The latter was watching us out of the corner of her eye and trying discreetly to attract our attention. We could feel her watching us with a kind of innocent slyness. Her eyes, half-hidden behind long locks of hair, made one think of a look-out post. It occurred immediately to Dido that she would be perfect for the part of Harriet in *The River*, on which I was then doing the preparatory work. I asked Dido to go and speak to her, but the train started at that moment and we had to go to our respective compartments. I tried to catch a glimpse of her on the train, but the doors of the sleeping compartments were closed for the night. The next day the Gare du Nord was packed and all I saw of her was her long hair as it vanished amid the crowd.

Our next meeting was in Los Angeles, at the house of the painter Pierre Sicard. The Sicards had also invited the dancers from the Roland Petit ballet. The first thing I saw was the little girl of Victoria Station, but this was some years later and the little girl had grown into a young lady whom I could not fail to recognize because of the way she sat, hidden behind her hair. At the same time I recognized *Lili* and the dancer in *An American in Paris*. We greeted each other like old friends and I noticed that she was like a cat. When next we saw her it was on the sidewalk in Times Square, waiting for something in the pouring rain. This time she looked like a soaked cat. And this was typical of my meetings with Leslie – she always looks as though she were expecting something.

Leslie Caron does not only resemble a cat. She also reminded me of the little girl who had been with the poachers who picked me up at the roadside after my accident with Pierre Champagne. I did not hesitate: with the thought of the Forest of Fontainebleau in mind I wrote *Orvet* and asked her to play the lead. She liked the play and consented.

'Orvet' is the name of the leading character; it is also the name of a small, harmless snake that lives in vegetable gardens and feeds on insects. It is welcomed by gardeners who call it the 'glass snake' because of its fragility, for it breaks like glass. Its only defence is its speed of movement. It vanishes into the grass as soon as anyone approaches. The country people in Essoyes, the village of my childhood, are apt to say of a particularly lively and nimble child that he is *'comme un orvet'*.

In 1955 Jean Dercante, the manager of the Théâtre de la Renaissance, undertook to produce *Orvet* and rehearsals began. They took place first in my apartment in Montmartre, and then on the stage of the theatre, strictly in the Italian fashion. This system had given me good results in films, and for a stage production it proved even better. Generally speaking, the lines in a film-script are short and terse: it is difficult for the actor to develop a character in dialogue consisting only of a few words. The extended dialogue of a stage-play affords him space in which to get to know more about the role he is playing. It is fascinating to watch the character being born in the actor. The monotony of the rehearsals has a subconscious effect not only on the actors but on the director.

Leslie entered into her part with a beginner's enthusiasm, and certain of her reactions recalled her bourgeois background. After a few rehearsals I realized that the problem where she was concerned was to make her forget the high-class convent where she had been educated. That had already been the problem with Janie Marèze in *La Chienne*, and I came to the theatre one day convinced that I had the answer. It lay in the pronunciation of the word '*bois*' (wood) in the way a little poacher's daughter would do it, making it sound something like '*bouah*' – '*J'va aller dans les bouahs*'. Leslie at once grasped what I had in mind, and the other, actors, witnessing the rehearsal, were themselves influenced by the effect it had upon her. Before long they had all adopted a key-word pronounced in a manner suited to their part as they conceived it and, finally, as I myself conceived it. All that remained was to blend together the results so that they did not clash. The world is one; I take this opportunity of saying it for the last time.

Paul Meurisse, in the role of the writer, symbolized the tangible reality as opposed to the characters he had imagined. The forest supplied the background of this fairy-tale. At certain moments in the play trees protruded into the setting created by Wakhevitch. It was quite mad but the public liked it.

Le Testament du Docteur Cordelier is an experimental film arising out of my work in the theatre. My conviction that the system of quick shots in the cinema hampers the actor's performance prompted me to try a system of direction in which the actor would determine his own speed. Under normal direction the actor has no sooner got into the skin of his part than the director cuts him short and the take is over. It costs him a great effort to get back into the rhythm. Unfortunately film equipment and particularly the length of the reels does not allow of takes without cuts. Hitchcock came nearest to that method in *The Rope*, in which there are no cuts, except at the end of each reel. I was less ambitious. In *Le Testament du Docteur Cordelier* I was content only to cut at the end of each sequence. I worked as a rule with three or four cameras, and sometimes, in order to get the necessary close-ups, I had as many as eight going simultaneously. You can imagine the miles of film that had to be thrown away. The editor and her assistants were nearly off their heads. The actors, on the other hand, were delighted. They saw it as a victory over that exasperating director's cry of 'Cut!' *Le Testament du Docteur Cordelier* is an adaptation in contemporary terms of Stevenson's *Dr Jekyll and Mr Hyde*. Jean-Louis Barrault played the dual role like a dancer, using no make-up for the transformation of Jekyll into Hyde. His only accessories were a set of false teeth and a shaggy wig. The film, shot in almost a single sequence, enabled Kosma to compose music with a single motif; and its unity once again illustrated my perpetual hobby-horse, the one-ness of the world.

I made one other film after the same method, *Le Déjeuner sur l'Herbe*, which was shot in 1959 almost entirely at Les Collettes, and in which I had the immense pleasure of filming the olive-trees my father had so often painted. That film was like a bath of purity and optimism. We felt, in its making, that we had been transformed into fauns and nymphs. Catherine Rouvel made her debut in it, and Paul Meurisse lent his authority to a coldly comic part. After this I abandoned that particular method, so profitable to the celluloid manufacturers.

I have tried in this book to give some idea of my productions, but I have only mentioned those marking a significant stage in my development as a maker of films· I will conclude these recollections of an out-of-sync film director with a mention of my very last work, *Le Petit Théatre de Jean Renoir*, made for television in 1969, after seven years of unwilling inactivity. In it I propounded my beliefs and my doubts, passing in its four episodes from realism to artifice and back again. The first episode portrays the importance of their dream life to two destitute vagrants; it was shot entirely in the studio, and is treated in a spirit of realist reconstruction. The second episode, *The Electric Floor-Polisher*, is treated like an opera and describes the sacrilegious passion of a modern respectable housewife for the machine which polishes her floor. Her husband throws it out of the window, and she follows it, plunging to her death. In the third episode Jeanne Moreau takes us for a little while outside our century of sleazy progress. The fourth episode, strictly realistic, is shot on location in natural surroundings.

It deals with a betrayed husband who refuses to be parted from his wife's lover, his penitent best friend. The chief actor in this little drama is the game of *pétanque*, which I firmly believe to be an instrument of peace.

Whether the setting is natural, or imitates Nature, or is deliberately artificial, is of little importance. I used external truth in so-called 'realistic' films like *La Chienne* and *La Bête Humaine*, and apparently total artificiality in films like *La Petite Marchande d'Allumettes* and *Le Carrosse d'Or*. I have spent my life experimenting with different styles, but it all comes down to this: my different attempts to arrive at the inward truth, which for me is the only one that matters.

An End to Nationalism

My French friends all ask me the same question: 'Why have
you chosen to live in America? You're French and you need
a French environment.' My answer to this is that the environment which has made me what I am is the cinema. I am
a citizen of the world of films.

With the development of new means of communication
we are back in the state of horizontal compartments, just as
in the Middle Ages the Western world was united by the
Latin language and Christianity. Our present-day religion
is the bank, and our language is publicity. The key-word is
output, by which we produce more. When the world
market is saturated we start another war to get new customers. The aim of warfare is no longer conquest but con-
struction. When the building is destroyed the wheels turn
again. We build skyscrapers on the ruins of pagodas, and
this fills the belly of the working-man, who would otherwise revolt.

I can well imagine a telephone conversation between the
Russian head of state and the American president. The
president: 'Can you help us out, my dear fellow? Arms
production is falling off in a most disturbing way.' The
Russian: 'We're having the same trouble. For the time being
the manufacture of the XYZ super-jet is keeping us going,
but that can't last much longer. We shall have to think up
something else.' . . . 'Can't we start a small war somewhere?
That would save the arms industry.' . . . It sounds like a joke,
but things must happen in much that kind of way.

India and the Indians have helped to rid me of the last

traces of nationalism. I spent two unforgettable years there.
From the moment when our plane arrived at Dum-Dum,
the Calcutta airport, before we had even left the gangway,
Dido and I found ourselves surrounded by some twenty
young people who greeted us with a touching warmth.
One of them took us to his home where his widowed
mother received us with Indian ceremony. Then she
vanished into the depths of the kitchen. They no longer
burn widows in India; the funeral pyre is reserved for the
dead. But the surviving wife does not leave the house or
show herself; she lives a life as near as possible to death
until she is claimed by her own funeral pyre. This lady was
making a great sacrifice when she welcomed us in person.
It is rare for a foreigner to enter an Indian home; but not
only were we admitted, we were cherished like children
returned from a long journey. The words of Mowgli in *The
Jungle Book* had preceded us: 'We are of the same blood, you
and I'; and the bond of blood which made us members of
one family was the cinema.

If a French farmer should find himself dining at the same
table as a French financier, those two Frenchmen would
have nothing to say to each other, each being unconcerned
with the other's interests. But if a French farmer meets a
Chinese farmer they will find any amount to talk about.
This theme of the bringing together of men through their
callings and common interests has haunted me all my life
and does so still. It is the theme of *La Grande Illusion* and it
is present, more or less, in all my works.

The nation, as we now know it, is an invention of the
French Revolution. Men who had been merely subjects
were raised to the rank of citizens. Systems crumble
slowly. The carcass of the Roman Empire remained stand-

ing long after the death of the last emperor. Many years will have to pass before an Italian cabinet-maker proclaims himself a citizen of his craft, and we are still very far from the day when every man will accept the fact that he is a citizen of the world. The nation is like an outworn house, but we like it and we prefer it to a more modern dwelling.

It was a fine thing, the nation. Behind its frontiers we could preserve our separate customs and languages, and the world did not present that tiresome unity towards which we are so rapidly progressing. Before long we shall travel round the world without even noticing. The plane will put us down in an airport identical with the one we left. The hotel room will be the same, and the restaurant menu will be like the menu in every restaurant on earth. Why not organize non-stop air tours around the world. We would embark and disembark in New York, having spent the time watching a film, and companies priding themselves on their originality will sometimes make it a film of the countries over which we are supposed to have flown.

Yes, the nation was a pleasant thing. It was the window of the local grocer's shop, the Auvergne accent of the man bringing the coal, the smell of frying coming from the concierge's lodge, the song of the house-painter reaching us through the leaves of chestnut trees. It is the hair of a beloved woman, the caress of a family pet. A very pleasant thing, but it is dying, and we cannot bring the dead to life.

We forget that while in a foreign land we try to re-live the country of our childhood, the shape of that country is constantly changing. And with it the spirit changes. We return after a few years to the scenes of our youth and find that we cannot recognize them. That is why, for our peace of mind, we must try to escape from the spell of memories. Our salvation lies in plunging resolutely into the hell of the new world, a world horizontally divided, a world without passion or nostalgia. We must forget the bistro in Magagnosc. The chances are, in any case, that we won't find it; it has probably vanished under a mountain of cement. We must never let ourselves be separated from the beloved, because after a long absence she will have become another person.

As I bid farewell to the landscape of my childhood I think of Gabrielle. Certainly it was she who influenced me most of all. To her I owe Guignol and the Théâtre Montmartre. She taught me to realize that the very unreality of those entertainments was a reason for examining real life. She taught me to see the face behind the mask, and the fraud behind the flourishes. She taught me to detest the cliché. My farewell to my childhood world may be expressed in very few words: 'Wait for me, Gabrielle.'

Index

By the same author

Renoir, My Father
The Notebooks of Captain Georges

Printed in the United States
209166BV00002B/190-210/A

9 780306 804571